Basketball Analytics

Objective and Efficient Strategies for Understanding How Teams Win

Stephen M. Shea   Christopher E. Baker

Contents

About the Authors

Stephen Shea is an associate professor of mathematics at Saint Anselm College in Manchester, New Hampshire. He earned a Ph.D. in mathematics from Wesleyan University in Middletown, Connecticut and a B.A. with a major in mathematics from The College of the Holy Cross in Worcester, Massachussetts. For years, Professor Shea has used his ability and interest in mathematics and statistics to analyze professional and amateur sports. At Saint Anselm College, he teaches a course titled Quantitative Analysis in Sports. He has participated in the MIT Sloan Sports Analytics Conference. His work has been featured as a finalist in the annual Stat Geek Idol competition on TeamRankings.com and in the Journal of Quantitative Analysis in Sports. As a mathematician, he specializes in dynamical systems, probability and statistics, and he is actively researching and publishing in these areas. Professor Shea's education and experience is reflected in his sports analytics. He lives with his wife (Cara), two sons (Miles and Gavin) and daughter (Eloise) in Hooksett, New Hampshire.

Christopher Baker received his Bachelor of Science degree in Computer Engineering from Washington University in St. Louis, Missouri. As a software developer, Mr. Baker has focused on Microsoft .NET Web Development and Microsoft SQL Server Database Architecture and Engineering. As a sports analyst, he has spent the past eight years developing advanced player projection algorithms, new concepts, and new metrics in Hockey and Basketball. He is a member of the Society for International Hockey Research (SIHR) and the Hockey Summary Project, where he has studied the development of the game of Hockey statistically over its vast history. Mr. Baker uses his combination of knowledge in sports and software engineering to design and develop efficient methodologies for calculating and visualizing metrics used in real-time systems. He was most recently published with Stephen Shea in the Journal of Quantitative Analysis in Sports for their work entitled "Calculating Wins Over Replacement Player (WORP) for NHL Goaltenders." Christopher lives with his wife (Francine), son (Michael) and daughter (Annabella) in Lake St. Louis, Missouri.

Preface

For decades, National Basketball Association (NBA) fans have been subjected to the same dull, insufficient and often misleading statistics. Our minds have been warped. We hallow the great point scorers and judge defense by blocks per game. If you have picked up this book, you are probably interested in the current movement for more intelligent analytics.

Baseball was the first sport to seriously use and celebrate advanced analytics. In retrospect, this was appropriate. Baseball has always been the easiest sport to model with mathematics. The game moves incrementally, one pitch at a time. The contributing players in each event can be easily identified and isolated.

Basketball is the other extreme. The game is fast; all five players are almost always a factor. In each play, a number of contributions go unnoticed by the traditional box score, such as screens away from the ball, and help defense that dissuades the opponent from driving.

Basketball teams, the media and fans have made great strides in recent years in the use of advanced metrics, in spite of the statistical challenges. NBA.com now presents shot charts, clutch scoring, and complete lineup data. Basketball-reference.com is the casual analyst's dream come true, with team and player data easily organized and converted to personal spreadsheets.

In this book, we will design a number of new statistics and conduct a series of new analyses. Our work is not ignorant of past and current practices; they often inspire us. We will survey John Hollinger's Player Efficiency Rating (PER), Winston and Sagarin's adjusted plus-minus, and the Wins Produced model popularized by David Berri. We characterize types of role players currently employed in the NBA in a chapter that was motivated by Muthu Alagappan's revolutionary redefinition of the positions on a basketball team. We mention Kirk Goldsberry's recent work that uses SportVU spatial tracking software to find new measures of interior defense. Other sections reference presentations at recent MIT Sloan Sports Analytics Conferences. This book could not have been written even one year ago. It reflects an awareness of the best ideas to date.

No metric is perfect, especially if it is attempting to measure the total ability, production or contributions of a basketball player. Imperfection does not imply futility. The key is to interpret the statistic appropriately. To interpret, we need to understand, and simplicity helps in understanding. The mathematics and statistics used in this book attempt to strike a balance between simplicity and performance. The exceptions are rare and always justified by a significant return when compared to simpler procedures. When we do introduce a more complicated technique, such as the use of Shannon's entropy from information theory, we will do our best to motivate and explain the mathematics.

A chapter of this book stems from Stephen Shea's Stat Geek Idol submission to TeamRankings.com. That piece analyzed NCAA basketball. We thank Mark Cuban for requesting that we pursue the topic in the NBA. We also thank everyone at TeamRankings.com who assisted in the initial analysis in the NBA.

Each section of the book should be read in succession. Later chapters depend on definitions given in earlier chapters. In its interdependence, the text delves deeper than could have been accomplished through disparate blog entries or magazine articles. We hope you enjoy reading what we believe is a thorough analysis of team success in the NBA as much as we enjoyed writing it.

As mentioned above, no metric is perfect, and the same holds for what we have created here (although we do hope to have provided new and significant insights). We will continue to work with these metrics and will post updates at our webpage BasketballAnalyticsBook.com. We also look forward to your comments and ideas, and we will use the webpage as a portal to answer reader questions, share reader feedback and generally progress the field of basketball analytics.

Introduction

In Clint Eastwood's blockbuster movie *Trouble with the Curve*, the Atlanta Braves are questioning the ability of their once hailed, but now aging scout, Gus (played by Eastwood). The Braves own the second pick in the upcoming draft and their top choice is a prized hitting prospect. The batter is in Gus' geographic region, and so reluctantly, the Braves assign the now nearly blind scout to his case. While Gus is on the road, a young data driven scout, Philip, is tapping away at his keyboard. Philip's analytics say the Braves can't miss on the hitter. At the park, Gus' ears tell him otherwise. In a dramatic scene, Gus *hears* a flaw in the batter's swing. He predicts that the prospect will not be able to hit a curve in the majors. Philip says take the kid, and Gus says don't. The data, math, statistics, and algorithms—*the analytics*—say the kid can't miss, and the trained ear of a great scout says he can't hit. It is new against old, modern analytics versus tradition. In the end, the Braves take the prospect, but Gus is proven correct. Gus' daughter brings in an undrafted pitcher that upstages the hitting prospect. (The movie is really about the relationship between Gus and his daughter.)[1]

Trouble with the Curve is fiction, but there is some wisdom in the story. Analytics will never replace the traditional methods of player evaluation. Unlike the portrayal in Eastwood's film, however, analytics and on-site scouting are not in competition with each other. Instead, each perfectly complements the other.

There is no replacing the value of getting into the gym or out to the field to see that college prospect play, to see how he interacts with his teammates and to see how he responds to his coach's demands in the huddle. Player interviews are also important. A lot can be learned about a player's knowledge of the game, attitude and professionalism from sitting down with the athlete in front of his game film. Looking at a player's statistics will never replace these more traditional scouting methods. The good scouts have eyes (and ears) trained to know when a player's production will likely translate to the next level or if there is that flaw in the mechanics that will be a project to correct. It is the human element that yields so many benefits. Unfortunately, the same human element creates the practice's major flaws.

Brian Burke has held many executive positions in the National Hockey League (NHL). He was the general manager for the Vancouver Canucks, the Anaheim Ducks and the Toronto Maple Leafs. He has built a reputation as a good eye for talent. In Vancouver, he drafted Henrik and Daniel Sedin, and the brothers are now superstars for that franchise. Anaheim won the Stanley Cup under his watch. So what does this great hockey mind think of modern analytics? "Statistics are more like a lamp post to a drunk… useful for support but not for illumination."[2] Clearly, this is not glowing praise for the analytics industry. The quote comes from the 2012 Hockey Analytics Panel at the MIT Sloan Sports Analytics Conference. Strangely, during that same panel discussion, Burke provides two examples that illustrate precisely the two weaknesses of traditional scouting.

Burke admitted underestimating the Boston Bruins' top line left wing (and Stanley Cup Champion) Milan Lucic's overall value, because Burke could not get over Lucic's awkward skating

---

[1] *Trouble with the Curve*. Dir. Robert Lorenz. Warner Bros., 2012. Film.
[2] The quote is at 5:31 in the video at http://www.sloansportsconference.com/?p=4550.

style.[3] Scouts evaluate players, and the great ones generally provide an accurate report. They identify the talent and predict the busts, but history tells us that they do not always get it right. A scout will travel to the rinks, see players skate, shoot and hit a certain way. They will watch how the players interact with their teammates and note body language. Eventually the scout will see which players pan out, and which ones never make it. This experience is invaluable. Trusting the lessons learned from these experiences will lead to successful scouting reports in the future. Unfortunately, the experience also creates biases. Over time, an observer will develop notions of what a future good player should look like. When someone like Lucic comes along that does not fit the mold, it is difficult to believe he can be successful. Live scouting's first weakness is subjectivity.

    In the same panel, Burke recalls a scouting trip where he went to watch Bobby Ryan (who he later drafted for Anaheim). While on-site, he also took a look at Ryan's teammate, Wayne Simmonds. Burke watched eight games. In his eyes, Simmonds was not very good. Burke is a great judge of talent, and so it is likely that Simmonds was not very impressive for that stretch. Today, Simmonds is a good player for the Philadelphia Flyers, but Burke "never saw that." In his words, "I watched him eight times, and I didn't see anything where I got in the car afterwards and said geez I gotta try and get that guy."[4] The problem is that eight games do not define a player. If Ryan were not on the team, Burke probably would not have been at the rink for even eight of Simmonds' games. Scouting is costly and time consuming. Burke might want to be at every game for every prospective player in the draft class, but this is not feasible. The second weakness of live scouting is its inefficiency.

    We present sports analytics as the objective and efficient counterpart to live scouting and evaluation. Where traditional methods suffer, modern algorithms excel. Analytics will measure a player's production ignorant of how ugly he looks doing it. Running advanced statistics on every player over decades can take only a few seconds. Teams still need scouts in the seats, but analytics can tell the organizations who to visit, what to look for, and when a scout's biases are influencing his reports. Analytics and live scouting collaborate to arm teams with the most information.

Baseball Leads the Way

This is a book about NBA analytics. It may appear as though we have gotten sidetracked talking about baseball and hockey. The fact is that basketball has a lot to learn from other sports, and the education begins with the baseball analysis of Bill James. James started a statistical revolution with his baseball abstracts.[5] Perhaps James' most fundamental principle was that the box score statistics of the day were not accurately capturing the value a player brings to his team. If a team could find a better way to measure a player's contributions, one distinct from what other teams are doing, it is likely they would rate and rank players differently than their opposition. In such a scenario, the team could have a significant advantage over the rest of the league. They could find players on the cheap that others underappreciated, while avoiding overpaying the overvalued options. This is part of why Billy Beane has been able to produce a competitive ball club in Oakland while on a limited budget. The best-selling book, *Moneyball*, by Michael Lewis,[6] and a movie starring Brad Pitt by the same name,[7] famously portrayed Beane's success.

---

[3] The quote is at 25:40.
[4] The quote is at 27:20.
[5] James, B. *Baseball Abstract*. self-published, 1980.
[6] Lewis, M. *Moneyball: The Art of Winning an Unfair Game*. W.W. Norton and Company, 2004.
[7] *Moneyball*. Dir. Bennett Miller. Columbia Pictures, 2011. Film.

In comparison to baseball's statistical advances, other major sports have lagged behind. This is not surprising. Baseball can be reasonably partitioned into a series of discrete events. The outcome of any one at-bat is largely the responsibility of the batter and pitcher involved. Of course, factors such as who is on base and who is on deck are important, but even these are easily identified. With some effort and creativity, these influences can be factored into most models.

In stark contrast, basketball is fluid. Each event is the result of a series of contributions (and mistakes) from a number of players on the floor. A team's basket could be the result of hard-nosed defense by all five players on the team, several timely and accurate passes in transition, and a solid screen away from the ball in the offensive zone.

To be an objective and efficient counterpart to coaching and scouting, analytics must be based on data or statistics. Basketball is far more difficult to analyze statistically than baseball. For this reason, the fundamental principle that pervaded the revolution led by James applies to an even greater extent in our situation. The statistics typically captured in an NBA box score are not sufficient. As Houston Rockets General Manager Daryl Morey once said, "Someone created the box score, and he should be shot."[8]

The Plan

In this book, we design and test advanced statistics on the NBA. Our goal is to better understand how teams win. We divide the projects and metrics into three categories. First, we evaluate players. We introduce a classification system of player value metrics, which helps identify the strengths and weaknesses of each approach. In this context, we survey some of the most popular statistics in the public domain, including Player Efficiency Rating (which was designed by John Hollinger), adjusted plus-minus as created by Wayne Winston and Jeff Sagarin, and the Wins Produced model popularized by David Berri. In Chapters 3 and 4, we introduce new measures of offensive efficiency and defensive quality. These innovative measures offer value that rivals that of any publicly available statistic while providing a simplicity that will allow you to understand their functionality and practical application in a matter of pages. We use these new measures to quantify and compare the value of NBA legends including Michael Jordan, Larry Bird and Magic Johnson, to today's stars such as LeBron James and Kevin Durant. Where certain players excel, others trail behind. We combine our offensive and defensive evaluations to approximate the total contributions of an individual to his team. With this metric, we can determine who is the most valuable player in today's NBA.

In Chapter 5, we discuss ways to best visually represent the statistics we introduce. Mathematics and statistics have historically used a variety of methods for visual representation. These disciplines use graphs to represent functions and pie charts for percentages. Our minds can often better process these visualizations than a table of values or an algebraic expression. The same holds true for sports analytics. How can we best represent a player's value? Players contribute in a variety of ways, such as rebounding, perimeter shooting, playmaking, and interior defense. How do we represent the specific ways in which a player impacts the game as well as his total contribution? Can we capture a player's development over multiple seasons in one image, or perhaps a movie? Our visualizations would have great value on web sites that feature NBA statistics. Chapter 5 explains how to turn tables of player statistics into useful visualizations.

---

[8] Lewis, M. "The No-Stats All-Star." *The New York Times*. February 13, 2009. <http://www.nytimes.com/2009/02/15/magazine/15Battier-t.html?pagewanted=all&_r=0>.

After player evaluations, we move to team evaluations. NBA analytics now offer a variety of metrics measuring team production. Not nearly as prevalent are measures of team style. We have measured what teams have done, but we have not well quantified how they did it. The latter is just as important to the team looking to build success in the future. Here, we introduce balance metrics, groundbreaking measures of player involvement in the many tasks required of a successful basketball team (such as scoring, rebounding and passing). Balance metrics are a quick way to approximate a team's style of play, such as how much the team shares the ball on offense. Should Kobe Bryant be concerned with getting his teammates shot opportunities? We correlate style of play with team success, and find results that, at first glance, would please your neighborhood ball hog.

The outcome of an NBA game can sometimes feel so arbitrary. Consider the following end of game example. A team is down by one. Their star launches a last second shot. As the buzzer sounds, the ball bounces around the rim a few times then slowly slides into the center. Then, as if yanked by an imaginary string, the ball that was halfway down and halfway to victory rises back up and slides out the side. It seemed so close. Victory was foiled by millimeters, a small breeze, or a scuff on the ball. Could there be an element of randomness in the game? Certainly odds-makers and gamblers lack perfect predictive power. Unpredictability is a factor when predicting the outcome of games or seasons, determining which prospects will develop into impactful NBA players, or understanding where the prized free agent will sign. In Chapter 10, we discuss unpredictability in basketball, how it impacts team analytics, and how teams can use this to their advantage. In particular, we discuss how the Houston Rockets have used a high variance approach to quickly rebuild their roster.

By this point in the text, we will have discussed how to evaluate NBA teams and how to identify their strengths and weaknesses. We will have shown which style of play has been the most successful in recent history. Lastly, we present analytics to help teams build their rosters. First, we present a draft pick value chart. The chart averages the production of players according to draft position. We also chart the probability each pick leads to a premium player, and the likelihood each pick results in a solid role player. We believe these probabilities are at least as important as the average production by pick when assessing the value of draft positions. Teams can use these charts to approximate the value of picks in future drafts.

We also take a serious look at the idea of rebuilding through the draft. This has been viewed as a cost effective strategy for acquiring talent. Talent is certainly available in the draft, especially at the higher picks. Historically, teams have parlayed high picks into championships. In 1979, the Los Angeles Lakers drafted Magic Johnson. They then went on to win 5 championships in the '80s. In 1984, the Houston Rockets selected Hakeem Olajuwon. Hakeem "the Dream" led the Rockets to two titles in the '90s. The Rockets' titles were sandwiched between Jordan's six titles. Jordan was the third overall selection of the Bulls in that 1984 draft. As we will show, the high draft pick to championship road has become the one less travelled.

Our analysis of the rebuilding through the draft strategy shows that the NBA landscape is changing. The way teams are constructing champions has evolved. When LeBron James decided to take his talents to South Beach, the Heat transformed into a "super team." By our measures, the best player in the league joined forces with two other premier players. The union came when all three athletes were just entering their primes. The combination of the three then became a magnet for capable veterans looking to win a title. In the 2012 offseason, Ray Allen reportedly spurned more money and a spot with a still competitive Celtics team (where he had won his first championship just a few years earlier) to join the Heat as a role player off the bench. LeBron's decision to join the Heat changed the game. The Heat have been to the finals in each year since his big decision and have won the last two titles. In the '80s, Bird and Magic spent their offseasons preparing to defeat the other. Today, players prepare to join each other. We have entered a super team era, and organizations must adjust. In Chapter 13, we discuss team strategies in this new age of competition. This includes less focus on player development and more on cap management.

After Chapter 13, we present most of the statistics introduced in this book organized by team. This includes team and player metrics. While reading the book, you can use this section to check your team's production in each newly defined statistic. After completing the text, this section can serve as an easily navigated reference.

Sports analytics is a rapidly evolving industry. The available data is expanding, and the methods used to analyze this data are improving. Throughout the book, we will identify future directions that can be explored. In particular, we will discuss SportVU spatial tracking technology, and how it can be used to further our analysis.

Analytics is the objective and efficient arm of information gathering. We introduce new metrics for player evaluation, team evaluation and team construction. The insights gleaned from our metrics may forever change the way you view the NBA.

Searching for the I in Team:
Player Evaluation

"One man can be a crucial ingredient on a team,
but one man cannot make a team."

-Kareem Abdul-Jabbar[1]

---

[1] Abdul-Jabbar, K. Athleticpoet.com. Retrieved August 15, 2013.
<http://athleticpoetics.com/post/30416493837/one-man-can-be-a-crucial-ingredient-on-a-team>.

1
Top Down vs. Bottom Up Metrics

How does one quantify the value or production of a basketball player? A number of statistics on the individual are readily available, such as points, rebounds, assists, blocks, steals, and turnovers. As fans, we are most familiar with these numbers. They are tracked in newspaper and in online box scores, highlighted in television broadcasts, placed on the back of trading cards, and tallied for fantasy sports. In the Introduction, we talked about how experience can create biases in scouts. The past emphasis on traditional box score statistics can make it difficult to not rely on these metrics when evaluating a player's performance.

A bottom up metric is a measure of an individual's production built upon records of individual accomplishments (such as a shot made or a rebound).

All of the stats mentioned above are what we classify as bottom up metrics. A bottom up metric is a measure of an individual's production built upon records of individual accomplishments (such as a shot made or a rebound). The sports industry has a long running infatuation with these types of numbers. In Major League Baseball (MLB), we root for single season home run records to be broken (at least when we do not suspect the player is pumped full of steroids or using HGH), we are amazed at triple crowns, and we wonder if anyone will ever hit .400 again. Recently, baseball has found new combinations of simple statistics such as OPS (On-base plus slugging percentage). The popularity of bottom up metrics might lead us to believe that they are the only way to measure an individual's contribution to his team.

Since the 1967-68 season, the NHL has tracked a statistic for a skater called plus-minus (+/-). It is the total goals scored by the skater's team while he is on the ice (provided his team is not on the power play) minus the total goals scored against his team while he is on the ice (and not on the penalty kill). Recently, the NBA has started tracking this stat as well. (In the NBA, we need not be concerned with power plays.) Players in hockey and basketball accumulate more positive (and thus better) plus-minus numbers when their team is outscoring the opponent. This

A top down measure of an individual's production is a statistic built only upon the production of whole lineups.

is an example of a top down metric. A top down measure of an individual's production is a statistic built only upon the production of whole lineups.

Comparing the Strengths and Weaknesses

Since we are more familiar with the bottom up approach, let's begin by analyzing the strengths and weaknesses of this philosophy. A bottom up metric gives credit to the specific individual completing the task. If Michael Jordan pulls down the board, he gets the rebound in the stat book. Teams need players to score, pass and rebound. Clearly, a player posting 25 points a night in the NBA knows how to score. If you assembled a team with the 2012-13 leaders in each of points, rebounds and assists per game, your team would feature Carmelo Anthony, Dwight Howard and Rajon Rondo (an excellent trio). So, where might bottom up metrics lead us astray?

Basketball is the ultimate team sport. It is a fluid and fast-paced game. Each made basket or defensive stop is generated through the combination of a series of contributions from all players on the court. For example, four players can be playing fantastic defense, but if that last defender loses his man, it can result in an easy dunk for the opponent, nullifying the efforts of the other four.

The first problem with a bottom up metric is that it gives all of the credit to the end result. A star player could draw a double team and make a great pass crosscourt to set up a teammate who then dishes the ball to the post. The center finishes off the sequence with a thunderous dunk. That star whose reputation drew the double team and made the pass that started the sequence to the easy basket gets no credit in the box score. However, the other two, who possibly performed far easier tasks, earn an assist and two points, respectively.

The situation on the defensive side of the ball is even worse. A great defensive player may rarely allow a shot attempt by his opponent. Thus, it is difficult to accumulate blocked shots. Like a cornerback in the NFL that cannot get interceptions because quarterbacks choose not to throw to him, sometimes ability makes it difficult to accrue box score statistics. Also, a great defender might force a player to make a bad pass. The pass could sail out of bounds or end up stolen by another player. Either way, the initial defense goes unnoticed with traditional statistics.

We identified the first problem of bottom up metrics as giving too much credit to the end result. A very closely related second issue is that bottom up metrics are incomplete. Let us walk through an example. On the defensive side, we record blocked shots. However, a defender can significantly alter a shot without blocking it. As mentioned above, sometimes great defense prevents the shot altogether. In the next chapter, we will discuss new ways to measure interior defense that account for these other contributions.

The two problems of incompleteness and bias towards the end result are linked. Dwight Howard is a beast on the boards. The Celtics fans appreciate when Kevin Garnett puts his body on the line, boxes out and clears Dwight Howard out from under the hoop. The Celtics appreciate it even if the rebound does not land in Garnett's hands, but rather is easily scooped from the open space by Rajon Rondo. We could say the problem here is that the rebounding statistic gives too much credit to Rondo. We could also say that the set of bottom up metrics is incomplete in that we do not currently keep a record of great box outs.

Where bottom up metrics fall short, top down approaches excel. If a player sets a screen away from the ball freeing his man for the wide-open lay-up, plus-minus credits the scorer and the screen setter. Top down metrics are complete in the sense that they give credit and blame for all activities on the court.

Top down metrics have their flaws as well though. They suffer from a bias towards players that play on good teams. To demonstrate the bias, Table 1.1 presents the NBA's top 20 players in plus-minus from the 2012-13 season. The top six includes three from Oklahoma City and three from Miami. LeBron James and Dwyane Wade are great players. Led by these two, Miami has had several very successful seasons. Mario Chalmers is not a bad player, but no one would argue that he is a top five NBA talent. It is more likely that Chalmers has a great plus-minus because he plays with great players.

Table 1.1: Top 20 +/- for the NBA's 2012-13 Regular Season

Rank	Player	+/-	Rank	Player	+/-
1	LeBron James (MIA)	720	11	Tony Parker (SA)	448
2	Kevin Durant (OKC)	717	12	Kevin Martin (OKC)	441
3	Russell Westbrook (OKC)	631	13	Marc Gasol (MEM)	432
4	Dwyane Wade (MIA)	571	14	Chris Paul (LAC)	431
5	Mario Chalmers (MIA)	569	15	George Hill (IND)	417
6	Thebo Sefolosha (OKC)	505	16	Kendrick Perkins (OKC)	403
6	Mike Conley (MEM)	505	17	Roy Hibbert (IND)	390
8	Serge Ibaka (OKC)	490	18	Blake Griffin (LAC)	387
9	Chris Bosh (MIA)	477	19	Tiago Splitter (SA)	378
10	Tim Duncan (SA)	457	20	Lance Stephenson (IND)	377

The greatest weakness of a top down metric is that it does not give enough credit (or blame) to the end result. While Kobe Bryant is making a fantastic move to beat his man and score, his teammate could be flirting with the pretty lady in the first row or fighting with her boyfriend. Either way, the aloof teammate will get credit in plus-minus. This effect can work against a player as well. If a player is part of a particularly poor defensive club, his teammates' mistakes will reflect negatively on the individual's plus-minus. As Brian Burke once said (speaking about hockey), "If you play on a horseshit team, you're going to be a minus player. It's that simple. If you play a lot of minutes on a horseshit team, you're going to have a real bad plus-minus rating."[1] If a player makes a mistake (in a top down metric like plus-minus) all the players on the court suffer.

Perfect Complements

The greatest weakness of the bottom up approach is the lack of regard for positive and negative activities that are not recorded in the box score. A top down approach will take note of this impact. Top down stats are strong where bottom up metrics are flawed. A top down metric does not differentiate the types of contributions and may not give enough credit to the end result. Bottom up approaches are precise where top down measures are ignorant. Top down and bottom up approaches are perfect complements of each other.

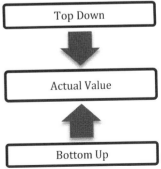

Ultimately, we want to identify the individual's value to his team. We picture the relationship between top down, bottom up and true value as in the diagram to the right. Both methods are working towards the same goal. Improvement in bottom up metrics comes mainly from developing and recording more advanced individual statistics, and we will discuss some of these in the next

---

[1] 2012 Hockey Analytics Panel at the Sloan Sports Analytics Conference. The quote is at 5:40 in the video at http://www.sloansportsconference.com/?p=4550.

chapter. Top down strategies improve as we develop better ways to account for and extract the team pull bias.

Both approaches are flawed, but have the good fortune of being flawed in distinct ways. For a given player, we can look at the top down number to see if good things are generally happening while he is on the floor. We can then look at his points, assists and rebounds, for example, and get a sense of how the individual is contributing to his team's successes or failures.

In the next chapter, we survey some of the best and most popular measures of an individual's ability. There will be examples of top down and bottom up methods. There will also be a hybrid of the two. In our survey, we will make note of how the different metrics try to account for the weaknesses in the respective approaches.

2

Surveying Player Value Metrics

It is naïve to think that a single statistic can tell us everything we need to know about a player. It is ignorant to believe that a single statistic can provide a ranking of the best players in the NBA. However, single statistics can approximate overall value. A single number that reasonably approximates total contribution has value. It can be an objective mechanism for identifying undervalued players. It can be an efficient means to group players into tiers based on performance and understand how many players in each tier the NBA currently employs. Constructing, viewing and evaluating attempts at a total evaluation of a player can also be quite enjoyable.

We will begin our study on player contribution by surveying some of the most well-known measures of a basketball player's value. We will be brief (whenever possible) in the descriptions. We will not spend a lot of time on motivating definitions and will leave out minor details. A more complete introduction to these metrics can be found in the original sources (cited throughout the chapter). In each case, the original source provides depth and insight on basketball statistics beyond the player value metric introduced here and is a must read for anyone interested in sports analytics.

Adjusted Plus-Minus

Plus-minus is the best-understood example of a top down metric. We have already discussed its major flaw. Plus-minus is heavily biased towards players that play with good teammates. If we can adjust plus-minus for the quality of teammates, perhaps the end product will be an unbiased result. Suppose we restrict ourselves to purely top down approaches. There is good reason for this restriction. Bottom up measures would rely on an incomplete portfolio of statistics recording individual accomplishments. Using a bottom up measure to assess the quality of teammates might undermine the goals of the top down approach. If we restrict ourselves to top down approaches, comparing team production with different lineups is the only way to distinguish teammates.

For example, suppose we notice that when LeBron James and Mario Chalmers are on the court together, the Miami Heat are productive. This is reflected in their plus-minus statistics, as they were both in the top 10 in the league in 2012-13. (See Table 1.1 for the top 20 players in plus-minus for the 2012-13 NBA season.) Additionally, the pair of James and Chalmers was plus 571 on the season, a higher total than any other pair from Miami (including the James and Wade pairing). With each of these pairings, our goal is to determine what percentage of the credit should be given to one player versus the other when they played together. One approach to differentiating each player's contribution is to see how Miami performed when LeBron played and Chalmers did not, and vice versa. Unfortunately, Chalmers played 1922 (92.9%) of his 2068 minutes with James. In the remaining 146 minutes (which is a small sample size), Chalmers was -2. James played a total of 2877 minutes, and he was +149 in the 955 minutes he played without Chalmers. We can reasonably conclude that James did not need Chalmers to be successful. While our good sense as fans of the game tells us that Chalmers benefited a great deal from James, the data on Chalmers without James is too limited to confidently support our intuition. Accounting for quality of teammates by looking at production when the teammates are not together is a fundamental idea behind the adjusted plus-minus statistic of Wayne Winston and Jeff Sagarin.[1]

Wayne Winston is well known in the basketball analytics community for his work with Mark Cuban and the Dallas Mavericks. A professor at Indiana University, Winston has a master's degree in mathematics from MIT and a Ph.D. in operations research from Yale. Sagarin's ratings for a variety of sports on USA Today are quite popular.[2] Sports analytics owes a great deal of gratitude to Winston and Sagarin for the many contributions they have made.

Here, we summarize the description of adjusted plus-minus as presented in Winston's book, *Mathletics*. Adjusted plus-minus is a value assigned to each player. The average player is given a value of 0. We interpret an adjusted plus-minus of 5 for player A to mean that player A is worth 5 points more than the average player for every 48 minutes of play. Here, the contributions from player A could be offensive or defensive. For example, player A may be worth an additional 2 points scored and -3 points against. To arrive at the adjusted plus-minus, Winston and Sagarin analyze time frames in games where there are no substitutions. For example, a time frame might look like the following.

Players on the Court

Home Team	Away Team
Kevin Garnett	Chris Bosh
Brandon Bass	Udonis Haslem
Paul Pierce	LeBron James
Avery Bradley	Dwyane Wade
Rajon Rondo	Mario Chalmers
Duration:	**5 Minutes**

To make the math simple, let's suppose each player is given the round (and not so accurate) adjusted plus-minus as labeled after his name.

Players on the Court

Home Team	+/-	Away Team	+/-
Kevin Garnett	10	Chris Bosh	5
Brandon Bass	0	Udonis Haslem	0
Paul Pierce	5	LeBron James	10
Avery Bradley	0	Dwyane Wade	10
Rajon Rondo	5	Mario Chalmers	5
Duration:		**5 Minutes**	

---

[1] Winston, W. *Mathletics, How Gamblers, Managers, and Sports Enthusiast Use Mathematics in Baseball, Basketball, and Football.* Princeton University Press, 2009.

[2] For Sagarin Computer Ratings, see http://usatoday30.usatoday.com/sports/sagarin.htm.

These numbers are points over average replacement per 48 minutes. In 48 minutes, we expect this Celtics lineup to be 10+5+5=20 points over replacement and the Heat lineup to be 5+10+10+5=30 points over replacement. Adjusted plus-minus also gives the home team 3.2 points per 48 minutes. In 5 minutes of play, we would expect the home Celtics to be (5/48)23.2=2.42 points over replacement and the away Heat to be (5/48)30=3.13 points over replacement. Therefore, the Heat lineup would be 3.13-2.42=.71 points better than the Celtics in those 5 minutes. For every time frame in the game between the Celtics and Heat, we can make a similar calculation. The goal is to have the actual end score as close to the projected score as possible. Label the difference of the projected home score minus the projected away score as PROJ and label the actual observed difference in the game as OBS. To determine adjusted plus-minus for all players in a season, Sagarin wrote a program called WINVAL that minimizes

$$\sum (PROJ - OBS)^2,$$

where the sum is taken over all games in the season. By squaring the errors (PROJ-OBS) in the projection, positive and negative mistakes cannot cancel each other out.

Players will earn high adjusted plus-minus numbers if they are consistently on the court for positive play (when their team is outscoring the opponent). With top down metrics, we determine who is largely responsible for the production by seeing whether that production typically follows the individual regardless of whom they are playing with and playing against. Adjusted plus-minus is fairly successful in this regard.

As we explained earlier, both top down and bottom up metrics have their strengths and weaknesses. What are the weaknesses of this specific system? For one, adjusted plus-minus is not very reliable for players that play limited time. Winston openly admits this in his book. Additionally, adjusted plus-minus lacks reliability when distinguishing between two players that play a significant proportion of their time together. Remember, purely top down procedures will use the time two individuals play without each other to determine which player is more responsible for the production. The smaller the sample of this time apart, the less confidence we should have in the difference in adjusted plus-minus between the two. In Chapter 7, we design a metric (Lineup Entropy) that specifically quantifies variation in teammates. Anyone interested in adjusted plus-minus or similar top down metrics should use our quantification of variation as a confidence check on the top down statistic. Players that play with a number of different teammates for significant periods of time have less opportunity to see their top down numbers pulled or inflated by a particularly good teammate or lineup.

The final problem with adjusted plus-minus is that it does not at all account for style of play or provide any mechanism by which it can be adjusted to account for style of play. We will see in Chapter 8 that certain teams are far more balanced on offense than others. Some teams share responsibility in scoring equally while others largely depend on a few individuals.

Player Efficiency Rating (a.k.a. PER)

John Hollinger designed Player Efficiency Rating (PER) as a means to aggregate the many ways a player can contribute to his team. He wanted a way to compare a 20 point and 5 rebound per game player with a 15 point and 10 rebound per game player. PER is a rate statistic and is meant to represent production per minute played. The formula is not simple. Still, we will reconstruct it here for comparison. PER is best classified as a bottom up procedure. As a means of combining typical box score stats, it is reasonable.

As we have already discussed, bottom up metrics are limited by the available statistics. Top down metrics such as adjusted plus-minus are not perfect either. To get the most complete picture of a player, we need to consider both top down and bottom up metrics. We need to see when and understand why the metrics agree and disagree with each other. We value a player that is an elite passer, defender and rebounder. In almost any system, this player will have value (at least when measured by plus-minus). However, an entire team of players that cannot shoot will not succeed, even if they are excellent in other respects. Typical box score stats have value. While top down metrics give the allure of being all encompassing, all teams need players who can actually accomplish the difficult tasks in the game. The value of PER is in its use of statistics that try to acknowledge the players who are accomplishing these tasks for their teams. We present PER as one of the better bottom up approaches to date. We will not justify or motivate each component in PER. We refer the reader to Hollinger's Pro Basketball Forecast for a complete presentation.[3]

Many of the inputs in the PER formula are more advanced metrics with some value in their own right. Hollinger defines Value of Possession (VOP) to be

$$VOP = \frac{(lgPTS)}{(lgFGA - lgORB + lgTO + (.44)lgFTA)}.$$

VOP takes as inputs league points (lgPTS), league field goal attempts (lgFGA), league offensive rebounds (lgORB), league turnovers (lgTO), and league free throw attempts (lgFTA). The denominator is an approximation of the offensive possessions in the league in the given time frame. If you are wondering where the .44 coefficient on lgFTA comes from, it is because players do not always take 2 free throws. Occasionally they take 3, but more often than 3, they attempt 1 (in a missed front end of a one-and-one or a basket-and-the-foul situation). Every possession ends in a field goal attempted, a turnover or a trip to the free throw line. Hollinger wants to consider the activity after an offensive rebound as a continuation of the same possession. So, ORB is subtracted in the denominator. Since the denominator closely approximates the league's possessions in a given time frame and the numerator is the total points scored, VOP is a close approximation of the average points scored per possession in the league.

Hollinger also defines a defensive rebound percentage (DRBP) for the league. It is the percentage of total rebounds for the league that are defensive rebounds (as opposed to offensive rebounds).

Before defining PER, Hollinger defines an unadjusted PER (uPER). The unadjusted number will then be adjusted for team pace and set to a scale where the league average is 15. Adjusting for pace is important as teams that play at a faster pace have more opportunity to accumulate stats such as rebounds and points scored.

The uPER formula is complicated. Do not expect to comprehend all aspects of the formula at first glance. Hollinger has written books detailing the motivation and construction of each component in PER. For those that are not interested in digging deeper into the mechanics of PER, simply understand that it is a bottom up metric that combines a player's contributions in what we call traditional box score metrics such as points, rebounds, assists, blocks and steals. In contrast to the construction of PER and some of the other metrics surveyed in this chapter, our individual

---

[3] Hollinger, J. *Pro Basketball Forecast 2004-05 Ed.* Potomac Books, 2004.

measures of player production will be simple. We believe that simplicity helps in the understanding of statistics and thus, the interpretation. **Those dismayed by the complexity of adjusted plus-minus and PER can take solace in knowing that simplicity is on the horizon.** Here is the formula for uPER.

$$
\begin{aligned}
uPER = {}& (1 \ / \ MP) \ [\ 3PT \ + \ (2/3) \ AST \\
& + (2 \ - \ factor \ (teamAST \ / \ teamFG)) \ FG \\
& + (FT \ * \ 0.5 \ (1 \ + \ (1 \ - \ (teamAST \ / \ teamFG)) \ + \ (2/3) \\
& * \ (teamAST \ / \ teamFG))) \\
& - VOP \ * \ TO \ - \ VOP \ * \ DRBP(FGA \ - \ FG) \\
& - VOP \ * \ 0.44(0.44 \ + \ (0.56 \ * \ DRBP))(FTA \ - \ FT) \\
& + VOP \ (1 \ - \ DRBP)(TRB \ - \ ORB) \\
& + VOP \ * \ DRBP \ * \ ORB \ + \ VOP \ * \ STL \\
& + VOP \ * \ DRBP \ * \ BLK \ - \ PF((lgFT \ / \ lgPF) \ - \ 0.44(lgFTA \ / \ lgPF)VOP)],
\end{aligned}
$$

where

$$
factor = (2/3) - (0.5 * (lgAST/lgFG))/(2 * (lgFG/lgFT)). \text{ [4]}
$$

The label "team" before a statistic denotes the team total, "lg" a league total, and otherwise the statistic is the individual's.

Since uPER has some team statistics as inputs, we might mistake it for a partially top down metric. The team statistics here are not at all dependent on the individual. The difference in uPER totals for different individuals on the same team comes only from the individual contributions and not any sort of team production while the individuals are on the court.

The unadjusted PER is then adjusted for team pace and the league average is set to 15. This is done by first multiplying uPER by the ratio of the league's average pace divided by the team's pace. Then that product is multiplied by 15 and divided by the league average uPER. We refer the reader to Hollinger's book for more details on the calculation of pace. Table 2.1 presents the top 20 in PER for the 2012-13 season (according to ESPN.com).[5]

Table 2.1: Top 20 PER for 2012-13 Regular Season

Rank	Player	PER	Rank	Player	PER
1	LeBron James	31.67	11	James Harden	23.00
2	Kevin Durant	28.35	12	Blake Griffin	22.44
3	Chris Paul	26.43	13	Amar'e Stoudemire	22.16
4	Carmelo Anthony	24.83	14	Andray Blatche	21.98
5	Brook Lopez	24.81	15	Anthony Davis	21.80
6	Tim Duncan	24.45	16	Anderson Varejeo	21.71
7	Dwyane Wade	24.04	17	Andre Drummond	21.69
8	Russell Westbrook	23.98	18	Kyrie Irving	21.51
9	Tony Parker	23.10	19	Stephen Curry	21.34
9	Kobe Bryant	23.10	20	Brandan Wright	21.03

---

[4] The formula can also be found at http://www.basketball-reference.com/about/per.html.

[5] http://insider.espn.go.com/nba/hollinger/statistics.

There have been criticisms of PER. To be fair, Hollinger admits, "that PER is not the final, once-and-for-all evaluation of a player's accomplishments during the season. This is especially true for defensive specialists—such as Quinton Ross and Jason Collins—who don't get many blocks or steals."[6] As we have already discussed, the available individual statistics are limited. As Hollinger is pointing out, this is especially true for defensive statistics. Bottom up approaches will improve as the statistics we gather improve.

There have also been concerns with the actual construction of PER. David Berri points out that if a player shoots above 30.4% on 2-point attempts, he can improve his PER simply by taking more shots (provided he continues to shoot above 30.4%).[7] Most players in the NBA shoot at a percentage above 30.4% on 2-pointers. The problem is that PER could be rewarding high quantities of poor quality shots. There are constraints in the game that prevent a poor shooter from taking too many shots. For one, his coach would likely bench him. Consequently, this may be more of a theoretical problem than a practical one. Also, quantity and quality are not independent. For example, the team's primary offensive option may be asked to take tough shots when the shot clock is winding down. Still, since PER is meant to be a rate statistic, Berri's criticism is valid.

Hollinger justifies his measures by saying the output is consistent with common perceptions of NBA production. In the same article where Berri points out that PER rewards volume of shots, he also criticizes Hollinger for not taking a particularly scientific approach.

> "Unfortunately, this is not the way science works. We do not begin with our beliefs, play with the numbers until our beliefs are confirmed, and then call it a day. Models are not evaluated in terms of whether they are consistent with what we believe, but in terms of their ability to explain what we purport to explain (and furthermore, provide predictive power)."

We do not believe that Hollinger was simply playing with coefficients until the output matched his perception. Still, the lack of a scientific approach is concerning. Our biases can easily sneak into the construction of a formula.

We see PER as an intelligent aggregation of largely box score statistics. As such, it will be limited in its ability to properly assess players that contribute in ways not captured by a box score. In particular, PER struggles to properly assess the defensive contributions of NBA players.

As we explained above, Berri wishes that PER had taken a more scientific approach. Berri's attempt at defining a metric with that approach is called Wins Produced.

Wins Produced

In *The Wages of Wins*, Berri, Martin Schmidt, and Stacey Brook define a measure of a player's value in Wins Produced.[8] There is a summary of how to calculate this number at The Wages of Wins

---

[6] Hollinger, J., "What is PER?" August 8, 2011.
<http://espn.go.com/nba/columns/story?columnist=hollinger_john&id=2850240, 2011>.
[7] "A Comment on the Player Efficiency Rating." *The Wages of Wins Journal.* November 17, 2006.
<http://wagesofwins.com/2006/11/17/a-comment-on-the-player-efficiency-rating/, 2006>.
[8] Berri, D., Schmidt, M. and Brook, S. *The Wages of Wins: Taking Measure of the Many Myths in Modern Sport.* Stanford Business Books, 2007.

Journal.[9] The summary in the Wages of Wins Journal is more up to date and slightly different than that presented in the original book. We will summarize the presentation in *The Wages of Wins*. Certainly, the general methodology in the calculation of Wins Produced has not changed, and thus the book's presentation is sufficient for an understanding of the metric's principles.

One of the main purposes of this section is to provide context for the development of our own metrics in later chapters. To truly understand what is new about our statistics, we need to know what has already been done. We will restrict ourselves to that which is necessary for context.

For Berri, et al., a team's offensive efficiency is their points scored per possession. A team's defensive efficiency is the points allowed by the team per opponent's possession. Basketball analysts Dean Oliver[10] and Hollinger both considered these metrics prior to *The Wages of Wins*. Berri, et al. take the analysis a step further and use a regression from efficiencies to team wins in their calculation. They found that team efficiencies explain 95% of wins. Furthermore, from the regression, they were able to determine a value (coefficient) in terms of wins to assign to each popular individual statistic (except assists). For example, a blocked shot is .021, a turnover is -0.034 and a 3-point field goal is .066 wins.

The next step in the calculation is to take a player's individual statistics, multiply each by the associated wins produced coefficient and sum the total value. If a player made ten 3-point shots, he would add 10(.066) wins or .666 wins. If the same player committed two turnovers, he would add 2(-.034)=-.068 wins. In other words, he would cost his team .068 wins. Call the sum of these values for a player his gross total.

Then Berri, et al. adjust the numbers dependent on the position the player plays. For each player, they calculate what we will call a net total by taking the individuals gross total and subtracting the league average gross total among players that played the same position. We will comment more on this adjustment at the end of this section.

They are not done yet. The goal of the next step is to have the eventual sum of the Wins Produced for the players equal to (or closely approximate) the sum of wins on the season in the NBA. To do this, they set each player's baseline or starting point from which to add or subtract value at the "league average wins per player." The average number of wins in the regular season in the NBA is 41 (since there are 82 games). Each team plays 5 players at a time. If we take 41 and divide by 5, we get 8.2. Thus, the average player playing all minutes is worth 8.2 wins. Berri, et al. take the net total and add 8.2 wins per 82 full games played prorated to the player's playing time. If a player played 50% of his team's time on court, we would add .5 times 8.2 or 4.1 wins to his net total.

To get unassisted wins produced (which is still not the final number), the authors adjust for team statistics. These are largely measures of defense that are not otherwise incorporated in the statistics. This includes, for example, opponents' turnovers that are not steals. Each of these stats can provide or take away value from a player. If a player's team is slightly better in these statistics than the average team in the league, the player will get a slight boost in value. This is a small adjustment and typically does not change the rankings of the players. Berri, et al. found a .99 correlation coefficient between the rankings with the team adjustment and those without. In summary, the effect of the team adjustment does not have enough of an impact to focus on it here. If you need further information on the team adjustments, see *The Wages of Wins*.

---

[9] "How to Calculate Wins Produced." *The Wages of Wins Journal*. Retrieved October 28, 2013. <http://wagesofwins.com/how-to-calculate-wins-produced/>.

[10] Oliver, D. *Basketball on Paper: Rules and Tool for Performance Analysis*. Potomac Books, 2004.

Finally, a separate analysis was done to determine that an assist is worth about .022 wins. They do not simply add .022 times the player's assists. Instead, the value is added in wins relative to the league average assists for the position. The final number is called Wins Produced (WP). Table 2.2 displays the top 20 in WP this past season.[11]

Table 2.2: Top 20 Wins Produced (WP) for 2012-13 Regular Season

Rank	Player	WP	Rank	Player	WP
1	Kevin Durant	20.6	11	Andrei Kirilenko	10.8
2	LeBron James	20.0	11	Jimmy Butler	10.8
3	Chris Paul	16.9	13	Kenneth Faried	10.7
4	James Harden	13.5	13	Thabo Sefolosha	10.7
5	Tyson Chandler	13.3	15	Shawn Marion	10.6
6	Serge Ibaka	11.5	16	Jose Calderon	10.5
7	Stephen Curry	11.4	16	Amir Johnson	10.5
7	Joakim Noah	11.4	18	Nicolas Batum	10.4
9	Mike Conley	11.2	18	Andre Iguodala	10.4
10	Dwyane Wade	11.1	20	Marc Gasol	10.2

Obviously, we have glossed over some of the details in the calculation. This metric certainly will not win any awards for simplicity. Except for the team adjustments (which were minimal), this metric is bottom up. Recall that one of the weaknesses of PER was that it lacked a truly scientific approach. WP was built upon a series of regressions. In this way, it had a scientific approach.

It is interesting that the construction of WP must adjust for position. Berri, et al. admit that without this adjustment, the rating would have a bias towards big men. Guards tend to handle the ball more and play on the perimeter. As a result, they accumulate more turnovers and fewer rebounds. They also take lower percentage shots on average.

Why bother with these guards that turn the ball over more and don't rebound as effectively? Why not field a team with all centers? That is not likely to succeed. Teams need players to play different positions. Why? Different positions have different responsibilities. Now, let's be clear. Certain power forwards can perform some of the tasks of a shooting guard, while certain guards can do the same for power forward. Perhaps the most spectacular example of position flexibility was demonstrated in the 1980 NBA finals. Kareem Abdul-Jabbar was out for Game 6 with a sprained ankle. Magic Johnson started at center in his place. One could argue that Magic played all five positions on the court that night. He played everywhere, and everywhere he played, he was magnificent. He finished with 42 points, 15 rebounds and 7 assists. The Lakers won the game and the championship. Magic could play anywhere on the court, but typically guards are responsible for perimeter play and perimeter defense, while centers patrol the interior. Teams need both to be successful. If a team cannot knock down a perimeter jumper, the opponent will pack their defense close to the lane, preventing drives and high percentage shots. If a team has stellar 3-point shooters, they can spread the floor, allowing a post player room to maneuver and finish around the hoop. In return, an effective post player can draw a double team freeing up an open jumper for the player on the wing. In a very tangible way, the post player deserves some credit for

---

[11] These stats are according to http://www.thenbageek.com/players, and were retrieved August 15, 2013.

the perimeter player's offensive production and vice versa. This sounds like an argument for a top down metric.

The greatest weakness of the Wins Produced model is the same weakness that troubles all bottom up metrics. The available individual statistics are incomplete. The fact that the authors had to adjust for position to eliminate the bias towards frontcourt players may reflect this problem. Perhaps we are not quantifying a way in which guards bring more value to the game (such as the effect of solid perimeter shooting on post scoring) or the strengths and weaknesses of post play both offensively and defensively. If there is one area where current bottom up metrics are particularly deplorable, it may be in measuring interior defense. At the end of this chapter, we discuss a new and particularly promising approach to quantifying a player's ability to defend the rim.

There are also likely flaws in the logic behind the construction of WP. When adding assists into the WP equation, a player only gets credit for his assists relative to the league average in assists for the position. The position adjustment in WP was due to the unadjusted version's bias towards big men. Again, this reflects the metric's inability to measure the guards' influence on the big man's production. In general, guards get more assists than their frontcourt teammates. An assist is by definition feeding a teammate the ball for a basket. The disparity in assists between backcourt and frontcourt players is a reflection of how backcourt players are contributing more to the offense of their forward and center teammates than these big men are giving back to the perimeter players. Maybe assists should not be adjusted for value relative to position before their inclusion in the player metric. One of the updates to the WP formula since the book was released was a revised adjustment for assists. It appears that the authors agreed with our assessment that the previous method for including assists was not appropriate.

Overall, we appreciate the scientific approach taken in the Wins Produced model. However, the series of adjustments after the initial calculation feel a bit like patchwork, plugging holes left by incomplete individual statistics. We like the initial methodology. As we continue to develop better measures of individual production (particularly on defense), we should go back and revise the set of inputs in the WP model. Eventually, certain adjustments such as the one for position may be unnecessary (or have minimal effect).

82Games.com Simple Ratings

We have talked about the strengths and weaknesses of top down and bottom up metrics. The weaknesses do not overlap. Bottom up and top down metrics complement each other well. Would it make sense to define a metric that takes as its main components a bottom up metric and a top down metric? This is precisely how the Simple Ratings at 82Games.com are defined.[12]

To be honest, we do not know exactly how Simple Ratings are calculated. The site explains, "This rating is actually more of a placeholder until the more sophisticated analysis we produce is made public." However, they do divulge that it has two main components. One of these components they refer to as a variant of PER. So, we will assume it is largely bottom up. The second component is on/off the court plus-minus. For on/off the court plus-minus, you take a player's plus-minus per 48 minutes of play and subtract the team's plus-minus per 48 minutes when the player is off the court. This net plus-minus number is sometimes referred to as a Roland Rating, named after Roland Beech (the founder of 82Games.com and now analytics expert for the Dallas Mavericks). Table 2.3 presents the top 20 in Simple Rating.

---

12 Sortable "Simple Ratings." Retrieved October 27, 2013.
<http://www.82games.com/1213/ROLRTG8.HTM>.

Table 2.3: Top 20 in Simple Rating (SR) for 2012-13 Regular Season

Rank	Player	SR	Rank	Player	SR
1	LeBron James	18.6	10	Mike Conley	8.5
2	Kevin Durant	15.8	12	Russell Westbrook	8.1
3	Dwyane Wade	12.2	13	Marc Gasol	7.6
4	Tim Duncan	10.6	14	Paul George	7.0
5	Chris Paul	10.1	15	James Harden	6.6
6	Brook Lopez	9.7	16	Vince Carter	6.4
7	Tony Parker	9.4	17	Jamal Crawford	6.1
8	Carmelo Anthony	9.3	18	Lamarcus Aldridge	6.0
9	David West	9.1	18	Paul Pierce	6.0
10	Kobe Bryant	8.5	18	Al Horford	6.0

Comparing PER, WP and SR

We have now covered three popular measures of player production. These were PER, WP and SR. Table 2.4 puts the top 20 of each metric side-by-side. There are differences in the goals of these three metrics. PER is meant to be rate statistic, while WP is measuring cumulative production. Still, PER, WP, and SR are all roughly approximating a player's ability. The metrics are (for the most part) in agreement at the top. James and Durant are in the top 2 in each. Paul is in the top 5, and Wade is in the top 10 across the board.

Table 2.4: Comparing the Top 20 in PER, WP and SR for 2012-13

Rank	PER	WP	SR
1	LeBron James	Kevin Durant	LeBron James
2	Kevin Durant	LeBron James	Kevin Durant
3	Chris Paul	Chris Paul	Dwyane Wade
4	Carmelo Anthony	James Harden	Tim Duncan
5	Brook Lopez	Tyson Chandler	Chris Paul
6	Tim Duncan	Serge Ibaka	Brook Lopez
7	Dwyane Wade	Stephen Curry	Tony Parker
8	Russell Westbrook	Joakim Noah	Carmelo Anthony
9	Tony Parker	Mike Conley	David West
10	Kobe Bryant	Dwyane Wade	Kobe Bryant
11	James Harden	Andrei Kirilenko	Mike Conley
12	Blake Griffin	Jimmy Butler	Russell Westbrook
13	Amar'e Stoudemire	Kenneth Faried	Marc Gasol
14	Andray Blatche	Thabo Sefolosha	Paul George
15	Anthony Davis	Shawn Marion	James Harden
16	Anderson Varejeo	Jose Calderon	Vince Carter
17	Andre Drummond	Amir Johnson	Jamal Crawford
18	Kyrie Irving	Nicolas Batum	Lamarcus Aldridge
19	Stephen Curry	Andre Iguodala	Paul Pierce
20	Brandan Wright	Marc Gasol	Al Horford

Where do the metrics differ? There are a number of players that are in the top 20 in WP that do not score well according to one or both of the other metrics. For example, Thabo Sefolosha is ranked 14th in WP. He is 210th among qualified players in PER. Sefolosha shoots a high percentage from the field (.481). He also does not attempt many shots (5.8 FGA in 27.5

minutes a game). Durant and Westbrook lead Oklahoma City's offense. It is reasonable to assume that Sefolosha benefits from the occasional easy bucket when the defense is overcommitting to the Thunder's big two. We do give Sefolosha credit for not taking bad shots, and for contributing in other ways. His efficiency on offense makes him an excellent role player. We will talk about the importance of role players in Chapter 9.

In Chapter 3, we will define a metric we call Offensive Efficiency. We believe looking at how efficiently players produce offense can be very telling. At the same time, we recognize the importance of quantity in scoring. Star players like Durant are often asked to take challenging shots. These situations can drain efficiency. In Chapter 3, we define Efficient Offensive Production, a measure of both quality and quantity of offense. WP is telling us that Sefolosha is very good at what he is asked to do for the Thunder. Given Sefolosha's limited field goal attempts, we cannot be certain that Sefolosha would be as valuable as the primary offensive option for an NBA team. WP may be overvaluing Sefolosha's efficiency given his limited quantity of offense. We are not the first to question WP in this way.[13]

Ultimately, no measure of player value is perfect. Each has its strengths and weaknesses. WP perhaps overrates offensive efficiency in instances where the player is not one of the first options in his team's offense. Hollinger admits that PER is not great at capturing defensive contributions from players that play good defense, but do not necessarily accumulate steals and blocks. Much of the limitations of these statistics stem from the limited set of data on the game that is currently available. We will define our own measure of player production (which we call Approximate Value) in Chapter 4. It will also not be perfect. We believe there are advantages to taking a variety of perspectives. The challenge is to understand each metric so that we can properly assess its strengths and weaknesses.

When developing a metric, one should prioritize simplicity. Specifically, increasing complexity in the formulation should always be justified by significant returns in the output. We believe we have been successful in striking the right balance in simplicity and accuracy with the metrics we define in Chapters 3 and 4. For more complicated stats, our classification as top down and bottom up helps us to truly understand where the measures are likely to be flawed.

New Measures of Interior Defense

At the 2013 MIT Sloan Sports Analytics Conference, Kirk Goldsberry presented his paper (coauthored with Eric Weiss) titled, "The Dwight Effect: A New Ensemble of Interior Defense Analytics for the NBA."[14] Goldsberry is an assistant professor at Michigan State University and a contributor at Grantland. He also maintains courtvisionanalytics.com.

Goldsberry uses SportVU data, which provides optically tracked data in the NBA.[15] At the time of the conference, it was reported that 15 NBA teams currently have SportVU technology in their arenas.

Goldsberry and Weiss looked at which interior defenders reduce their opponents' shooting percentage near the basket when the defender is around the rim. They found that Larry Sanders and Roy Hibbert were particularly strong in this regard. Then they looked at which interior

---

[13] "Jose Calderon: An Example of How Wins Produced Fails." *A Screaming Comes Across the Court.* October 15, 2012. <http://ascreamingcomesacrossthecourt.blogspot.com/2012/10/jose-calderon-example-of-how-wins.html>.

[14] The paper and presentation can be found at http://www.sloansportsconference.com/?p=10179.

[15] For more information on SportVU, see http://www.stats.com/sportvu/sportvu.asp.

defenders actually deter opponents from attempting shots near the hoop. Dwight Howard was the best in this category.

There are many ways in which an interior defender can impact opponents' shots. Blocked shots are only capturing a small piece of the total defensive contribution. They do not record the other ways in which defenders alter shots or account for situations when the center's presence under the hoop is enough to coax opponents into taking lower percentage perimeter shots. Goldsberry and Weiss introduce some new statistics that take a large leap forward in measuring the defensive value of a big man. We mention their work here because we believe that future bottom up metrics should incorporate these improved defensive metrics. This study also presents hope that spatial tracking technology will yield a whole new generation of individual statistics, improving the way we measure all contributions on the court. This in turn, could lead to a new generation of bottom up metrics that improve on WP and PER and provide a better overall measure of a player's value to his team.

Conclusions

When constructing or reviewing a player value metric, we should be mindful of whether the measure is top down or bottom up. The classification helps to identify strengths and weaknesses of the metric and assists in locating comparable statistics already in use. We have also shown that metrics can have components that are both top down and bottom up. There is some merit to this approach given that the strengths of the two methods complement each other well.

There are two obvious components to the game of basketball, offense and defense. Any statistic that hopes to capture all of a player's production or value must account for both sides of the ball. The two are very different endeavors. On the offensive side of the ball, teams can clear out for one player (as in LeBron James) to essentially go one-on-one to the hole. Having a few good 3-point shooters (such as Ray Allen and Mike Miller) on the floor to keep the defense from shading too far into the paint and double-teaming LeBron helps, but still the offensive activity can be very unbalanced. In fact, we will show in Chapter 8 that the best teams are the least balanced offensively. Meanwhile, strong defense must be a team effort. Players need to rotate to cover for each other. One missed assignment is two (or three) points for the opponent.

Red Auerbach once said, "Basketball is like war in that offensive weapons are developed first, and it always takes a while for the defense to catch up."[16] The same is true for offensive and defensive metrics. Whether it is the independent nature of the offensive game in the NBA or simply our affinity for scoring, current bottom up metrics for measuring offense are far superior to those measuring defense.

We have classified two approaches to measuring a player's value and recognize that combining the two could have merit. We understand that there are two components—offense, which is far better suited for bottom up approaches, and defense, where at this point, a top down methodology is almost essential. In Chapter 3, we introduce a new bottom up metric for player offense. In Chapter 4, we introduce a new top down measure of a player's defense. We then combine the two for an advanced metric defining a player's value. To our knowledge, it is the first measure of player value that is entirely bottom up in its evaluation of offensive contributions and solely top down in its evaluation of an individual's defense.

---

[16] Auerbach, R. BrainyQuote.com. Retrieved August 15, 2013.
<http://www.brainyquote.com/quotes/quotes/r/redauerbac100531.html>.

3

Measuring Efficient Offensive Production

Efficient – def. "Achieving maximum productivity with minimum wasted effort or expense."[1]

Allow us to make an obvious statement. The team that scores the most points wins the game. If you cannot score, you cannot win. However, there are several ways to score. Some players like Shaquille O'Neal and Hakeem Olajuwon dominated the post. LeBron James is at his best when he is driving to the hoop. Stephen Curry and Ray Allen are elite 3-point shooters. More important than how a player chooses to score is whether or not his scoring is efficient. This concept was the impetus behind our first original metric, Efficient Offensive Production (EOP).

No one ruins a pick-up game like the gunner (except maybe the guy who calls a foul on every play). To the gunner, every shot is a good shot, and passing is not an option. When he hits the court, it is bombs away from downtown with bricks clanging in every direction. Don't bother setting a screen away from the ball. By the time you set your feet, the gunner will be back peddling, holding the follow through and not at all discouraged by another air ball.

The NBA has its version of the gunner as well, although not typically sporting as many sweat bands. Some players in the NBA score more from quantity of shots than from quality of shots. More shots likely mean more points in the scorebook, but not necessarily so many wins in the standings.

Basketball has common measures of shooting efficiency. Those trading cards referenced earlier typically carry free throw, field goal, and three-point field goal percentages. NBA.com now carries effective field goal percentage, which is field goals plus 0.5 times three-pointers all divided by field goal attempts, or $(FG+.5(3P))/FGA$. This accounts for the difference in value between a three-point basket and a two-pointer. These metrics are decent, but we can do better. We want a more complete measure of offensive efficiency, one that goes beyond shooting percentages. We also want a metric that considers both quality and quantity of production.

We designed our measure of Efficient Offensive Production (EOP) under several assumptions. We will highlight these as we define the statistic, but it may also be useful to have them clearly delineated at the top. Here are our fundamental assumptions.

---

[1] *Oxford Dictionary.* Oxford Univerity Press. 2013

Assumptions in the EOP Design

1. Taking more shots does not necessarily help your team. Taking and making more shots does.
2. Prolific scorers may have to take tougher shots in general than their teammates. Quality is not independent of quantity.
3. There is value in passing off a difficult shot to set up a teammate.
4. A turnover is at least as bad as a missed field goal.
5. Offensive rebounds extend offensive possessions, and their value in doing so should be weighted appropriately against activities that end possessions (such as a turnover).

We will define our new statistic in three steps. First we design a measure of efficiency (a quality rating), which we will call Offensive Efficiency (OE). Then, we introduce Efficient Points Scored (EPS), which adjusts a player's points scored based on their efficiency. Finally, we use OE to adjust offensive production in both points and assists. This measure of both offensive quality and quantity is what we have titled Efficient Offensive Production (EOP).

Offensive Efficiency

Hollinger[2] and Oliver[3] both looked at a team's points per possession. The number of team possessions (POSS) can be approximated by the formula POSS=FGA+.45*FTA+TO-ORB. Points per possession (literally, PTS/POSS) is a good predictor of wins. In 2012-13, the team with the higher points per possession in each game won 97% of the time. This is not so surprising (or impressive) a result, however. The team with more points wins 100% of the time. In basketball, possessions alternate (for the most part). At the end of the game, both teams will have approximately the same number of possessions. In fact, in 2012-13, the average POSS was 94.79, and the average absolute value of the difference in POSS between the winner and loser was 2.17.

It may have not been surprising that points per possession at the team level was a good predictor of wins, but that does not mean that teams should not value individuals who produce offense efficiently. Our measure of Offensive Efficiency (OE) will be constructed in the spirit of what Hollinger and Oliver studied at the team level. OE will be the total number of successful offensive possessions the player was directly involved in divided by that player's total number of potential ends of possession. We believe efficient players make for efficient teams, and efficient teams win. We define OE to be

We believe efficient players make for efficient teams, and efficient teams win.

$$OE = \frac{FG + A}{FGA - ORB + A + TO}$$

Players score higher in OE by making shots, accruing assists and pulling down offensive rebounds. Players decrease their OE by missing shots and turning the ball over.

[2] Hollinger, J. *Pro Basketball Prospectus 2002 Ed*. Potomac Books, 2002.
[3] Oliver, D. *Basketball on Paper: Rules and Tools for Performance Analysis*. Potomac Books, 2004.

Before we go into great detail on the motivation for the OE formula, let us emphasize again that OE was designed to be a part of EPS and then EOP. OE does not account for the difference between a two-pointer and a three-pointer. It also does not give credit for free throws made. These will be components in the construction of both EPS and EOP.

One major difference between the team level efficiency designs of Hollinger and Oliver and our design for the individual is not accounting for total points scored. The other significant difference is that we include assists. At the team level, assists are redundant. Every time a team gets an assist, they also score points. If the team metric is already accounting for points scored or field goals made, it need not account for assists. This is not true for the individual. An individual cannot assist on his own hoop. At the player level, assists are an important part of the efficiency equation.

Motivation and Justification for the OE Formula

We could have made other choices in the construction of the OE formula. Since OE will be an important part of what we will do in later chapters in the book, let us take some time to properly motivate and justify the OE design.

The construction of OE began with a series of objectives. We first present these as a list. We will then detail why these goals were set and how OE meets them.

OE Objectives

1. OE should intelligently measure quality of offensive production. It should penalize the players that score points or otherwise fill a box score in ways that do not necessarily help their team win. In particular, it should give lower scores to "gunners" (players that miss a number of poor quality shots) and inefficient protectors of the ball (players that turn the ball over at high rate relative to their involvement in the offense).
2. The formula should be simple. We want it to have a minimal set of inputs or variables. In doing so, OE should identify the core statistics that reflect true efficiency.
3. An OE of 1.0 should correspond to 100 percent efficiency for the individual. The requirements to achieve an OE of 1.0 should be easily recognizable and appropriate given the desired interpretation.
4. Even though OE will not measure quantity of points scored, OE should be a good predictor of wins at the team level.

As stated earlier, we believe that how efficiently a player produces points is at least as important as how many points they score. This hypothesis will be confirmed when we get to objective 4 and study how accurately a team's OE can predict wins. With objective 1, we hoped to find a measure that accurately reflects individual offensive efficiency.

OE has field goals attempted (FGA) in the denominator. With each missed shot, a player's OE decreases. OE also has turnovers in the denominator. With each errant pass or dribble off the toes, the player's OE will decrease. OE is more intelligent than a formula that simply subtracts each missed shot or turnover from the sum score. Instead, the impact of a missed shot or turnover is dependent on the total production of the individual. Consider the following example where we determine the effect of an additional turnover on the OE score of two teammates. Our teammates are Mike and Scottie. On a given night, Mike and Scottie might produce the following stat line.

Scenario 1

Mike   Scottie
10 field goals made   4 field goals made
18 field goal attempts   6 field goal attempts
5 assists   2 assists
2 turnovers   2 turnovers
5 offensive rebounds   2 offensive rebounds
OE=.75   OE=.75

In Scenario 1, Mike and Scottie had the same OE. However, Mike was more involved in the offense. He took and made more shots and had more assists than Scottie. One offensive opportunity represents a smaller percentage of Mike's total involvement in the offense than Scottie's total involvement. An additional missed field goal or turnover should be less detrimental to Mike's OE than to Scottie's OE. If we had a formula that simply subtracted a constant value for every field goal missed or turnover, such a failure would have the same impact on the scores of Mike and Scottie. Let's see what an additional turnover does to each teammate's OE. An additional missed field goal would have the same effect.

Scenario 2

Mike   Scottie
10 field goals made   4 field goals made
18 field goal attempts   6 field goal attempts
5 assists   2 assists
3 turnovers   3 turnovers
5 offensive rebounds   2 offensive rebounds
OE=.71   OE=.67

As it should, the additional negative play had less of an effect on the teammate that was asked to do more in the offense. In summary, OE is a true rate statistic that is measuring the quality of offense produced by the individual. OE meets objective 1.

In Chapter 2, we surveyed some very complicated measures of player production in Player Efficiency Rating, adjusted plus-minus and Wins Produced. We even covered Simple Ratings, a metric that has become relatively popular despite its formula not having been released publicly. We are positive that a great deal of care was put into the design of each metric. All of these formulas are after a measure of total production. Yet, we see that different formulas can yield shockingly different assessments of the same player. We do not believe that one metric is correct while the others are wrong. They are all different and each gives a different insight into the value of a player. To properly use and get the most information out of each metric, we need to truly understand how each arrives at its output. Due to the complexity of the formulas for the metrics surveyed in Chapter 2, it can be very difficult to ascertain specifically why one metric might be fond of Andre Iguodala while another is not. How can we properly utilize the information provided if we do not completely understand how it is gathered, aggregated and presented?

We can only pull as much value out of a statistic as we can properly interpret the outputs. Understanding is the foundation of interpretation. Simplicity is the key to understanding. We see simplicity as of the utmost importance in analytics. It is the virtue above all other virtues. We wanted OE to be a simple and straightforward statistic. This allows OE to be understood and the output properly interpreted.

We know that teams should try to score more points per possession than their opponents, but how does a team do this? OE attempts to reflect a player's ability to make the most rudimentary decisions and rates their ability to succeed on the tasks required by those decisions. Does the player choose to take high percentage shots? Do they make those shots? Is the player a bit too daring in trying to thread the needle between two defenders, or are they creating space and making a crisp pass that assists on their teammate's bucket? Are the players shooting when they are supposed to be shooting and passing when passing is more advantageous?

OE is certainly simple, but to say it accurately assesses the player's ability to fulfill the core requirements of a successful offense, we need to know that OE is important at the team level. This will be addressed when we get to objective 4. After we demonstrate OE's ability to predict wins, we will have shown that OE meets objective 2.

Individually, OE has tremendous value, but OE has a higher calling. It was constructed as a means to adjust points and assists for efficiency. If a complete individual measure of offensive production recognizes that the end goal of every possession is points, then it must account for a player's ability to score. Unfortunately, points scored can be misleading. We have already outlined our belief that scoring more points does not necessarily help your team. Rather, the scoring must also be efficient. We believe that in meeting our first two objectives, OE properly assesses a player's efficiency in the team's offense. Ideally, we want to be able to think of OE as a percentage. If a player had an OE of .90, we might think of that player as performing at 90% of excellent efficiency. Then if they scored 30 points, we can easily adjust the points scored and arrive at .90 times 30 or 27 efficient points scored. In other words, we have a new total that is still roughly on a points scored scale and that reflects the actual value provided by the individual on offense. Now, if a player scores twenty points by "gunning," they might produce an OE of .2. We then can interpret their production as a contribution closer to .2 times 20 or 4 efficient points scored than the 20 points the box score reflects. Given the prevalence of points scored as a reported metric, we already have developed notions of what a 20 point performance or 30 point performance is worth. We wanted OE to be part of a formula that can alter points scored so that the total better reflects the actual value of the production.

It is difficult for a player to produce an OE above 1. In general, multiplying by OE will decrease points scored. To truly put the adjusted total on a points scored scale, we will multiply the adjusted total by a coefficient that brings the sum of the league's adjusted points back to the sum of the league's points that season. This will be described in greater detail later in the chapter when we define EPS.

Assuming a player has no offensive rebounds and at least one field goal made or assist, the player will have an OE of one if he did not miss a shot or turn the ball over. This is truly 100% efficiency. Each offensive rebound pulled down by the individual extends a possession and negates a potential end of possession for the team. A player can have an OE above one if his offensive rebounds exceed the sum of missed FG and TO. In other words, a player will be more than 100% efficient if he creates more possessions than he personally terminates without a made basket. The interpretation of OE as a percentage is reasonable, and the standard to reach an OE of one is clearly defined. Thus, OE meets objective 3.

A player will be more than 100% efficient if he creates more possessions than he personally terminates without a made basket.

To meet objective 4, we need to show that OE is important for teams. We will do this in two ways. First, we will look at the impact of an individual's OE on his team's success. Then, we will look at team OE as a predictor of wins.

Posting an OE above 1 is rare for a player asked to shoulder much of his team's offense. But, how rare is it? Even LeBron never posted an OE above 1. He did produce an OE above .70 18 times. By comparison, Kevin Durant and James Harden each achieved an OE above .70 five times. Kobe Bryant, Carmelo Anthony and Stephen Curry did it four, three and two times, respectively. **In the 37 games when one of the above leading scorers had an OE above .70, the teams were 37-0.**

Let us continue with some more anecdotal evidence. The Heat were 5-9 when LeBron had an OE below .58. They were 61-7 otherwise. The Lakers were 2-10 when Kobe had an OE below .42. They were 11-23 when his OE was below .52. They were 31-13 in games Kobe played and had an OE at or above .52. OE does not account for quantity of production, give credit for getting to the free throw line, nor differentiate between two and three point shots. It has stripped away those details (although they will return when we create our total measure of offensive production). Still, it appears that when a team's top scorer produces a high OE, the team is more likely to win, and a low OE tends to predict a loss. To test the degree to which the extremes of this simple statistic predict a team victory, we looked at players that were their team's leading scorer and averaged more than 16 points per game (PPG) in the 2012-13 season. We also restricted the list to those that qualify (played 70 games or scored at least 1400 points). The data is collected in Table 3.1.

Clearly, teams are doing a lot better when their leading scorer is efficient. The teams were 127-38 when the teams' leading scorers on the season had an OE greater than .7. The teams were 43-136 when the teams' leading scorers had an OE less than .4.

Some of the games that bucked the trend can be easily explained, further supporting the value of OE. On April 17, Pierce had an OE of .75, but only played 14 minutes and 21 seconds. This was one of the examples where Pierce had an OE above .7 and the Celtics lost. He scored 11 points on the night. Clearly, he was not the centerpiece of the offense. Remember that OE is just the first step of our metric for total offensive value, and in the next section, we will address these quantity related problems.

In Table 3.1, we looked at the effect of an individual's production at the extremes of OE on a team's win percentage (W%). We can also look at the importance of the team's OE. Team OE is defined in the same way as player OE, only we use the team's totals. Note that team OE is redundant in the numerator and denominator. As we discussed earlier, an assist at the team level will also be a field goal made. (This is not a problem on the individual level, because a player cannot assist on his own basket.) We only use team OE for justifying player OE. Since this is the sole purpose, we kept the team formula consistent with its individual counterpart.

The more efficient teams have been more successful. The top five teams in OE in the 2012-13 season all won at least 56 games. Two of these teams were the Miami Heat and San Antonio Spurs. These teams met for the NBA Championship. Chart 3.2 plots W% to team OE for 2012-13. Chart 3.3 presents W% to OE for the last ten seasons. Recall that OE does not account for team defense, a big part of winning basketball games. Three of the top six OE seasons in the last ten years came from Steve Nash's Phoenix Suns. Those teams had an efficient and high scoring offense, but lacked the team defense to win a title.

The top five teams in OE in the 2012-13 season all won at least 56 games.

Table 3.1: Individual OE and Team Record

Player	PPG	Team	Rec.	Rec. OE>.7	Rec. OE<0.4
Carmelo Anthony	28.7	NY	54-28	3-0	5-5
Kevin Durant	28.1	OKC	60-22	5-0	3-0
Kobe Bryant	27.3	LAL	45-37	4-0	1-6
LeBron James	26.8	MIA	66-16	18-0	0-0
James Harden	25.9	HOU	45-37	5-0	4-10
Stephen Curry	22.9	GSW	47-35	2-0	1-3
LeMarcus Aldridge	21.1	POR	33-49	4-6	1-5
Brook Lopez	19.4	BKN	49-33	13-5	4-5
Monta Ellis	19.2	MIL	38-44	2-1	3-8
Paul Pierce	18.6	BOS	41-40	2-2	2-6
DeMar Derozan*	18.1	TOR	34-48	1-1	4-14
Blake Griffin	18.0	LAC	56-26	25-3	1-2
Al Jefferson	17.8	UTA	43-39	11-2	1-5
Kemba Walker	17.7	CHA	21-61	3-2	0-4
Jrue Holliday	17.7	PHI	34-48	2-2	0-5
Josh Smith	17.5	ATL	44-38	7-1	2-8
Paul George	17.4	IND	49-32	1-0	5-9
DeMarcus Cousins	17.1	SAC	28-54	5-5	0-11
Ty Lawson	16.7	DEN	57-25	8-1	1-3
Luol Deng	16.5	CHI	45-37	3-1	3-9
Ryan Anderson	16.2	NOH	27-55	3-6	2-18
			TOTAL:	**127-38 (.770)**	**43-136 (.240)**

*Rudy Gay played for both Toronto and Memphis and averaged 18.2 PPG on the season. Since Gay did not play more than 42 games for either team, the next highest scorer for Toronto was chosen. The next highest scorer for Memphis averaged less than 16 PPG.

Chart 3.2: Team W% to OE for 2012-13

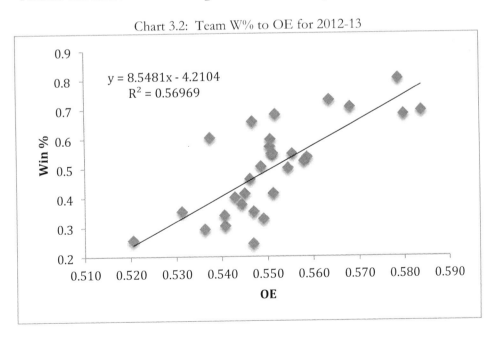

$$y = 8.5481x - 4.2104$$
$$R^2 = 0.56969$$

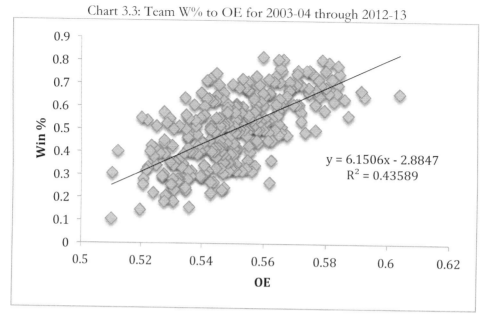

Chart 3.3: Team W% to OE for 2003-04 through 2012-13

$$y = 6.1506x - 2.8847$$
$$R^2 = 0.43589$$

How does OE compare as a predictor of win percentage to points scored alone? This is in some sense the ultimate test of the value of OE. Which is more important, how many points a team scores, or how efficiently they score? To answer this question, we turn to linear regressions. Simply put, regressions are a statistical tool used to measure the linear correlation between a set of inputs and its corresponding set of outputs. The R-squared term on a regression is a measure of how good a predictor those inputs are for the outputs. The value of R-squared ranges from 0 to 1. 0 represents no predictive power, and 1 would be a perfect linear correlation. In Chart 3.2, we see that the regression from OE to win percentage for 2012-13 had an R-squared of .57. The regression from points to win percentage for 2012-13 provides an R-squared of .36. When we look at the larger sample set of seasons from 2003-04 to 2012-13, OE to win percentage has an R-squared of .44. Points per game to win percentage provides an R-squared of .15. We use points per game because of the shortened season in 2011-12. Points to win percentage provides a worse R-squared of .05. In conclusion, we can safely say that a team's Offensive Efficiency is far more important than their total points scored.

One additional study we ran was to see if the team with the higher OE in a given game was more likely to emerge victorious. Of the 1229 games in the 2012-13 season, there were four games where the competing teams had equal OEs. Of the remaining 1225 games, the team with the higher OE won 1066. OE predicted the winner in 87% of those 2012-13 games. There were 677 games where the difference in OE was greater than .05. The team with the higher OE won 98% of those games. **OE has a simple formula that successfully assesses whether or not an individual has the basic decision making skills and efficiency in production required by winning teams in the NBA.**

OE is everything that we had hoped for. It meets all of our objectives. Could we have defined OE differently and still met the same four objectives? Is there a different OE formula that accomplishes our four objectives and more? The answer to both is *probably*. In fact, we strongly encourage the inclined reader to try and define his or her own measure of "offensive efficiency," to expand on our methodology and philosophy, and to find new insights beyond what we will present here. In this light, we will now present our thoughts as to what might be incorporated in other OE definitions.

First, recall that OE is designed to fit in two larger equations to be defined later. Those larger formulas, EPS and EOP, will incorporate quantity as well as quality of production. They will specifically account for the difference in a three-pointer and a two-pointer. They will also incorporate free throws made. Since these statistics will be included at the next steps, we will not address adding them to OE.

We believe that a very reasonable critique of OE is that it does not have attempted assists in the denominator. OE has field goals in the numerator and field goals attempted in the denominator. It has assists in the numerator. Why does it not have attempted assists in the denominator? Unfortunately, complete passing data is hard to come by. We simply do not have a record of passes made or even passes made immediately prior to a shot attempt. This data is available with SportVU tracking software. We do recommend that those with access to passing data consider running a more detailed OE that includes some measure of attempted assists. However, if we were to use the data through SportVU, we would encounter a new problem. We want to be able to calculate OE back several decades. As far as we know, even SportVU could not provide this. We simply did not have the option of using a reasonable approximation of attempted assists.

The other problem with attempted assists is that it may unfairly penalize players whose teammates make poor choices. If Carmelo Anthony takes a bad shot, we should not necessarily penalize Raymond Felton for passing him the ball. In a model with attempted assists, this could be seen as a failed attempt for Felton.

OE among the Elite

Table 3.4 presents the top 20 players in total points in 2012-13 and their season OE. Notice how particularly efficient James was given his high total of points produced. In contrast, Carmelo produced a particularly low OE. The Heat pair of James and Wade was very efficient, while the Knicks pair of Anthony and Smith had two of the lowest OE scores on the board. The league OE was .55. We see that some players in Table 3.4 were more efficient than the league average, while others were not. Remember that one of our assumptions at the beginning of this chapter was that quality and quantity of offense are not independent. The more a player is asked to do, the harder it becomes to produce with high efficiency. If a player had an OE below the league average, it does not imply that he was a below average offensive player.

Table 3.4: 2012-13 Top 20 in Total Points with OE

Rank	Player	Pts	OE	Rank	Player	Pts	OE
1	Kevin Durant	2280	0.54	11	DeMar DeRozan	1485	0.49
2	Kobe Bryant	2133	0.53	12	Deron Williams	1476	0.57
3	LeBron James	2036	0.65	13	Dwyane Wade	1463	0.59
4	James Harden	2023	0.51	14	David Lee	1459	0.62
5	Carmelo Anthony	1920	0.49	15	Kemba Walker	1455	0.54
6	Russell Westbrook	1903	0.56	16	J.R. Smith	1446	0.48
7	Stephen Curry	1786	0.55	17	Blake Griffin	1440	0.64
8	Monta Ellis	1577	0.51	18	Brook Lopez	1437	0.59
9	Damian Lillard	1562	0.54	19	Paul Pierce	1430	0.52
10	LaMarcus Aldridge	1560	0.56	20	Brandon Jennings	1397	0.53

We are always trying to compare today's players to those in past generations. In Table 3.5, we see that the range of OE among the top 20 scorers in 1991-92 is comparable to that in 2012-13. Jordan was efficient, posting an OE of .59, a number higher than Durant and Bryant last year, but short of LeBron.

Table 3.5: 1991-92 Top 20 in Total Points with OE

Rank	Player	Pts	OE	Rank	Player	Pts	OE
1	Michael Jordan	2404	0.59	11	Reggie Lewis	1703	0.55
2	Karl Malone	2272	0.58	12	Reggie Miller	1695	0.58
3	Chris Mullin	2074	0.57	13	Drazen Petrovic	1691	0.55
4	Patrick Ewing	1970	0.57	14	Ricky Pierce	1690	0.52
5	Clyde Drexler	1903	0.58	15	Jeff Malone	1639	0.54
6	Tim Hardaway	1893	0.60	16	Joe Dumars	1635	0.54
7	Mitch Richmond	1803	0.53	17	Jeff Hornacek	1632	0.61
8	Glen Rice	1765	0.51	18	Kendall Gill	1622	0.56
9	Charles Barkley	1730	0.67	19	Danny Manning	1579	0.64
10	Scottie Pippen	1720	0.63	20	David Robinson	1578	0.66

At this point, we are not noticing any extreme bias in OE towards a particular position or style of play. If anything, players that do a lot of their scoring around the rim with high percentage shots score a little better than the rest. Blake Griffin and David Robinson are examples of this.

We decided to go back and look at the career of perhaps the greatest all-around offensive talent of all-time, Magic Johnson. Table 3.6 presents the season and career OE for Magic. The highest OE among the players in Table 3.4 was .65. That belonged to LeBron James. Magic had an OE at or above .65 for the first 12 years of his career. It was only when he came out of retirement at age 36 in 1995-96 that he finally produced an OE below .65. That year, his OE was .62. Even then, he was more efficient than most of the elite scorers from 2012-13 and 1991-92.

Table 3.6: Magic Johnson Career OE

Season	Age	FG%	AST	PTS	OE
1979-80	20	0.530	563	1387	0.65
1980-81	21	0.532	317	798	0.66
1981-82	22	0.537	743	1447	0.72
1982-83	23	0.548	829	1326	0.72
1983-84	24	0.565	875	1178	0.71
1984-85	25	0.561	968	1406	0.71
1985-86	26	0.526	907	1354	0.69
1986-87	27	0.522	977	1909	0.67
1987-88	28	0.492	858	1408	0.66
1988-89	29	0.509	988	1730	0.67
1989-90	30	0.480	907	1765	0.66
1990-91	31	0.477	989	1531	0.67
1995-96	36	0.466	220	468	0.62
Career		0.520	10141	17707	0.68

Magic saw an improvement in OE in each of his first three seasons. The OE trend that we see in Magic's career is typical. Young players can score, but even the great ones tend to be less efficient in their first few seasons. Larry Bird had an OE of .57 in his first two seasons. He then had a string of seven seasons where he posted an OE of .60 or better. Unfortunately, not all players, and not all perceived superstars improve in this way. Chart 3.7 tracks the first ten seasons of LeBron and Carmelo. Carmelo's two lowest season OE scores were in his first two seasons. However, the improvement since then has been minimal, and in recent seasons, his OE has regressed to numbers comparable to his rookie season. Carmelo was always a less efficient offensive player than LeBron and the margin is growing. LeBron has worked hard on improving his jump shot. The results of his hard work are evident in his improved OE. His jump shot was on display in game seven of the 2012-13 NBA finals. The San Antonio Spurs backed off of LeBron on defense, daring LeBron to shoot and taking away his drive. LeBron knocked down five three-pointers. The Heat won the game and series.

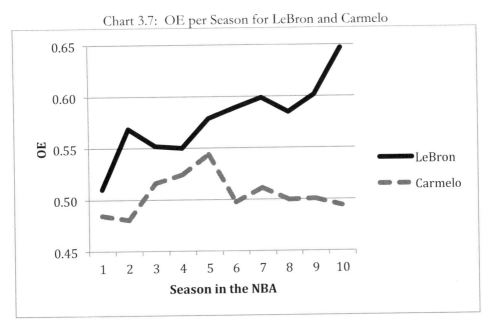

Chart 3.7: OE per Season for LeBron and Carmelo

The trends up in OE are another reminder that players develop. A big part of constructing an NBA team is to find and sign players that will improve. We will focus on player improvement in Chapter 6.

OE is just the first step in our new measure of Efficient Offensive Production. It is built on simple and readily available box score statistics. This bottom up metric uses these statistics in a new way and yields new information. The still simple formula is distinguishing what appear to be two prolific scorers in LeBron and Carmelo. The latter is far less efficient than the former. We would think that teams looking to acquire players that are entering their prime would be interested in the OE career trends. A player's trend up can reflect maturity and a good work ethic, traits that teams want in players and that are difficult to quantify.

Efficient Points Scored (EPS)

Before we define EOP, we stop at a sort of halfway point between OE and EOP, a metric we call Efficient Points Scored (EPS). To calculate EPS, we adjust points scored based on the individual's OE. The difference between EOP and EPS is that EOP will also account for quantity of assists.

In Game 1 of the 2012-13 NBA finals, Boris Diaw came off of the bench for the Spurs. He played nine minutes, made one basket in one attempt, had one assist, grabbed no offensive rebounds, and committed no turnovers. His OE was 1.0. By comparison, Tony Parker played 40 minutes, went 9 for 18 from the floor, had six assists, and committed no turnovers. He also had no offensive rebounds. Parker's OE on that night was .63. Clearly, Parker provided more offense to his team than Diaw. OE measures how efficiently the offense was produced, but pays no attention to the quantity of production.

Teams need players to score more than 2 points a night and play more than nine minutes. The teams' top scorers must play when fatigued and typically draw the opponent's best defenders. Top scorers sometimes have to take difficult shots as the shot clock is running down or at the end of the game. For example, see Tony Parker's desperation bank shot at the end of Game 1 in those same 2012-13 NBA finals. To get a true measure of a player's value to his team's offense, we have to incorporate the amount of production a player provides.

OE did not give credit for free throws. It also counted all field goals equally. We want a more complete measure of offensive production. Points scored counts free-throws, 2 point field goals and 3-pointers for what they are worth to the team. Let's not look beyond the obvious choice of statistic. We will use points scored. We have already seen that players score in different ways, and some far more efficiently than others. We want a metric that rewards efficient production. The more efficient the scorer, the higher his OE will be. So, we combine OE and points in the simplest manner that reflects the value of each. We take the product of the two. Besides the product of OE and points, there will be one more factor in the calculation of EPS. This last factor (labeled F) will be the same for all players in a given season. It does not affect rankings in EPS within a season. The factor's sole purpose is to place the output on a points scored scale. We define Efficient Points Scored (EPS) to be

$$EPS = F * OE * Points$$

Let us define and motivate this factor F. In basketball, football, and baseball, we have great examples of advanced statistics that are used to globally evaluate each sport's players. Some generally understood statistics that come to mind are QBR (a rating that measures the performance of a quarterback in football), OPS (the sum of slugging percentage and on-base percentage for a batter in baseball), and in basketball, the already discussed PER. All of these metrics produce numbers on scales that initially are hard to comprehend. The results are unfamiliar. The difficulty in interpreting OPS prompted Bill James[4] to put the outputs on a sort of Likert Scale[5]. Here, he attached classifications like "average" and "great" to ranges of outputs. We do not want to have to group a performance of 25 efficient points scored and 30 efficient points scored into a single category titled "great." We already understand the points scored scale. If we are going to adjust

---

[4] James, B. "The 96 Families of Hitters." *The Bill James Gold Mine.* 2009.
[5] Likert R. "A Technique for the Measurement of Attitudes." New York: Archives of Psychology. 1932.

points scored for efficiency, would it not make sense to kick back a number that could be placed on the standard points scored scale? With the adjustment F, the sum of the EPS scores for all players in a given season will be equal to the sum of the points scored in that season. We define the factor F as follows.

$$F = \frac{League\ Points}{\sum(OE * points)}$$

where the denominator sums each individual's points times OE for the given season.

EPS is points adjusted for the player's efficiency. Table 3.8 displays the top 20 in EPS for the 2012-13 season. When compared to points scored alone, there were both perimeter players and post players that saw significant improvements in ranking after the adjustment. Al Horford was ranked 32nd in the league in points scored and 14th in EPS. Chris Paul was ranked 42nd in points scored and 20th in EPS. Going the other direction, J.R. Smith was ranked 16th in the league in points and 38th in EPS.

EPS is points adjusted for the player's efficiency.

Table 3.8: Top 20 in EPS for 2012-13 Regular Season

Rank	Player	Pts	EPS	Rank	Player	Pts	EPS
1	LeBron James	2036	2340	11	Dwyane Wade	1463	1541
2	Kevin Durant	2280	2193	12	Deron Williams	1476	1503
3	Kobe Bryant	2133	2001	13	Brook Lopez	1437	1503
4	Russell Westbrook	1903	1878	14	Al Horford	1289	1492
5	James Harden	2023	1846	15	Damian Lillard	1562	1489
6	Stephen Curry	1786	1753	16	Dwight Howard	1296	1487
7	Carmelo Anthony	1920	1684	17	Tony Parker	1341	1473
8	Blake Griffin	1440	1636	18	Monta Ellis	1577	1430
9	David Lee	1459	1599	19	Al Jefferson	1391	1420
10	LaMarcus Aldridge	1560	1556	20	Chris Paul	1186	1400

As we did with OE, we decided to look back at a past season's leaders in EPS. Table 3.9 displays the top 20 for the 1979-80 season. Boston Celtics forward Cedric Maxwell received the biggest bump up the ranking with the OE adjustment. He had 1350 points on the season, but his OE of .73 rated well compared to his peers. Maxwell shot over 60% from the field that year. He was known for being a solid low post scorer. Since Maxwell produced most of his scoring near the hoop, it is not surprising that he was an efficient scorer. In the next section, we incorporate quantity of assists in our measure of offensive production. Maxwell was a prolific and efficient scorer. He did not, however, accumulate a great deal of assists. He is an example of a player that ranks higher in EPS than EOP.

Over the last few decades, the league average points per game has changed dramatically. Between the 1977-78 and 2012-13 seasons, the average points per game for a team has ranged from around 91 to 110. It would be naïve to compare the EPS of a player in 2012-13 to that of a player in 1979-80 without accounting for the difference in scoring between the two eras. After we define EOP in the next section, we will discuss methods for factoring out the differences in scoring rates in the different years for our offensive metrics.

Table 3.9: Top 20 in EPS for 1979-1980 Regular Season

Rank	Player	Pts	EPS	Rank	Player	Pts	EPS
1	George Gervin	2585	2430	11	Gus Williams	1816	1787
2	Moses Malone	2119	2368	12	Otis Birdsong	1858	1787
3	Kareem Abdul-Jabbar	2034	2266	13	Ray Williams	1714	1764
4	Julius Erving	2100	2113	14	Mike Mitchell	1820	1762
5	Adrian Dantley	1903	1998	15	Jamaal Wilkes	1644	1736
6	Dan Issel	1951	1987	16	Cedric Maxwell	1350	1701
7	World B. Free	2055	1859	17	Larry Bird	1745	1696
8	Marques Johnson	1671	1832	18	Walter Davis	1613	1650
9	Bill Cartwright	1781	1805	19	Reggie Theus	1660	1630
10	Paul Westphal	1792	1802	20	Elvin Hayes	1859	1623

Efficient Offensive Production

We are now ready to define our complete measure of offensive production. (Defense will be addressed in the next chapter.) We have a measure of efficiency. We have seen how this can be used to modify a player's point total. Lastly, we want to include the player's quantity of assists in the calculation.

Before we can include assists in our metric, we are faced with the following perplexing question. What is the value of an assist relative to a point scored? Not all assists are equal. In his career, Steve Nash was excellent at setting up his teammates for easy looks. Nash deserves a great deal of the credit on the baskets in which he assists. LeBron James might draw double or triple-team coverage while driving to the hoop. James has the ability to pass out of the triple-team and find an open teammate such as Udonis Haslem slashing to the hoop. James' historical ability as a prolific scorer drew the extra defenders and created the open space for Haslem. Here, it is LeBron that created the scoring opportunity. These are situations where the assist was the better half of the scoring equation. There is also the other side of the coin. While standing a yard behind the three-point line, Westbrook might toss an easy pass to Durant on the wing. Even with a defender in his face, Durant can pull up and knock down the three. In this hypothetical scenario, Westbrook did very little to assist in Durant's offense.

Let's begin with the undeniable facts. First, an assist is not worth more than the points scored as a result of that pass. Second, there are instances when the assist deserves at least some (if not all) of the credit for the score. Finally, there are instances when the assist deserves very little to no credit for the score. All of this tells us that the average assist to a two-point field goal is worth somewhere strictly between 0 and 2 points.

Ideally, we would want a rating attached to each assist. A high rating would tell us the assist was something special. A low rating would tell us that the assist was not the source of the offense. This does not exist, and if it did, it would almost certainly be highly subjective.

Thanks to Hoopdata.com, we do know where the bucket resulting from the assist was scored. They have detailed passing data that breaks down whether or not the score occurred at the rim, within 10 feet, between 10 and 15 feet, between 15 and 23 feet, and when it was a 3-point field goal.

Shots around the rim are the highest percentage shots. These are precisely the type of shot that great playmakers look to create for all of their teammates. Certainly, LeBron might look to kick out to Ray Allen for an open three, but this is only a good pass because Ray Allen is an excellent 3-point shooter. If it were Udonis Haslem on the perimeter, the pass would be worthless. Even on a good assist to a 3-point shot, a lot of the responsibility of the basket has to go to the shooter. In contrast, just about any NBA player can finish around the hoop. It is far more likely that the assist deserves more credit on the pass to the shot at the hoop than to the one on the perimeter. Furthermore, the greatest limitation of EPS as a measure of offensive production is that it gives too much credit to the players that score around the rim and not enough credit to the teammates that set-up the dunks and layups. While not every assist on a bucket near the rim was a magnificent pass, and there are certainly valuable assists to scores elsewhere, our belief remains that the best approximation of the percentage of assists that are meaningful should be tied to the percentage of assists that lead to the high percentage shots around the rim. If we create EOP on this assumption, it overcomes the greatest limitation of EPS.

According to Hoopdata.com, about 38% of assists in the 2012-13 season led to a basket at the rim. We will give playmakers full credit (2 points) for these 38% of assists. So, we will think of a player with some number N assists as having created 2*.38*N points. For example, if a player had 100 assists, we would say he created 2*.38*100=76 points.

By saying 38% of every player's assists are meaningful, we are making a high level assumption. While we have detailed assist data for players in recent seasons, we would not be able to use individual percentages of assists to buckets at the rim for all players going back several decades. We like the simplicity of the high level assumption; however, we chose not to be more detailed, because the historical data to do so simply does not exist.

FUTURE DIRECTION

We believe that in the next five years or so, great advances will be made towards a better understanding of how teams play, the value of getting players involved in the offense, and specifically the value of good passing. We will present some of our ideas on these topics in Chapters 7 and 8. Thanks to technology such as SportVU spatial tracking software, NBA teams are now recording detailed data on player passing and positioning on the floor. New metrics will be developed to classify shapes of defense. From this data and these new metrics, we will learn how particular players change the shapes of defenses and create space for their teammates. After all of this work, we will have a good approximation of the value of an assist relative to a point. We will also have more years of passing data particular to each individual. Since the analytics industry is close to significant advances in this area, any present study on the value of an assist will quickly become outdated. We settle for the simple coefficient of .76 and predict that we will be able to revisit this topic armed with far more information in the near future.

As we did with EPS, we want EOP to be output on the points scored scale. This will require multiplying all outcomes by a constant. Before that step, we define Raw EOP to be

$$RAW\ EOP = (.76 * Assists + Points) * OE$$

So that the sum of player EOP in a given season equals the points scored in that season, we define

$$EOP = G * (RAW\ EOP)$$

where G is a factor defined as follows.

$$G = \frac{League\ Points}{\sum(OE * (points + .76 * assists))}$$

The factor G is defined analogously to the factor F in the EPS formula. In the denominator of G, we are summing the RAW EOP over all individuals that played in the given season. For a given season, the factor G is constant. Therefore, the player rankings according to EOP are the same as the rankings according to Raw EOP.

The factor G will change with the different scoring rates in different seasons. We ran the totals for G in the 1977-78 through 2012-13 seasons. Table 3.10 displays this data in addition to the points per game and assists per game for each team in the respective seasons. We have also included the league's OE for the season (LOE). Not surprisingly, the highest scoring seasons were also the years with the highest efficiency.

Table 3.10: League OE and Coefficient from 1977-78 through 2012-13

Season	PPG	APG	LOE	G	Season	PPG	APG	LOE	G
1977-78	108.5	25.0	0.56	1.51	1995-96	99.5	22.7	0.56	1.49
1978-79	110.3	25.8	0.57	1.47	1996-97	96.9	22.0	0.56	1.50
1979-80	109.3	25.8	0.58	1.45	1997-98	95.6	22.0	0.56	1.50
1980-81	108.1	25.5	0.58	1.45	1998-99	91.6	20.7	0.54	1.54
1981-82	108.6	25.2	0.59	1.44	1999-00	97.5	22.3	0.55	1.52
1982-83	108.5	25.9	0.58	1.45	2000-01	94.8	21.8	0.55	1.53
1983-84	110.1	26.2	0.59	1.43	2001-02	95.5	21.9	0.55	1.52
1984-85	110.8	26.3	0.59	1.43	2002-03	95.1	21.5	0.54	1.54
1985-86	110.2	26.0	0.58	1.44	2003-04	93.4	21.3	0.54	1.54
1986-87	109.9	26.0	0.59	1.43	2004-05	97.2	21.3	0.55	1.53
1987-88	108.2	25.8	0.59	1.43	2005-06	97.0	20.6	0.55	1.53
1988-89	109.2	25.6	0.58	1.45	2006-07	98.7	21.3	0.55	1.52
1989-90	107.0	24.9	0.58	1.45	2007-08	99.9	21.8	0.56	1.50
1990-91	106.3	24.7	0.58	1.44	2008-09	100.0	21.0	0.55	1.52
1991-92	105.3	24.5	0.58	1.44	2009-10	100.4	21.2	0.56	1.52
1992-93	105.3	24.7	0.58	1.44	2010-11	99.6	21.5	0.55	1.52
1993-94	101.5	24.4	0.57	1.44	2011-12	96.3	21.0	0.54	1.54
1994-95	101.4	23.4	0.57	1.47	2012-13	98.1	22.1	0.55	1.52

Table 3.11 presents the Top 20 in EOP for the 2012-13 season. There are significant differences in rankings according to EOP and points scored. Chris Paul was ranked 42nd in points scored, but was ranked 7th in the league in EOP. Greivis Vasquez was ranked 58th in points scored and was ranked 18th in EOP. EOP directly accounts for assists. Not surprisingly, it ranks highly the prolific passing point guards.

It appears the points guards will in general rate more highly in EOP than big men. Obviously, the average starting point guard in the NBA generates more offense than the typical starting big man. Many of the league's centers earn their playing time through stellar interior defense. In the next chapter, we will define a defensive measure that will accurately assess these contributions.

Table 3.11: Top 20 in EOP for 2012-13 Regular Season

Rank	Player	Pts	EOP	Rank	Player	Pts	EOP
1	LeBron James	2036	2408	11	Damian Lillard	1562	1599
2	Kevin Durant	2280	2105	12	Jrue Holiday	1383	1571
3	Kobe Bryant	2133	1994	13	David Lee	1459	1563
4	Russell Westbrook	1903	1992	14	Dwyane Wade	1463	1556
5	James Harden	2023	1845	15	Carmelo Anthony	1920	1535
6	Stephen Curry	1786	1840	16	Monta Ellis	1577	1513
7	Chris Paul	1186	1714	17	Kemba Walker	1455	1477
8	Deron Williams	1476	1682	18	Greivis Vasquez	1083	1459
9	Blake Griffin	1440	1616	19	Al Horford	1289	1454
10	Tony Parker	1341	1613	20	LaMarcus Aldridge	1560	1453

Al Horford was the only true center to make the top 20 in EOP in 2012-13. EOP recognizes the offensive contributions from centers when they exist. Let us return to the 1979-80 season, where center Kareem Abdul-Jabbar ranked third overall in EPS. Table 3.12 lists the top 20 in EOP for the 1979-80 season. Three centers (Kareem, Moses Malone and Dan Issell) were ranked 1st, 3rd and 7th respectively.

Previously, we specifically mentioned the EPS of Cedric Maxwell. Maxwell was rated just above his teammate, Bird, in EPS in 1979-80. We suggested that Maxwell did most of his damage around the rim. Bird was ranked 16th in EOP for that season, while Maxwell falls out of the top 20. Bird's higher ranking in EOP demonstrates that Bird created more offense for his teammates than Maxwell.

Table 3.12: Top 20 in EOP for 1979-80 Regular Season

Rank	Player	Pts	EOP	Rank	Player	Pts	EOP
1	Kareem Abdul-Jabbar	2034	2182	11	Micheal Ray Richardson	1254	1740
2	George Gervin	2585	2178	12	World B. Free	2055	1737
3	Moses Malone	2119	2109	13	Norm Nixon	1446	1706
4	Julius Erving	2100	2017	14	Reggie Theus	1660	1704
5	Ray Williams	1714	1831	15	Magic Johnson	1387	1704
6	Adrian Dantley	1903	1819	16	Larry Bird	1745	1666
7	Dan Issel	1951	1810	17	Jamaal Wilkes	1644	1638
8	Paul Westphal	1792	1793	18	Otis Birdsong	1858	1636
9	Gus Williams	1816	1763	19	Bill Cartwright	1781	1634
10	Marques Johnson	1671	1743	20	Walter Davis	1613	1618

Today's NBA does not feature the superstar offensive centers that the game featured in 1979-80. Still, teams need to play centers, and having a center that is good offensively relative to others for the position can have a great deal of value for a team. We will revisit this idea later in the chapter when we consider EOP relative to the position. For now, we present the top 20 centers in EOP for 2012-13.

The most interesting case in Table 3.13 is that of Tyson Chandler. Chandler only put up 689 points in 2012-13. He also only had 62 assists. His high ranking among centers is due to his high OE. Chandler's OE is largely due to his field goal percentage of .640 and his ability to grab offensive rebounds.

Table 3.13: Top 20 Centers in EOP for 2012-13 Regular Season

Rank	Player	Pts	EOP	Rank	Player	Pts	EOP
1	Al Horford	1289	1454	11	J.J. Hickson	1018	1171
2	Greg Monroe	1298	1363	12	Nikola Vucevic	1008	1136
3	Dwight Howard	1296	1349	13	Nikola Pekovic	1011	1050
4	Marc Gasol	1127	1336	14	Joakim Noah	784	1042
5	Brook Lopez	1437	1330	15	Robin Lopez	929	996
6	Al Jefferson	1391	1320	16	DeAndre Jordan	724	952
7	Tyson Chandler	689	1264	17	Kevin Garnett	1004	949
8	DeMarcus Cousins	1280	1194	18	Omer Asik	832	935
9	Chris Bosh	1232	1190	19	Spencer Hawes	905	930
10	Tim Duncan	1227	1181	20	Roy Hibbert	937	922

The Appendix contains more of the EOP data, including top 100 charts for the 2012-13 season and several past seasons. It also contains the career OE and EOP data for LeBron, Jordan and Bird.

EOP Relative to the Position

In the current NBA, guards tend to put up the highest EOP numbers. However, teams need to employ players that play other positions. Teams need players to rebound and defend the interior, even if these players are not go-to offensive weapons. Teams must play centers. Having a center that is very good offensively relative to other centers in the league could have great value to a team.

To measure a player's production relative to the position he plays, we introduce the idea of a replacement player. The idea of considering production relative to a replacement player has become quite popular in recent years. ESPN.com now carries Wins Above Replacement (WAR) for MLB players. In WAR, the replacement is a hypothetical approximation of what could be picked up off of waivers at the respective position. In general, a replacement could be a real player. For example, a team considering not resigning their starting point guard might compare the starter's production relative to the current backup. The team might also consider the starting point guard's production relative to an available free agent.

We can also look at production in any statistic relative to the league average in the given season. In this way, production across different eras can be compared. For example, scoring in the NBA is down significantly from what it was in the 1980s. This year, teams averaged 98.1 points per game. In 1985-86, teams averaged over 110 points per game. When comparing a 20-point scorer in today's NBA to one of the mid '80s, we should keep this difference in mind. Alternatively, we could attempt to factor out the difference and look at each individual's points per game relative to the league average of the respective season.

A replacement player could also be a team average. Consider the following plus-minus example. The worst player on a good team could have a positive plus-minus while the best player on the worst team could have a negative plus-minus. The plus-minus alone would not well represent each player's production. However, if we took the individual's plus-minus and subtracted the team's average plus-minus, the best player on the worst team now looks better.

In this section, we are interested in EOP relative to the general output at the position. We take the replacement player to be the weighted average EOP (by minutes played) of all players that qualified at that position (according to Basketball-Reference.com) in a given season. These averages are gathered in Table 3.14. As expected, the highest average is at the point guard position. Even though the 2nd ranked player in EOP was a small forward (Kevin Durant), this position had the lowest average.

Table 3.14: Average EOP by Position

Position	C	PF	SF	SG	PG
Avg. EOP	764	803	656	754	980

Let Efficient Offensive Production relative to position (EOPP) be the individuals EOP minus the average in Table 3.14 at the individual's position. Table 3.15 presents the top 20 in EOPP. Two centers, Horford and Monroe, made the list. Centers Dwight Howard, Marc Gasol, Brook Lopez and Al Jefferson were all in the top 25. The top 90 in EOPP can be found in Table A7 in the Appendix.

Table 3.15: Top 20 in EOPP for 2012-13

Rank	Player	Tm	Position	EOP	EOPP
1	LeBon James	MIA	PF	2408	1605
2	Kevin Durant	OKC	SF	2105	1449
3	Kobe Bryant	LAL	SG	1994	1240
4	James Harden	HOU	SG	1845	1090
5	Russell Westbrook	OKC	PG	1992	1011
6	Stephen Curry	GSW	PG	1840	860
7	Blake Griffin	LAC	PF	1616	813
8	Dwyane Wade	MIA	SG	1556	802
9	David Lee	GSW	PF	1563	760
10	Monta Ellis	MIL	SG	1513	758
11	Chris Paul	LAC	PG	1714	734
12	Carmelo Anthony	NYK	PF	1535	732
13	Deron Williams	BRK	PG	1682	702
14	Al Horford	ATL	C	1454	691
15	Paul Pierce	BOS	SF	1346	690
16	LaMarcus Aldridge	POR	PF	1453	650
17	Tony Parker	SAS	PG	1613	633
18	Damian Lillard	POR	PG	1599	619
19	Greg Monroe	DET	C	1363	599
20	Jrue Holiday	PHI	PG	1571	591

In the Clutch

There are times in a game when the game itself changes. Late in the game, with the score close, teams put their best lineups on the floor, defenses up their intensity, the coaches call the most effective plays, and star scorers demand the ball. In these situations, when the pressure is the greatest, we see which players are clutch and which players crack and crumble.

We restricted our attention to five minutes left in the game, and a difference of no greater than five points on the scoreboard. There were 113 players in 2012-13 that played at least 100 minutes in this situation.

No player played more than 218 minutes of clutch time. We are dealing with small sample sizes for this analysis. Small sample sizes for any statistical analysis can create problems. Here, we have to be aware that a player's performance in 150 minutes of clutch time is not necessarily representative of their typical clutch production. However, when one player was particularly "clutch" while another was particularly deplorable in clutch situations, we would rather have the player that performed well.

In this small sample size, we also have to deal with a mathematical inconvenience in the formula for OE. OE can be negative. For this to happen, a player must have more offensive rebounds than the sum of field goal attempts, turnovers and assists. Furthermore, the player must have had at least one field goal made or assist. As you might expect, this almost never happens. In the 2012-13 season, no player had a negative OE. If we were to try and imagine a player for which OE could be negative, we would picture a big man who is not typically a part of the offense. It would be a player that is not asked to handle the ball or pass. It would be a player that played almost exclusively around the rim on offense and was athletic and strong enough to gain a number of offensive rebounds. It would be a player like Tyson Chandler.

Chandler is an anomaly in our study. We saw in Table 3.13 that Chandler was ranked 7th among centers in EOP in 2012-13. He had this ranking in spite of scoring fewer points than any other center in the top 20. Chandler had an OE above 1 for the full season. He is not asked to shoot perimeter shots or create offense off the dribble. He is not put in positions where he could accrue negative statistics such as a turnover or missed jump shot. Instead, he hangs around the rim and grabs offensive boards. In the 116 minutes of clutch time he played last season, Chandler remarkably posted a negative OE. He made 7 of his 8 field goal attempts. He had 2 assists and 1 turnover. He also had 12 offensive rebounds. He had 1 more offensive rebound than the sum of his field goal attempts, assists and turnovers. Since Chandler was the only player to produce a negative OE in the full 2012-13 season or in clutch time, we will call instances where a player produces a negative or zero OE, a case of the "Tyson Chandler phenomenon." When players pull a "Tyson Chandler" we will make note and exclude them from the study.

Table 3.16 presents the top 20 players according to OE. There is an overwhelming presence of big men that are not necessarily the first option on offense for their respective teams and that have the ability to crash the boards on offense. These players did not produce nearly as efficiently in non-clutch situations. Clearly, the NBA's style of play changes at the end of close games. The OE of these players went up because they were asked to do less in terms of creating offense. Players like Serge Ibaka were asked to do less because more of a burden was placed on star scorers like Kevin Durant. So, we suspect that the increased responsibility in clutch time will decrease the OE of these great scorers. Sure enough, Durant, Carmelo, Deron Williams, Rudy Gay, J.R. Smith and Demar Derozan all had an OE in the clutch of below .40. In all of these cases, the player's OE was at least .10 beneath his season OE. The biggest exception to the trend of elite scorers seeing a decrease in OE in the clutch was LeBron James. LeBron's OE on the season was .65. His OE in the clutch was exactly the same. This truly classifies the greatness that LeBron brings to the game.

LeBron is at his best when he is driving to the hoop. This type of offense can take a toll on even the strongest players. LeBron simply cannot maintain this level of physicality all game for every game. However, when the stakes are high, and his team most needs his efforts, he has another gear. When defenses are at their best, and all effort is put towards stopping LeBron, he maintains his level of efficiency. It is more difficult for star players to score in the clutch. LeBron has demonstrated that his offensive game can rise to the challenge and can do so to an extent far beyond that of the other premier scorers in the NBA.

Table 3.16: Top 20 in OE During Clutch Time in the 2012-13 Season

Rank	Player	Min.	Pts	OE
1	Serge Ibaka (OKC)	120	25	1.43
2	Amir Johnson (TOR)	149	49	1.19
3	Larry Sanders (MIL)	125	43	1.19
4	Kenneth Faried (DEN)	122	49	1.15
5	JJ Hickson (POR)	138	43	0.94
6	Tristan Thompson (CLE)	143	48	0.91
7	Joakim Noah (CHI)	125	45	0.87
8	Chris Bosh (MIA)	162	76	0.86
9	Carlos Boozer (CHI)	126	67	0.85
10	Thaddeus Young (PHI)	120	38	0.81
11	Nikola Vucevic (ORL)	120	44	0.80
12	Dwight Howard (LAL)	131	43	0.78
13	Al Horford (ATL)	151	74	0.70
14	Roy Hibbert (IND)	140	27	0.68
15	Jimmy Butler (CHI)	118	39	0.68
16	Alonzo Gee (CLE)	153	28	0.68
17	Kawhi Leonard (SAS)	106	44	0.68
18	Marc Gasol (MEM)	143	55	0.68
19	Shawn Marion (DAL)	110	26	0.67
20	LeBron James (MIA)	161	130	0.65

Table 3.17: Top 20 in EOP During Clutch Time in the 2012-13 Season

Rank	Player	Min.	OE	EOP
1	LeBron James (MIA)	161	0.65	166
2	Kobe Bryant (LAL)	140	0.48	121
3	Chris Paul (LAC)	110	0.55	110
4	Tony Parker (SAS)	158	0.57	109
5	Kyrie Irving (CLE)	130	0.45	107
6	Ty Lawson (DEN)	177	0.53	102
7	Chris Bosh (MIA)	162	0.86	102
8	Jrue Holiday (PHI)	120	0.56	101
9	Paul Pierce (BOS)	218	0.47	101
10	Monta Ellis (MIL)	169	0.47	100
11	James Harden (HOU)	143	0.45	98
12	O.J. Mayo (DAL)	203	0.49	97
13	Amir Johnson (TOR)	149	1.19	97
14	Kevin Durant (OKC)	145	0.39	96
15	Carlos Boozer (CHI)	126	0.85	94
16	Kenneth Faried (DEN)	122	1.15	91
17	Jarrett Jack (GSW)	141	0.53	89
18	Al Horford (ATL)	151	0.70	88
19	Al Jefferson (UTA)	157	0.55	86
20	Larry Sanders (MIL)	125	1.19	84

OE is a rate statistic, and players can score highly in OE because they are not asked to be a big part of the offense. Many of the players in Table 3.16 did not take many shots in clutch situations. We now look at EOP in these situations. Studying EOP in these situations allows us to account for production and give credit to the individuals who are consistently called on for late game heroics. Table 3.17 presents the Top 20 in EOP in the clutch. EOP is in part a product of opportunity, the team's opportunity to perform in the clutch and the player's opportunity to shoot or pass in those situations. It is not accurate to say that the top players on these lists are the most clutch in the NBA, as there may be other individuals who simply did not have the opportunity. Still, there is value in comparing two players who have had the opportunity to determine who had the better performance. We have found yet another part of the game where LeBron is outstanding. The data on all 113 qualified players can be found in Table A8 in the Appendix.

Era Independent EOP

Often, one wants to compare the production of players that played in different seasons or eras. We saw in Table 3.10, that scoring rates in the NBA have changed significantly over the last 36 years. To properly compare Michael Jordan's offensive production to LeBron James' offensive production, we need to account for these variations.

To put all EOP scores on a level playing field, we define Era Independent EOP (EOP$^+$). We still want EOP$^+$ to be output on a points scored scale. Since 2012-13 is the most recent season in our study, we will adjust all EOP numbers to align with the scoring rates that year. To do this, we define a player's EOP$^+$ as follows.

$$EOP^+ = EOP * \frac{2013\ Team\ PPG}{Season\ Team\ PPG}$$

where 2013 Team PPG is the average points per game for a team in the 2012-13 season and Season Team PPG is the average points per game for a team in the season in which we are calculating the individuals EOP$^+$. For example, in 1978-79, teams averaged 110.3 points per game. That year Bob Lanier had an EOP of 1139. To arrive at Lanier's EOP$^+$ we take the EOP of 1139 and multiply by the ratio 98.1/110.3. The result is that Lanier's EOP$^+$ is 1013. Since Lanier played in a higher scoring era, his EOP$^+$ is less than his EOP.

EOP$^+$ allows for era independent comparisons of player offensive production. We can now compare the total offensive contributions of Kareem to those of Shaq. These are the types of comparisons we will conduct in the next section.

Comparing the Great Offensive Players from the '80s, '90s and Today

We now look at EOP$^+$ for seasons dating back to 1977-78. 1977-78 was the first season that the NBA officially recorded turnovers. OE relies on turnovers in its calculation. Thus, this is the earliest season where EOP$^+$ can be calculated. We begin with the top 20 seasons in Table 3.18. Then we present the top 20 seasons for each position in Tables 3.19 through 3.23. While perusing the top 20 lists in Tables 3.18 to 3.23, note that certain players can best be classified at different positions at various points in their careers. Also, the season column is the year the season ended. For example, the 1999-2000 season is denoted as 2000.

Table 3.18: Top 20 EOP+ Seasons from 1977-78 through 2012-13

Rank	Season	First Name	Last Name	Team	Pos	Age	EOP+
1	2000	Shaquille	O'Neal	LAL	C	27	2665
2	1989	Michael	Jordan	CHI	SG	25	2547
3	1988	Michael	Jordan	CHI	SG	24	2518
4	1990	Michael	Jordan	CHI	SG	26	2507
5	1994	Shaquille	O'Neal	ORL	C	21	2490
6	2001	Shaquille	O'Neal	LAL	C	28	2485
7	2006	LeBron	James	CLE	SF	21	2459
8	2010	LeBron	James	CLE	SF	25	2451
9	2009	Dwyane	Wade	MIA	SG	27	2437
10	2009	LeBron	James	CLE	SF	24	2425
11	2013	LeBron	James	MIA	PF	28	2408
12	1995	Shaquille	O'Neal	ORL	C	22	2399
13	1997	Karl	Malone	UTA	PF	33	2398
14	2009	Chris	Paul	NOH	PG	23	2387
15	2006	Kobe	Bryant	LAL	SG	27	2375
16	1991	Michael	Jordan	CHI	SG	27	2370
17	2003	Kobe	Bryant	LAL	SG	24	2337
18	2008	Chris	Paul	NOH	PG	22	2329
19	2003	Tracy	McGrady	ORL	SG	23	2327
20	2005	LeBron	James	CLE	SF	20	2291

Michael Jordan, Shaquille O'Neal and LeBron James were the most impressive in our study. Together, they accounted for 11 of the top 12 and 13 of the top 20 seasons in Table 3.18. LeBron's five seasons in the top 20 were the most of any player. Karl Malone was the only player with a season at an age older than 28 to make the list. Malone was 33 in 1997, and his production that year was good enough for 13th on the board.

Shaq holds the top four seasons and six of the top nine among centers. David Robinson makes the list four times, Moses Malone made the list three times, and Amar'e Stoudemire and Hakeem Olajuwan each made it twice.

Charles Barkley, Karl Malone and Kevin Garnett had 16 of the top 20 seasons for power forwards. Eight of those 16 seasons belonged to Malone, five to Garnett and three to Barkley. LeBron was best classified as a power forward in 2012-13. Given his high involvement in generating the Heat's offense, it's not surprising that his performance in 2012-13 was the best season we have ever seen by a power forward.

Chris Paul holds the top two spots for point guards. These seasons came when Paul was 22 and 23 years old. Gary Payton has three seasons in the top 20. Payton was between 31 and 33 years old in those seasons. Magic Johnson and John Stockton each also had three seasons in the top 20. Allen Iverson and Steve Nash each made the list twice.

Just how good is LeBron James? We already saw James' 2013 season at power forward was the best among that position. James also had the six best seasons for small forwards. Larry Bird made the list of small forwards four times. Adrian Dantley made the top 20 three times, including the best two seasons by a player not named LeBron.

LeBron was impressive, but perhaps no player dominated his position like Michael Jordan. Jordan had ten of the top 17 seasons for shooting guards, a feat LeBron might match for small forwards before his career is over. Kobe Bryant had four seasons in the top 20. Dwyane Wade had three seasons.

Table 3.19: Top 20 Season EOP$^+$ for Centers

Rank	Season	First Name	Last Name	Team	Age	EOP$^+$
1	2000	Shaquille	O'Neal	LAL	27	2665
2	1994	Shaquille	O'Neal	ORL	21	2490
3	2001	Shaquille	O'Neal	LAL	28	2485
4	1995	Shaquille	O'Neal	ORL	22	2399
5	1994	David	Robinson	SAS	28	2219
6	1982	Moses	Malone	HOU	26	2183
7	2003	Shaquille	O'Neal	LAL	30	2108
8	1996	David	Robinson	SAS	30	2107
9	2002	Shaquille	O'Neal	LAL	29	2055
10	2005	Amar'e	Stoudemire	PHX	22	2053
11	1995	David	Robinson	SAS	29	2049
12	1979	Moses	Malone	HOU	23	1992
13	1980	Kareem	Abdul-Jabbar	LAL	32	1959
14	1994	Hakeem	Olajuwon	HOU	31	1956
15	2005	Shaquille	O'Neal	MIA	32	1934
16	1993	Hakeem	Olajuwon	HOU	30	1934
17	2008	Amar'e	Stoudemire	PHX	25	1929
18	1991	David	Robinson	SAS	25	1920
19	1990	Patrick	Ewing	NYK	27	1918
20	1981	Moses	Malone	HOU	25	1908

Table 3.20: Top 20 Season EOP$^+$ for Power Forwards

Rank	Season	First Name	Last Name	Team	Age	EOP$^+$
1	2013	LeBron	James	MIA	28	2408
2	1997	Karl	Malone	UTA	33	2398
3	2004	Kevin	Garnett	MIN	27	2272
4	2003	Kevin	Garnett	MIN	26	2262
5	1998	Karl	Malone	UTA	34	2217
6	1988	Charles	Barkley	PHI	24	2209
7	1989	Charles	Barkley	PHI	25	2205
8	1990	Charles	Barkley	PHI	26	2187
9	2002	Tim	Duncan	SAS	25	2146
10	2005	Kevin	Garnett	MIN	28	2135
11	1990	Karl	Malone	UTA	26	2131
12	1996	Karl	Malone	UTA	32	2090
13	1993	Karl	Malone	UTA	29	2068
14	2003	Tim	Duncan	SAS	26	2044
15	1991	Karl	Malone	UTA	27	2043
16	2000	Karl	Malone	UTA	36	2039
17	1995	Karl	Malone	UTA	31	1997
18	2006	Elton	Brand	LAC	26	1997
19	2000	Kevin	Garnett	MIN	23	1944
20	2001	Kevin	Garnett	MIN	24	1941

Table 3.21: Top 20 Season EOP$^+$ for Point Guards

Rank	Season	First Name	Last Name	Team	Age	EOP$^+$
1	2009	Chris	Paul	NOH	23	2387
2	2008	Chris	Paul	NOH	22	2329
3	1987	Magic	Johnson	LAL	27	2283
4	2000	Gary	Payton	SEA	31	2276
5	2006	Allen	Iverson	PHI	30	2270
6	2002	Gary	Payton	SEA	33	2232
7	1989	Magic	Johnson	LAL	29	2179
8	2006	Gilbert	Arenas	WAS	24	2165
9	1990	Magic	Johnson	LAL	30	2145
10	2005	Allen	Iverson	PHI	29	2144
11	2006	Steve	Nash	PHX	31	2125
12	1991	John	Stockton	UTA	28	2124
13	1985	Isiah	Thomas	DET	23	2118
14	2001	Gary	Payton	SEA	32	2117
15	2007	Steve	Nash	PHX	32	2094
16	1989	John	Stockton	UTA	26	2090
17	2008	Deron	Williams	UTA	23	2088
18	2005	Stephon	Marbury	NYK	27	2078
19	1996	Anfernee	Hardaway	ORL	24	2075
20	1990	John	Stockton	UTA	27	2074

Table 3.22: Top 20 Season EOP$^+$ for Small Forwards

Rank	Season	First Name	Last Name	Team	Age	EOP$^+$
1	2006	LeBron	James	CLE	21	2459
2	2010	LeBron	James	CLE	25	2451
3	2009	LeBron	James	CLE	24	2425
4	2005	LeBron	James	CLE	20	2291
5	2008	LeBron	James	CLE	23	2275
6	2011	LeBron	James	MIA	26	2215
7	1982	Adrian	Dantley	UTA	25	2181
8	1981	Adrian	Dantley	UTA	24	2141
9	2013	Kevin	Durant	OKC	24	2105
10	1985	Larry	Bird	BOS	28	2084
11	2007	LeBron	James	CLE	22	2074
12	1983	Alex	English	DEN	29	2068
13	1988	Larry	Bird	BOS	31	2053
14	1984	Adrian	Dantley	UTA	27	2049
15	1997	Grant	Hill	DET	24	2003
16	1987	Larry	Bird	BOS	30	1986
17	1982	Alex	English	DEN	28	1981
18	2001	Vince	Carter	TOR	24	1976
19	1986	Larry	Bird	BOS	29	1966
20	1987	Alex	English	DEN	33	1960

Table 3.23: Top 20 Season EOP$^+$ for Shooting Guards

Rank	Season	First Name	Last Name	Team	Age	EOP$^+$
1	1989	Michael	Jordan	CHI	25	2547
2	1988	Michael	Jordan	CHI	24	2518
3	1990	Michael	Jordan	CHI	26	2507
4	2009	Dwyane	Wade	MIA	27	2437
5	2006	Kobe	Bryant	LAL	27	2375
6	1991	Michael	Jordan	CHI	27	2370
7	2003	Kobe	Bryant	LAL	24	2337
8	2003	Tracy	McGrady	ORL	23	2327
9	1996	Michael	Jordan	CHI	32	2284
10	1997	Michael	Jordan	CHI	33	2276
11	1987	Michael	Jordan	CHI	23	2270
12	1992	Michael	Jordan	CHI	28	2202
13	1993	Michael	Jordan	CHI	29	2190
14	2006	Dwyane	Wade	MIA	24	2173
15	2007	Kobe	Bryant	LAL	28	2168
16	2008	Allen	Iverson	DEN	32	2139
17	2008	Kobe	Bryant	LAL	29	2082
18	1998	Michael	Jordan	CHI	34	2062
19	1988	Clyde	Drexler	POR	25	2048
20	2010	Dwyane	Wade	MIA	28	2040

When calculating EOP$^+$, we adjust EOP based on the scoring rates per game. We chose not to adjust based on the season scoring totals. This is important to note when trying to compare shortened season EOP$^+$ to typical EOP$^+$ numbers. The shortened seasons will have significantly smaller totals. One could adjust EOP based on the season point totals. We chose not to do this because it would imply full season production where it did not occur. We did not want to assume players would produce over a full 82 game schedule at the same rate as in any shortened season.

4

Defensive Stops Gained and Player Approximate Value

As promised, Efficient Offensive Production was an exclusively bottom up metric. Our defensive metric, however, will be top down. Again, offense can be far more individualistic than defense, and the available bottom up statistics on offense when compared to those available for defense reflect this.

A player can positively impact his defense in three ways. First, he can prevent shots by causing turnovers. Second, he can lower the opponent's shooting percentage by obstructing shots or forcing lower quality shots. Finally, he can snatch up extra rebounds, preventing the opponents from maintaining possession after a miss.

There is arguably a fourth way to significantly influence the defense. Certain players are better at contributing in the ways described above without fouling. Other players can get caught in a bad position and end up fouling to prevent the easy bucket. We chose not to include fouls in our defensive metric. There are many logical reasons to exclude fouls from a defensive metric. Sometimes teams foul solely for strategic reasons. At the end of games, teams foul to stop the clock. At other times, teams foul to prevent an easy bucket. Perhaps the most well-known fouling strategy was the "hack a Shaq" strategy where teams intentionally fouled Shaquille O'Neal to send him to the free throw line. Shaq shot over 58% from the field and below 53% from the free throw line in his career. The idea was that Shaq would on the average produce fewer points from the charity stripe than from around the basket. When incorporating fouls, one must also account for the difference in the frequency of potential opportunities to foul by position. Typically, interior defenders are more often in positions to foul than perimeter defenders. For all of the above reasons, we chose not to include fouling rates in our defensive metric.

The three components of our defensive metric are motivated by the three ways (outlined above) to positively impact a defense. Those are the opponents' effective field goal percentage (EFG%), offensive rebounding percentage (ORB%) and turnover percentage (TO%). Recall that EFG% is field goals plus 0.5 times three-pointers all divided by field goal attempts, or symbolically

$$EFG\% = \frac{FG + .5(3P)}{FGA}$$

ORB% is the percentage of rebounds the offense grabs out of the total number of available offensive boards. Turnover percentage is the percentage of possessions where the offense turns the ball over. For our defensive statistic, we are interested in these numbers for the individual's opponents. We want to know how well the opposition is shooting, how many extra chances they get from offensive boards, and how often they turn the ball over and get no shot at all.

In this section, we use a top down approach. As stated in Chapter 1, the greatest weakness of this approach is the tendency for the output to be biased towards players that play on good teams. One way to account for this is to look at production relative to the team in the individual's absence. We will use a so-called on/off the court metric in the same grain as the on/off plus-minus used in the calculation of Simple Ratings by 82games.com (discussed in Chapter 2).

Designate a player C. Let EFG%[On] be the opponents' EFG% when C is on the court. Let EFG%[Off] be the opponents' EFG% when C is off the court. Define EFG%[Net]=EFG%[On]-EFG%[Off]. Define analogously for ORB% and TO%. For LeBron James, the three net statistics in the 2012-13 season were as follows.

	EFG%[Net]	ORB%[Net]	TO%[Net]
LeBron James	-0.8	-1.2	2

When LeBron James is on the court, opponents of the Heat have an EFG% of .8 percent lower than when he is off the court. Opponents also grab 1.2% less offensive rebounds and turn the ball over 2% more. In all three cases, LeBron is helping the Heat.

We want to stress that these numbers are the effect LeBron has on the Heat's defense by stepping on and off the court. It is hard to argue that LeBron is benefiting from playing with good teammates when his teammates are not as effective without him.

We have identified statistics that help us understand a player's influence on his team's defense. By taking the net on/off the court numbers we have significantly reduced any team pull effect usually associated with top down statistics. Now, we would like to combine the three numbers into a single number.

Each of the net statistics is a percentage, but they are not percentages of the same events or quantities. To compare all three measures, we will think in terms of defensive stops. In 2012-13, an NBA team averaged 82 field goal attempts (FGA) per game and 20 of those were three point attempts (3PA). So, the league attempted about 62 + 1.5*20=92 "effective field goals" (EFG) per game. For every percent drop in EFG%, the opponent is missing an additional .92 EFGs per game. Effective field goal attempts, however, do not correspond with a single missed shot and thus a single offensive possession. We know that on the average, there are 82 FGA for every 92 EFGA. On the average, a percent drop in EFG% corresponds to the opponent missing an additional .82 field goals. Before we can convert this number to defensive stops, we need to know how many missed field goals turn into defensive rebounds (ending the possession).

We will work with field goal attempts as opposed to effective field goal attempts for the purposes of defining Defensive Stops Gained (our defensive metric). Why not start with opponents' field goal percentage as opposed to effective field goal percentage? Effective field goal percentage accounts for the difference in value between a two-point and three-point shot. By not accounting for this difference, field goal percentage could be misleading. For example, let us suppose that player A is a bad perimeter defender who often leaves his man open for a three-point attempt. While player A is on the court, the opposing team will have more open looks from behind the arc. If they take a higher percentage of three-pointers while player A is on the court, they may see their field goal percentage drop. However, since they are attempting more three-pointers, they may actually be scoring at a higher rate per offensive possession. In this scenario, taking FG%[Net] would make player A look like a good defender, when in fact, he is a detriment defensively to his team. If the opposition is scoring more points on field goals in this scenario, effective field goal percentage will go up. Thus, EFG%[Net] is more representative of player A's defensive contributions.

An NBA team averages 42 rebounds per game. Therefore, a percentage point drop in ORB% means .42 less offensive rebounds given up, or .42 ends of possession per game. About 73.5% of missed shots are rebounded by the defense. So, the .82 FG saved leads to .735*.82 defensive stops. Teams averaged 14.6 turnovers per game. The average TO% was 13.7. On average, teams had roughly 106 opportunities per game to turn the ball over. A percentage point in TO% is worth 1.06 defensive stops.

With the above information, we can calculate Defensive Stops Gained per full game (DSG/G) by the individual as

$$DSG/G = -(.82 * .735 * EFG\%[Net]) - (.42 * ORB\%[Net]) + (1.06 * TO\%[Net])$$

DSG/G is the number of defensive stops gained by the individual in a game if that individual played the whole game. We can convert this to the number of defensive stops gained per minute (DSG/M) by dividing DSG/G by the number of minutes in a game. There are approximately 48 minutes per game. Define DSG/M to be DSG/G divided by 48. DSG/M is a rate statistic. As we did with EOP, we now consider quantity of defensive stops.

Defense is work. A player that can be a quality defender for 35 minutes a night is more valuable than a player that can do the same in 5 minutes a night. Also, those that can guard the opponents' top offensive players will likely see more time. We have a statistic that measures Defensive Stops Gained per minute. To get the cumulative production for the season, we simply have to multiply DSG/M by the player's minutes (M) played. We define Defensive Stops Gained (DSG) as

$$DSG = \frac{DSG}{M} * M$$

FUTURE DIRECTION

All of the coefficients in the calculation of DSG are first level (rounded) approximations based on league average statistics. There is an obvious opportunity to improve the statistic by constructing coefficients particular to each team, or even each player. For example, suppose player A plays for team B. Opponents of team B might attempt 84 field goals a game, slightly above the league average of 82 field goals. In the computation of player A's DSG, we could use the coefficient of .84 as opposed to .82. Also, instead of using the league average defensive rebounding rate of 73.5%, we might use the actual defensive rebounding percentage of team B when player A is on the court. Using the percentages tied to a particular player's time on court can create small sample size issues, but there are statistical techniques to smooth out anomalies (such as the team that pulls down 100% of defensive rebounds in hypothetical John's forty total minutes of playing time on the season). All of these adjustments would produce a slightly more accurate, but far more complex formula. We encourage the inclined reader to run more detailed DSG calculations. The diminishing return on the results did not warrant the increased complexity in our formula and was therefore not appropriate for our purposes here.

Table 4.1 presents the top 20 players in DSG for the 2012-13 season. NBA Defensive Player of the Year Marc Gasol is third in DSG. LeBron James and Tony Allen, All-Defensive First Teamers, land in the top eight. The top DSG earner, Mike Conley, was selected to the All-Defensive Second Team. These types of season awards are not necessarily an indication that our metric is accurate. Still, it is interesting to note the overlap in the voters' opinions and DSG. Larry Sanders made the top 20. According to the Goldsberry article we discussed in Chapter 2, Sanders is particularly good at keeping down the opponent's FG% around the hoop when he is patrolling the area. This skill is probably contributing to his impressive EFG%[Net] of -4.1.

Computing the on/off the court net statistics necessary for DSG requires play-by-play data. We need to know what is happening when each player is on the court and off the court. Unfortunately, this is only available from the 2001-02 season forward. We cannot do the same kind of historical comparisons that we did for EOP.

Table 4.1: Top 20 in DSG for 2012-13

Rank	Player	EFG%[Net]	ORB%[Net]	TO%[Net]	DSG
1	Mike Conley	-2.4	-1.7	2.5	276
2	Kevin Garnett	-2.0	-3.8	2.4	225
3	Marc Gasol	-1.8	-2.2	1.5	210
4	LeBron James	-0.8	-1.2	2.0	186
5	Jrue Holiday	-1.1	0.2	2.3	184
6	Amir Johnson	-2.8	-3.6	0.5	181
7	Dwight Howard	-1.6	-2.0	1.3	180
8	Tony Allen	-1.1	-2.1	2.4	180
9	Lamar Odom	-5.8	2.1	2.3	170
10	Dwyane Wade	0.7	0.0	3.5	164
11	Metta World Peace	-0.7	-1.4	1.7	148
12	Vince Carter	-3.4	-3.6	-0.2	146
13	LaMarcus Aldridge	-0.7	-2.9	0.8	145
14	Andre Iguodala	-2.1	-2.8	0.0	141
15	Tiago Splitter	-2.1	-1.0	1.3	127
16	Larry Sanders	-4.1	-1.1	-0.1	114
17	Kemba Walker	0.4	-1.8	1.3	113
18	Brandon Knight	-3.7	-1.1	-0.4	112
19	Mario Chalmers	-0.1	0.0	2.3	108
20	Matt Barnes	-4.8	1.2	0.1	107

DSG Relative to the Position

As we did with EOP, we could now look at DSG relative to position to see if any players are particularly productive relative to their positional peers. The average DSG per position is presented in Table 4.2. These averages are weighted by the playing time of the individual.

Table 4.2: Average DSG for 2012-13 by Position

Position	C	PF	SF	SG	PG
Avg. DSG	4.19	-4.21	7.33	-15.83	-12.5

The averages by position range from positive 7.33 to -15.83. Teams do not always play exactly one player at each of the five positions. Teams occasionally "play small" and will run a lineup that does not include a center.   For example, Boston occasionally fielded the lineup of Brandon Bass (PF), Avery Bradley (PG), Jeff Green (PF), Paul Pierce (SF), and Rajon Rondo (PG). The average DSG of 4.19 for centers and average DSG of -4.21 for power forwards suggest that when teams play small, they are not as good defensively.   Another factor at play here may be the way in which we choose to label the position of a player. There are players that play more than the one position we have classified them to be. For example, many small forwards could also be considered shooting guards and vice versa. The positive average DSG for small forwards and the negative DSG for shooting guards may indicate that we typically label the offensive wing player a shooting guard, while the perhaps slightly taller and better defender on the wing is called a small forward. In other words, the differences in the average DSG per position may be a reflection of a bias in assignment of traditional positions.

In Chapter 9, we will discuss the notion of redefining the positions in the NBA. There, we will discuss the possibility of a better system for classifying player skill sets that would include more than five total positions. For example, we might distinguish big men by their ability to knock down threes or defend the interior. We believe that a more refined classification of player skills would be of great benefit when trying to calculate a player's DSG relative to his peer group.

Anytime we consider a statistic relative to the position, we are subject to the limitations of the original position assignments. This limitation is particularly troubling in this instance. When calculating DSG relative to position, shooting guards would get a significant boost as compared to small forwards. The problem is that we can often replace the player classified as a shooting guard with a small forward. Often, this is done when defense is prioritized. Thus, we will not present DSG relative to the position.

Combining EOP and DSG

We now have measures of offensive value and defensive value. Why not combine them for a more complete assessment of the player's contribution to his team? After all, DSG and EOP (at the team level) are highly indicative of a team's quality. We ran a multiple regression using opponents EFG%, TOV% and ORB% together with EOP and OE as inputs. For the output, we chose team win percentage. For the 2012-13 season, the regression had an R^2 of .81. In other words, at the team level our inputs for DSG and EOP are great predictors of team win percentage.

To combine DSG and EOP, we need to put the two on comparable scales. EOP measures efficient points added and is already on a points scored scale. DSG approximates the defensive stops added in the player's time on the court over what the team would earn otherwise. The alternative to a defensive stop would be allowing a score or sending the opposing team to the free throw line. For the sake of simplicity, we will suppose that each defensive stop prevents an average of two points. Let Defensive Points Saved (DPS) be 2 times DSG. We then define a player's Approximate Value (AV) to be

$$AV = DPS + EOP$$

Table 4.3 presents the Top 20 in AV for this past season. AV is not biased against any particular position. All five positions are represented in the top 7. It does not favor players that play on good teams. 11th ranked Kemba Walker played for the 21-61 Charlotte Bobcats. It recognizes defensive contributions. Marc Gasol, the Defensive Player of the Year, is ranked 7th despite being the 4th leading scorer (per game) on his own team.

Table 4.3: Top 20 in AV for 2012-13

Rank	Player	Tm	Pos	Age	DPS	EOP	AV
1	LeBron James	MIA	PF	28	372	2408	2781
2	Jrue Holiday	PHI	PG	22	368	1571	1939
3	Mike Conley	MEM	PG	25	553	1336	1888
4	Dwyane Wade	MIA	SG	31	328	1556	1884
5	Russell Westbrook	OKC	PG	24	-111	1992	1881
6	Kevin Durant	OKC	SF	24	-284	2105	1821
7	Marc Gasol	MEM	C	28	419	1336	1756
8	LaMarcus Aldridge	POR	PF	27	289	1453	1742
9	Tony Parker	SAS	PG	30	106	1613	1719
10	Dwight Howard	LAL	C	27	361	1349	1710
11	Kemba Walker	CHA	PG	22	225	1477	1703
12	Kobe Bryant	LAL	SG	34	-305	1994	1689
13	Stephen Curry	GSW	PG	24	-184	1840	1656
14	James Harden	HOU	SG	23	-228	1845	1617
15	Chris Paul	LAC	PG	27	-189	1714	1526
16	Monta Ellis	MIL	SG	27	3	1513	1515
17	Andre Iguodala	DEN	SG	29	283	1197	1479
18	Greg Monroe	DET	C	22	79	1363	1441
19	Paul Pierce	BOS	SF	35	77	1346	1423
20	David Lee	GSW	PF	29	-152	1563	1411

LeBron James is beyond great. His AV is over 800 points better than the 2nd best player in the NBA. This is greater than the margin from ranks 2 to 20. LeBron is ranked first in EOP, EOP relative to the position, and clutch EOP. He is also ranked 4th in our defensive metric, DSG. According to AV, LeBron is by far the best player currently in the NBA.

There are several ways to be valuable to your team, and there are several ways to post a high AV. Stephen Curry uses great offense to overcome not-so-stellar defense. Marc Gasol provided a lot of defensive value and was still solid, but not exceptional, on offense. Tony Parker was very good on both ends of the court.

Table 4.3 contains some of the NBA's biggest stars. Everyone recognizes the talents of LeBron, Paul, Howard, Bryant, Parker, Durant, Wade, Pierce, Harden and Westbrook. Table 4.3 also includes Curry and Aldridge who both perhaps took that step into the elite last year. If there are surprises in the top 20, they might be Jrue Holliday and Kemba Walker. Jrue Holliday was the only player in the NBA last year to average at least 17 points and 8 assists. He was recognized for his contributions by being selected to the all-star game and by being invited to the National Team's minicamp in the summer of 2013. At only 23, Jrue Holliday has a promising career in front of him. If he is not yet a household name, he will be soon. Kemba Walker made headlines by carrying an otherwise young University of Connecticut Huskies team to an improbable national championship in 2011. Entering the Big East Conference Tournament that season, the Huskies were not a guarantee to get an at-large bid in the NCAA tournament. The Huskies won five games in five days to take the Big East Tournament and the automatic bid in the NCAA tournament that accompanied it. Walker was in the top 25 in the NBA this past season in points per game and assists per game. He also received an invitation to Team USA's minicamp.

Table A9 in the Appendix presents the top 90 in AV for 2012-13.

Approximate Value (AV) Relative to Position

AV is the sum of Defensive Points Saved (DPS) and Efficient Offensive Production (EOP). EOP favors playmakers, and rightfully so. Point guards (if they are racking up assists) carry a great deal of responsibility in the offense. Thus, point guards tend to outperform other positions in EOP. This carries over into AV. Table 4.4 contains the average AV by position. As with EOP, these averages are weighted based on playing time.

Table 4.4: Average AV by Position

Position	C	PF	SF	SG	PG
Avg. DSG	772	795	671	723	955

We now present the top players in AV relative to position (AVP). We calculate AVP by taking the AV score and subtracting the average in Table 4.4 for the appropriate position. LeBron's AVP is almost double any other player's AVP. The Heat (who won the last two championships) have the top two players in AVP for 2012-13. See Table 4.5 for the top 20. Notable names that just missed the top 20 include Kevin Garnett, Carmelo Anthony, Al Horford and Chris Paul.

Table 4.5: Top 20 in AVP for 2012-13

Rank	Player	Team	Pos	Age	AVP
1	LeBron James	MIA	PF	28	1986
2	Dwyane Wade	MIA	SG	31	1161
3	Kevin Durant	OKC	SF	24	1150
4	Marc Gasol	MEM	C	28	984
5	Jrue Holiday	PHI	PG	22	984
6	Kobe Bryant	LAL	SG	34	966
7	LaMarcus Aldridge	POR	PF	27	947
8	Dwight Howard	LAL	C	27	938
9	Mike Conley	MEM	PG	25	933
10	Russell Westbrook	OKC	PG	24	926
11	James Harden	HOU	SG	23	894
12	Monta Ellis	MIL	SG	27	793
13	Tony Parker	SAS	PG	30	764
14	Andre Iguodala	DEN	SG	29	757
15	Paul Pierce	BOS	SF	35	752
16	Kemba Walker	CHA	PG	22	748
17	Paul George	IND	SF	22	713
18	Stephen Curry	GSW	PG	24	701
19	Greg Monroe	DET	C	22	670
20	J.R. Smith	NYK	SG	27	633

AV, EOP, DSG and the related relative-to-position metrics are cumulative statistics. To score highly in these statistics, players need to play significant minutes. Playing time can be diminished for a variety of reasons, including injuries. Production in general can be influenced by a number of factors including the quality of the system the player operates in. While a high AVP indicates great ability, it is possible for a very talented player not to post a top score. For the sake of identifying solid production in limited playing time, AV per minute, OE and DSG/M can be considered.

Rate Versions of AV and DSG

We now consider Approximate Value per minute (AV/M) and Defensive Stops Gained per minute (DSG/M). We use the rate statistics to find players that had value in limited playing time. We will also look at players that were traded midseason and compare their rate statistics with each team they played for.

One of the main reasons we consider rate statistics in addition to cumulative statistics is to find production in limited minutes played. Like any rate statistics, AV/M and DSG/M can be misleading on small sample sets. We will try to restrict our analysis to situations where the player played a reasonable amount of minutes. In all cases, we will mention the minutes played.

Let's start by looking at the best producers of AV/M among players that played at least 820 minutes (or 10 minutes per game played by the team). This will allow us to find players that were productive in shortened seasons or as a role player off the bench without worrying a great deal about small sample size anomalies. Table 4.6 presents the top 20 among this group in AV/M. The data shows that both John Wall and Rajon Rondo have high approximate value for their time played. Both missed significant time in 2012-13 due to knee injuries. Utah center Enes Kanter had a high AV/M in his 1078 minutes played. Kanter will likely see in an increased role in 2013-14 since Al Jefferson, the former starting center for Utah, was signed by Charlotte. Kanter has yet to demonstrate he can score like Jefferson. Kanter's high ranking here is because of his high DSG/M numbers. Out of the 291 players that played at least 820 minutes in 2012-13, Kanter ranked 8th in AV/M and Jefferson ranked 231st. If AV/M is any indication, the Jazz made the right decision in letting Jefferson walk and going with the younger Kanter.

Table 4.6: Top 20 in AV/M for 2012-13

Rank	Player	Tm	Pos	MP	DSG/M	EOP/M	AV/M
1	LeBron James	MIA	PF	2877	0.065	0.837	0.966
2	Tony Parker	SAS	PG	2174	0.024	0.742	0.791
3	Dwyane Wade	MIA	SG	2391	0.069	0.651	0.788
4	Kevin Garnett	BOS	C	2022	0.111	0.469	0.692
5	Mike Conley	MEM	PG	2757	0.100	0.485	0.685
6	John Wall	WAS	PG	1602	0.014	0.638	0.666
7	Jrue Holiday	PHI	PG	2926	0.063	0.537	0.663
8	Enes Kanter	UTA	C	1078	0.096	0.469	0.661
9	Russell Westbrook	OKC	PG	2861	-0.019	0.696	0.657
10	Chris Paul	LAC	PG	2335	-0.040	0.734	0.653
11	Dwight Howard	LAL	C	2722	0.066	0.496	0.628
12	Marc Gasol	MEM	C	2796	0.075	0.478	0.628
13	LaMarcus Aldridge	POR	PF	2790	0.052	0.521	0.624
14	Andray Blatche	BKN	C	1555	0.046	0.528	0.619
15	Rajon Rondo	BOS	PG	1423	0.017	0.584	0.619
16	Tiago Splitter	SAS	PF	1997	0.064	0.488	0.615
17	Kyrie Irving	CLE	PG	2048	-0.010	0.623	0.602
18	Vince Carter	DAL	SF	2093	0.070	0.462	0.601
19	Kemba Walker	CHA	PG	2859	0.039	0.517	0.596
20	Amir Johnson	TOR	PF	2325	0.078	0.438	0.593

Table 4.7 presents the top 20 in DSG/M. Notables that just missed the top 20 included Larry Sanders, Metta World Peace, Kawhi Leonard and Andre Iguodala. There are not so many

surprises on the list. Garnett, Conley, Tony Allen, Gasol, Howard, and James are all typically considered to be very good defenders. It may come as a bit of a surprise to see the now 36-year-old point guard Pablo Prigioni ranked 18th on the list. To get a better understanding of Prigioni's value to the Knicks, we looked at the team's three-man lineup data. We restricted to three man groups that played at least 82 minutes on the season (or 1 minute per team game). The top triple in +/- per 48 minutes was Chandler, Novak, and Prigioni. The trio of Felton, Prigioni and Smith tied for second. Prigioni is the common factor in the trios. None of New York's top three threesomes included Carmelo. Exactly how does Prigioni impact New York's defense? Ian Begley of ESPNNewYork.com wrote, "The end-to-end pressure he puts on opposing guards can disrupt and delay an opponent's offense."[1] Knicks point guard Raymond Felton had the following to say about Prigioni. "Pablo is very aggressive, a guy who just bothers you the whole game, stays on top of you, stays in you, is just always nagging you the whole game. And that's something that's big for us. He initiates our whole defense. When we see him out there working as hard as he does, playing as hard as he does, it makes us want to play, too."[2] Our numbers agree with what many have observed about Prigioni.

Table 4.7: Top 20 in DSG/M for 2012-13

Rank	Player	Pos	Tm	MP	DSG/M	EOP/M	AV/M
1	Kevin Garnett	C	BOS	2022	0.111	0.469	0.692
2	Lamar Odom	PF	LAC	1616	0.105	0.248	0.459
3	Mike Conley	PG	MEM	2757	0.100	0.485	0.685
4	Enes Kanter	C	UTA	1078	0.096	0.469	0.661
5	Tony Allen	SG	MEM	2109	0.085	0.302	0.472
6	DeMarre Carroll	SF	UTA	1111	0.082	0.379	0.543
7	Amir Johnson	PF	TOR	2325	0.078	0.438	0.593
8	Marc Gasol	C	MEM	2796	0.075	0.478	0.628
9	Devin Harris	SG	ATL	1421	0.074	0.420	0.567
10	Vince Carter	SF	DAL	2093	0.070	0.462	0.601
11	Dwyane Wade	SG	MIA	2391	0.069	0.651	0.788
12	Chuck Hayes	C	SAC	1209	0.068	0.299	0.434
13	Dwight Howard	C	LAL	2722	0.066	0.496	0.628
14	LeBron James	PF	MIA	2877	0.065	0.837	0.966
15	Tiago Splitter	PF	SAS	1997	0.064	0.488	0.615
16	Udonis Haslem	PF	MIA	1414	0.063	0.241	0.367
17	Jrue Holiday	PG	PHI	2926	0.063	0.537	0.663
18	Pablo Prigioni	PG	NYK	1263	0.061	0.366	0.487
19	Eric Bledsoe	PG	LAC	1553	0.060	0.452	0.572
20	Greg Stiemsma	C	MIN	1209	0.059	0.212	0.330

Prigioni was productive on defense in 1263 total minutes played on the season. In general, production in limited minutes does not imply the ability to produce in extended minutes. At 36

[1] Begley, I. "Reaction: Prigioni to re-sign with Knicks." ESPN.com. July 4, 2013. <http://espn.go.com/blog/new-york/knicks/post/_/id/46447/reaction-pablo-prigioni-to-re-sign-with-knicks.>

[2] Zillgit, J. "Pablo Prigioni key to New York Knicks' success." USA Today. April 30, 2013. <http://www.usatoday.com/story/sports/nba/2013/04/30/new-york-knicks-vs-boston-celtics-pablo-prigioni/2125169/>.

years old, it is unlikely Prigioni could produce the same DSG/M in over 2500 minutes on the season.

AV measures a player's value to his team. A player can have different value for different teams. Paul Pierce was often the first option on offense for the Celtics during his career. He and Garnett have been traded to the Brooklyn Nets, a team with Deron Williams, Joe Johnson and Brook Lopez. It is not likely that Pierce will be used to the same degree in the offense in Brooklyn as he was used in Boston.

Each year, players are traded. If the player plays significant minutes for both clubs, this can provide an opportunity to compare a player's value to two different clubs in the same season. In 2013, point guard Beno Udrih was traded from the Bucks to the Magic. In the same deal, J. J. Redick was sent from Orlando to Milwaukee. Also last season, Jose Calderon was traded from Toronto to Detroit, and Rudy Gay was dealt from Memphis to Toronto. All of these players played at least 700 minutes for each team they suited up for.

Table 4.8 details each player's production in DSG/M, EOP/M, and AV/M for each team in 2012-13. Udrih was slightly more valuable defensively and slightly less valuable offensively for Milwaukee than Orlando. Overall, Udrih provided approximately the same value to each club he played for. The largest discrepancy in the chart belonged to Gay. Gay was more valuable offensively and defensively for Toronto than he was for Memphis. We talked above about how Pierce will likely have a lesser role with Brooklyn than he did in Boston. In the trade, Pierce is leaving a team where he was the primary option on offense, and joining a team where he may be the 3rd or 4th option. Gay was dealt from a competitive team in Memphis to a less competitive club in Toronto. It seems that with less around him in Toronto, Gay had the opportunity to do more. Recall that DSG is computed by looking at net rates. It is not surprising that Gay's leaving the court had less of an impact on the defense in Memphis that featured stellar defenders such as Conley, Allen and Gasol, than it did in Toronto.

Table 4.8: Traded Players in 2012-13

Player	Team	Min.	DSG/M	EOP/M	AV/M
Beno Udrih	MIL	719	0.025	0.473	0.523
Beno Udrih	ORL	738	0.003	0.487	0.494
Jose Calderon	TOR	1273	-0.010	0.589	0.568
Jose Calderon	DET	887	-0.030	0.529	0.469
Rudy Gay	MEM	1541	0.004	0.365	0.373
Rudy Gay	TOR	1146	0.050	0.445	0.545
J.J. Redick	MIL	804	-0.039	0.372	0.295
J.J. Redick	ORL	1575	-0.022	0.477	0.433

Comparing AV to PER and WP

In Chapter 2, we surveyed some popular measures of player production. Two of these were Player Efficiency Rating (PER) and Wins Produced (WP). We want to emphasize some of the significant differences in the outputs of AV, PER and WP.

PER is a rate statistic. It is meant to capture production per 48 minutes. AV is a cumulative statistic. Thus, there are top performers in PER, such as Anderson Varejeo, that would not be ranked highly in AV. Varejeo had a PER of 21.71. That was good enough for 16th overall among players that played at least 6.09 minutes per game. Due to an injury, Varejao only played 25 games in 2012-13. As a result, he was ranked 177th in AV. (Varejao was 21st in AV/M among players that played at least 820 minutes.) The pattern demonstrated by Varejao is typical among players that rate highly in PER but were not on top of the AV board. It is more interesting to study players that were ranked high in AV, but not high in PER. To be high in AV, a player must produce in quantity, but also quality. PER should reflect the quality of production. Among players ranked in the top 20 in AV, the biggest difference in AV rank and PER rank was that of Andre Iguodala. Iguodala was 17th in 2012-13 in AV. He was ranked 137th in PER, just behind Chris Wilcox, a backup center in Boston. PER uses blocks and steals as the major defensive measures for an individual. Iguodala does get steals. He was ranked 11th in the league last season. Still, PER may be underrating Iguodala's other contributions on defense. Iguodala was ranked 14th in DSG. Offensively, EOP ranks Iguodala 41st overall, around players like Chandler Parsons and Paul Millsap. In other words, EOP sees Iguodala as a solid 2nd or 3rd option on offense, but not as a 1st option like James, Durant, Bryant, Westbrook or Harden. Iguodala's PER was 15.27 (just above the league average of 15). Is Iguodala an average player? Or is Iguodala a stellar perimeter defender and a solid (but not exceptional) contributor on offense as DSG and EOP suggest? There is no right or wrong here. In fact, the large discrepancy in the two metrics probably implies that AV overrates Iguodala while PER underrates him. Other players that were rated in the top 25 in AV but did not rate particularly well in PER included Jrue Holiday in Philadelphia, Mike Conley in Memphis, Monta Ellis in Milwaukee and Paul George in Indiana.

There are similarities in the outputs of AV and WP. First, we note that WP agrees with AV in regards to Iguodala. Iguodala was ranked 19th by WP. WP also agrees with AV in regards to another player that was rated high in AV but not PER. Houston small forward Chandler Parsons was ranked 34th by AV, 34th by WP and 135th by PER.

A number of players had high AV ranks but not so high WP ranks. WP agrees with PER on Jrue Holiday. PER ranks him 94th and WP ranks him 123rd. Recall that Holiday was ranked second in AV in 2012-13. PER and AV largely agree on LaMarcus Aldridge. AV ranks him 8th, and PER ranks him 24th. WP ranks him 108th. One of the more surprising differences to us was Kevin Garnett. Garnett was 22nd in AV but 131st in WP. The biggest difference among the top 25 was Carmelo Anthony. AV ranked Carmelo 21st. WP ranked Carmelo 200th! We did not hold back criticism of Carmelo for being inefficient as compared to other elite scorers in the NBA, but we do not believe that 199 players provided more value to their team in 2012-13. WP ranked Carmelo below his teammate Steve Novak.

There were many players that AV ranked highly, but WP ranked quite low. So, there must be players going the other direction. Jimmy Butler and Thabo Sefolosha were in the top 15 in WP and not in the top 100 for AV. Reggie Evans was ranked 25th by WP and 121st in AV. All of these examples played significant minutes and thus had the opportunity to produce a high AV score.

PER, WP, and AV are all computed in very different ways. In that respect, it is not surprising that the outputs can be so different. However, each metric is after some representation of player value. Given the relatively similar objectives, it is surprising to see that one metric (WP) ranked Reggie Evans 106 spots ahead of Kevin Garnett while another (AV) ranked Garnett 99 spots ahead of Evans.

PER, WP, and AV are all valuable. Each is an intelligent perspective on player production—a more advanced measure than looking at traditional box scores alone. There are obvious differences in the formulas of these metrics, but comparing and contrasting the value assigned to actual players yields another level of recognition. Ultimately, the goal is to best understand all of the metrics so that we can properly interpret the results.

5

Visualizing NBA Analytics

There are a variety of ways to visually represent statistics. Pie charts, line and bar graphs, box and whisker plots, and scatter plots are just a few options. Visual representations help our minds process the data and notice trends. The most appropriate choice of visual representation is dependent on the nature and purpose of the underlying statistics. Basketball data presents its own unique challenges when it comes to visual representations.

Visual representations of NBA data are popping up everywhere. NBA.com now presents shots charts for players.[1] They partition the floor into various regions. The user can look at the player's shot distribution as well as percentages. Muthu Alagappan uses visualizations and topological data analysis to redefine the positions on the NBA court.[2] He is certainly catching people's attention. He was named one of Forbes 30 most influential people under 30 in sports. He also gave a talk at TEDx.[3] His work maps the skill sets of players currently in the NBA, with very similar skill sets forming dense "cities." It is these dense spots that Alagappan identifies as the new positions. We will talk more about the idea of redefining NBA positions and Alagappan's work in Chapter 9. We mention his work now because we can learn a lot simply by looking at the visualizations of his analysis. See the references in the footnote for more details. In this chapter, we will stick with the theme of the first third of our book and focus on visual representations of individual measures of production.

When looking at measures of player performance, we often have single numbers such as OE, EOP, DSG and AV that have multiple components. If we care about the totals, we also care about the simple statistics on which the totals are built. This presents a challenge of how best to represent total production in conjunction with each component. Perhaps we can gather this information in a visual representation that will allow our mind to process the results more quickly than when the data is organized in a table.

We will begin with simple diagrams that are valuable in their own right. We then move to more complicated representations that use the simple diagrams as building blocks.

---

[1] NBA.com. <http://stats.nba.com/shotcharts.html>.
[2] Alagappan, M. "From 5 to 13: Redefining the positions in Basketball." 2012. <http://www.sloansportsconference.com/?p=5431>.
[3] Alagappan, M. "The new positions of basketball." 2013. <http://tedxtalks.ted.com/video/The-new-positions-of-basketball>.

Chart 5.1: Visualizing EOP for the 2012-13 Season

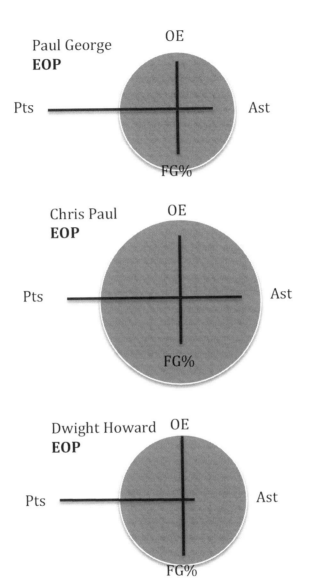

Visualizing Efficient Offensive Production (EOP)

Consider Chart 5.1. Here we compare EOP in the 2012-13 season for three players—Paul George of the Indiana Pacers, Chris Paul of the Los Angeles Clippers and Dwight Howard of the Los Angeles Lakers. George is a small forward/shooting guard, Chris Paul is a point guard, and Dwight Howard is a center. In the chart, the gray circle represents EOP. The radius of the circle is proportional to EOP for the season. Four lines come out of the circle in the four cardinal directions of north, south, east, and west. The four lines represent the player's OE, assists, points, and FG%. The length of the line from the center of the circle is proportional to the total production in each stat for the individual. This representation allows us to quickly compare the contributions of the individuals. George has a slight edge in points. Paul is by far the most prolific in assists. George is second, and Howard is a distant third in this category. George trails Howard and Paul in OE, and Paul takes top honors in EOP. The chart is constructed to draw the viewer's eye first to the cumulative impact, the EOP statistic, and then to the complementary numbers. The vertical alignment allows for an easy comparison of the east and west arms (points and assists). A horizontal alignment would allow for easier comparison of the rate statistics, OE and FG%.

There is nothing holding us to the choice of complementary statistics or the number of arms coming out of the center of the circle. Although, less arms is probably easier for the mind to interpret quickly. We could add or replace existing arms with free throw percentage or 3 point percentage for example. We can also run similar charts for other metrics. For example, we could create an image for Hollinger's PER with arms representing points, assists, rebounds, blocks and steals.

The goal of the visual representation is to allow the mind to quickly process the contributions of an individual or several individuals. This allows for ease of comparison between two players or to compare a player's production in different situations, at different times in a season, or across several seasons. We will use these representations in the next chapter when we consider player development.

Ultimately, we could see these charts having value on the player stat pages of sites such as Basketball-Reference.com, ESPN.com, or NBA.com. Perhaps a site could host a design your own image portal, where the user could pick the master and sub stats, and then call the picture for several players or for the same player in several seasons.

Visualizing Approximate Value (AV)

Recall that Approximate Value (AV) is the sum of Defensive Points Saved (DPS) and Efficient Offensive Production (EOP). DPS is just Defensive Stops Gained (DSG) times two. AV has an offensive and a defensive component. In Chart 5.2, we represent Approximate Value together with EOP for several players in the 2012-13 season. AV is represented with a circle with white interior. The radius of the circle is proportional to the player's AV for the season. EOP is a gray circle. Again, the radius of the circle is proportional to the player's EOP. Since AV is the sum of DPS and EOP, DPS can be discerned from the diagram. EOP is always positive, while DPS can be positive or negative. Marc Gasol and Larry Sanders had positive DPS. Thus, their AV circle has a larger radius than EOP. Kevin Durant and Al Jefferson had negative DPS. Their AV circles are smaller than their EOP circles.

Looking at Chart 5.2, we can quickly gather who had positive and who had negative DPS. We can also see who had the better AV. Gasol and Durant were more valuable than Sanders and Jefferson. Comparing Gasol and Durant, it is easy to see that Gasol contributes defensively while

Durant is a superior offensive player. Like Gasol, Sanders brings solid defense, but his total contributions are not near Gasol's. Jefferson is a far better offensive player than Sanders and a comparable offensive talent to Gasol. However, Jefferson is a detriment to his team on the defensive side. Overall, Jefferson provides the least value of the group.

As with the diagrams in Chart 5.1, we could add arms for complementary statistics to the circles in Chart 5.2. Reasonable choices could include the components of DSG or EOP. We could also include stats such as rebounds, blocks and steals. The most appropriate choices depend on what we are looking for. Are we interested in comparing defensive big men? If so, we might want to include blocks or the new measures of interior defense presented by Goldsberry and discussed in Chapter 2.

The visualizations in Chart 5.2 are simple. The simplicity allows for the diagrams to be pieces in a larger visualization without creating too overwhelming an image. Chart 5.3 demonstrates how we can use the AV/EOP pictures in a larger visualization.

In the 2013 offseason, Al Jefferson signed a three-year, 41 million-dollar deal with the Charlotte Bobcats.[4] Jefferson posts impressive box score statistics. In 2012-13, he averaged 17.8 points and 9.2 rebounds per game. His Player Efficiency Rating (PER) of 20.99 was 21st in the NBA. However, AV does not share the same affinity for Jefferson as Hollinger's PER. In particular, Jefferson flunks Defensive Stops Gained (DSG), the defensive component in AV. To learn more about Jefferson, we plotted his AV/EOP with minutes played by season in his career. The results are displayed in Chart 5.3. Again, gray circles reflect EOP and white circles reflect AV. Below the chart, we provide two points of reference, the 2012-13 AV/EOP of centers Tiago Splitter and Al Horford. We believe the most interesting trend that emerges from this visualization is that Jefferson appears to have the most value when he plays closer to 2000 minutes on the season. When his minutes approach 3000, he produces more offense, but his liabilities on defense more than cancel out the increased offensive production.

Team Crop Circles

All players are confined to playing within the limitations of their team. A limited number of minutes are dispersed across a given team's roster. A given player may be more or less involved in the offense than they would prefer to be based on the personnel that surround them. Furthermore, a team's style of play can greatly impact the individual statistics of players within that structure.

Due to the limited amount of opportunities that each team has to give, there are players that simply do not get enough opportunities to perform despite playing highly efficiently in limited time. To rate highly in EOP, one must be given the opportunity to take advantage of their efficiency over a large percentage of their team's time. Thabo Sefolosha had his highest EOP while with the Oklahoma City Thunder in 2012-13. We would be missing a major component of his increased production if we did not recognize the opportunity created when James Harden was traded to Houston the previous summer.

---

[4] Stein, M., "Sources: Al Jefferson to Bobcats." July 4, 2013.
<http://espn.go.com/nba/story/_/id/9450469/al-jefferson-sign-charlotte-bobcats-sources-say>.

Chart 5.2: Visualizing AV/EOP for the 2012-13 Season

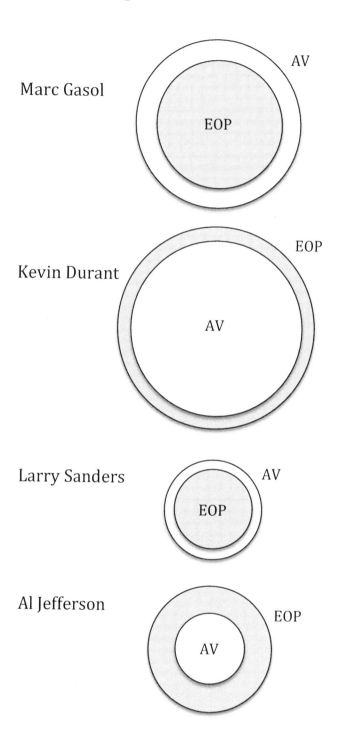

Chart 5.3: Al Jefferson AV/EOP by Season

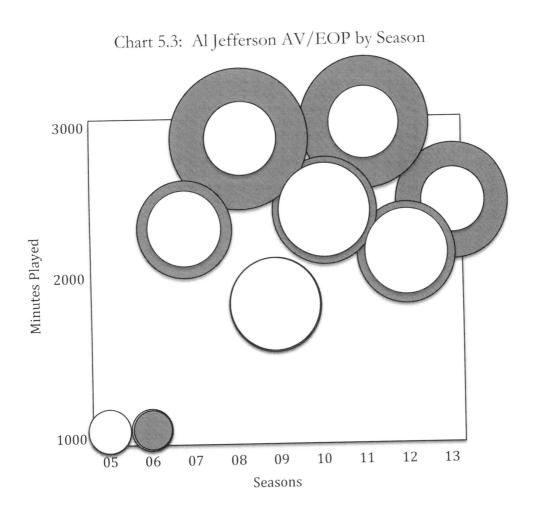

Points of Reference from 2012-13

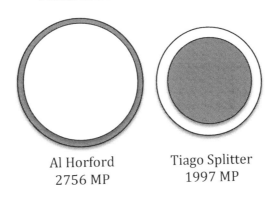

Al Horford
2756 MP

Tiago Splitter
1997 MP

A player will have a positive DSG when his team is better defensively with him on the court than they are with him off the court. When it comes to the individual calculation of DSG for players on a given team, players actually have a direct impact on their teammates' abilities to post high DSG scores. Teams sometimes have well-defined first and second units. In this situation, if the first unit has a negative DSG, the second unit will have a positive DSG and vice versa. The individual statistics are earned while playing for a team. To truly understand a player's numbers, we must analyze the individual statistics in the context of the entire team's performance.

Visualizing the individual contributions of an entire team is challenging. Our AV/EOP circle diagrams are simple enough to be used as a primary building block for a total team representation. They are also useful in that they reflect offensive and defensive contributions. Note that similar diagrams could be constructed on other metrics.

Chart 5.4 displays the AV/EOP diagrams for the major contributors to the Oklahoma City Thunder in the 2008-09 through 2012-13 seasons. We refer to the diagrams as Team Evolution Charts (TECs) since they reflect the growth and development of players as well as roster acquisitions and departures. We also refer to TECs as crop circles because of their resemblance to the eerie patterns that have riddled UFOlogists for decades.

The AV/EOP circles are organized as follows. Each column is associated with a season. The first column on the left represents the earliest season in the chart. Each successive column is the next season. If a player was a significant contributor to the team for the entire period in the TEC, one row will be assigned to that player. Otherwise, multiple players may exist in the same row. This will certainly be done if a particular player's role is immediately replaced. For example, all three players in the last row of Chart 5.4 served primarily as backup point guards. In these cases, we label the first season circle with the player's name. The 2009-10 circle in the last row of Chart 5.4 is labeled Maynor. There is no label with the 2010-11 circle in the same row. This was Maynor's production as well. The backdrop for the diagram is a line chart of the win % for the team. In this way, we can see if the changes at the individual level are reflected in the overall team production.

When looking at Oklahoma City's TEC, we first notice the extreme value of Durant and Westbrook. These two are the center of the offense. Next, we notice that the improvement in approximate value for these two stars largely mimics the increased win percentage of the time period. Later, we will study player involvement metrics. Those numbers will support the notion that the NBA is a star's league. As the stars go, so will the team. The crop circles here seem to tell the same story.

When Harden was traded from Oklahoma City to Houston in the 2012 offseason, there was an opportunity for other players to step up in the offense. Kevin Martin filled some of, but not the entire void left by Harden. (When comparing the players' production in 2011-12 to that of 2012-13, remember that 2011-12 was a shortened season.) Sefolosha also appears to have benefited from the void left by Harden.

Chart 5.4 nicely represents the transition from Jeff Green as the primary power forward to Serge Ibaka. When Ibaka was drafted in 2009, Green was a big part of the offense for the Thunder. As an undersized power forward, Green was a liability defensively. The Thunder did not have the option to play Green at small forward since Durant occupied that position. Ibaka had minimal impact his first year. However, he has developed to be more valuable overall than Green was for OKC in 2008-09 and 2009-10. Ibaka is still not the efficient offensive producer Green was, but he is a better defensive power forward than Green was for the Thunder.

The Thunder do not rely much on the production of their centers. Neither Krstic nor Perkins has done much in terms of EOP or AV for Oklahoma City. Instead, power forward Nick

Collison has provided extra value in the frontcourt while coming off the bench. The Thunder often play a smaller lineup without a traditional center. The third most common lineup for Oklahoma City in 2012-13 featured a frontcourt of Durant, Ibaka and Collison (with Martin and Westbrook at guard).

The starters for the Thunder were typically slightly negative in DSG, while the second unit was slightly positive. The second unit may generally play against second units and thus weaker opposition. We should not jump to the conclusion that the second unit is better defensively than the starting unit. However, there are plenty of starting units across the NBA with significantly positive DSG. Quality of opposition alone is not an excuse. The Thunder have a backup center in Hasheem Thabeet (who is not featured in the chart) that is very good defensively. Thabeet's DSG/M was the highest on the Thunder last season. In fact, his DSG/M more than doubled any other player on the team. Thabeet's defensive prowess with the second unit likely contributed to the positive DSG of that group and negative DSG of the starters.

Each year, younger players develop and improve, while the production of older players declines. Teams lose and acquire members. In any given season, there is only so much room for individual production. TECs (or crop circles) help us put together the moving and changing pieces of the team puzzle.

We are just scratching the surface of what could be accomplished with visual representations of NBA data. Sports analytics is a growing industry. New metrics are introduced seemingly every day, and the metrics themselves are becoming more complex. Fans and NBA front offices would both appreciate and sometimes require simple and easily interpretable representations of these new statistics. Tables filled with values may not always be optimal. We encourage those that design new metrics to be creative in their choice of presentation.

Chart 5.4: Oklahoma City Crop Circles

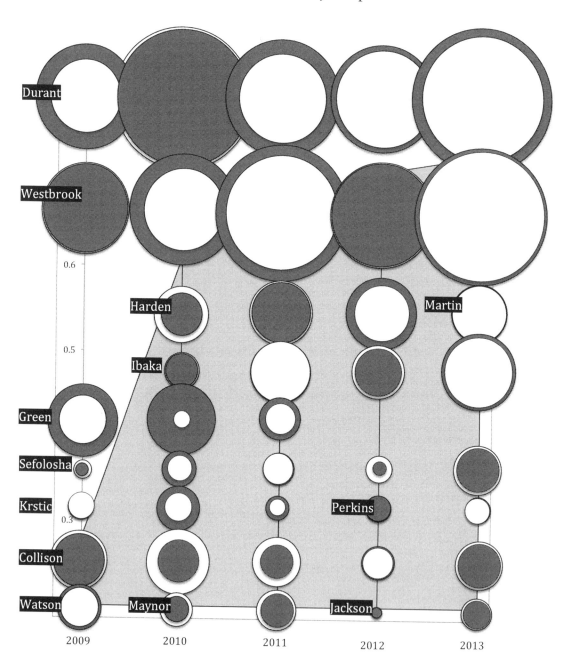

6

Player Development

A 2009 TrueHoop blog on ESPN.com discusses "The Kevin Durant Conundrum."[1] Kevin Durant entered the NBA after his freshman year at The University of Texas. At the time of the blog, Durant had just turned 21. The post acknowledges, "For players his age, his scoring is top-five all-time." The blog then continues with the following.

> "And yet, a shocking piece of news: The Thunder have, over the last two years, consistently performed worse than normal when Durant is on the floor. Any way you slice the +/- numbers, he's one of the Thunder's worst players."

The numbers are bizarre. How could the Thunder get worse when Durant is on the floor? There could be a number of reasons. One simple explanation is that Durant's teammates at the time were not capable of playing at his level. It is possible that Durant played at a different speed, and the disparity in quality when Durant was on the floor led to the poor overall team play. Another simple explanation is that Durant, while a prolific scorer, had yet to learn how to play reasonable defense. Perhaps he was still learning when to shoot and when to pass. Maybe he had yet to trust his teammates and was taking the more challenging shot when he should have given the ball up. It could be that he was still learning NBA defenses and how to create plays in the world's most competitive league. Durant came into the league with loads of potential. However, with only one year of basketball above the high school level under his belt, he had a lot to learn.

As we look at the results of our metrics, it is important to remember that players develop and mature. Many players play a very inefficient style of basketball when they enter the NBA. This does not imply that they will be inefficient for their careers. In fact, Durant's OE has risen from .45 his rookie season to .54 last season. Durant had all the makings of a player that would improve significantly as his career progressed. If we do not recognize players' ability to develop and improve, we might make the same mistake former adviser to the Mavericks and co-designer of adjusted plus-minus, Wayne Winston, made when asked about Durant. The following is from the same TrueHoop article.

---

[1] "The Kevin Durant Conundrum." TrueHoop Blog at ESPN.com. October 9, 2009. <http://espn.go.com/blog/truehoop/post/_/id/7047/the-kevin-durant-conundrum>.

"Knowing that just about any NBA general manager would trade his own children for a prospect of Durant's caliber, I asked Winston if he'd advise his team to accept if the Mavericks were (in some alternate universe) offered Durant for free. 'I'd say probably not,' he replied. 'I would not sign the guy. It's simply not inevitable that he'll make mid-career strides. Some guys do. But many don't, and he'd have to improve a lot to help a team.'"

Winston has produced a lot for NBA analytics, and so we will assume he was grandstanding (to a degree) here.

For the purposes of tracking a player's offensive development, we particularly like OE. We have already seen how LeBron has improved in OE, but Carmelo has not. See Chart 3.7. One of our favorite examples of a player improving efficiency is Robert Parrish. Parrish played in more NBA games than any other player, 1611 regular season games to be exact. To do this, Parish played until he was 43 years old. The Chief (as he was nicknamed) teamed with Larry Bird and Kevin McHale to form Boston's original big three. Those Celtics won titles in 1981, 1984 and 1986. It is not unusual for a player to improve his OE over his first few seasons in the NBA. Many players improve initially, and then plateau for the prime of their career. Parrish's OE steadily improved over the first 14 seasons of his career. Most NBA players do not play 14 seasons. When players his age were retiring, he was still improving his efficiency. Chart 6.1 tracks the Chief's OE over his 20 seasons in the NBA. As one would expect, his efficiency could not improve forever. At about the age of 40, the Chief's game and his OE declined. We also included the OE of Parrish's teammate Kevin McHale. Both players were skilled offensive big men. McHale's line is far more typical. He improved steadily early in his career. The decline for McHale began after his eighth season in the NBA. Parrish's OE is just another impressive statistic on his age-defying career.

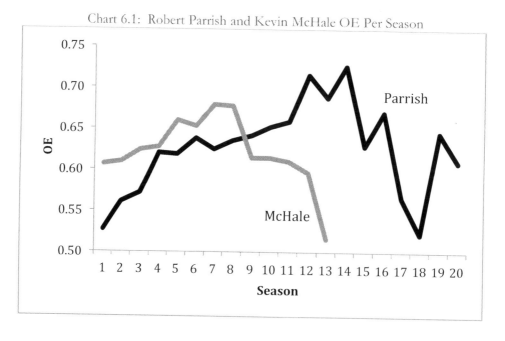

Chart 6.1: Robert Parrish and Kevin McHale OE Per Season

OE is an important stat to track when looking at a young player's development. However, it can sometimes be misleading. As a developing player becomes a better and more efficient scorer, he will draw tougher defenders and more of the opposing team's focus on defense. Teams will scout the player to understand what he does and does not do well. To get a better sense of the player's development and whether or not he is becoming one of his team's first few options on offense, we need to factor in offensive production as well as efficiency. We already have a statistic in Efficient Offensive Production (EOP) that does this well.

Chart 6.2 details the progression of Spurs center Tiago Splitter over his first three seasons in the NBA. Here we use the circle and arm visual representations presented in Chapter 5. Recall that the radii of the gray circles in the diagram are proportional to the player's EOP for the given season. The diagrams display significant improvement for Splitter. His EOP and points have improved each year. Even with an increased role in the offense as the years progressed, Splitter was able to maintain his level of OE. We also see that in 2012-13, Splitter started to earn assists as well. Splitter was not a young rookie. He was 26 years old in his rookie season for the Spurs, after playing several years professionally in Spain. Still, the development of Splitter bodes well for his future.

The NBA lockout shortened the 2011-12 season. The circle along with the east and west arms of the diagrams are cumulative statistics. As such, it is important to remember that the players had less opportunity to accumulate numbers in 2011-12. The north and south arms of the diagram are rate statistics and essentially indifferent to season length. For those particularly concerned with the cumulative numbers across multiple seasons, we recommend using the per-game relatives of EOP, points and assists in the charts.

Detroit's Greg Monroe is another player that has a positive trend in production. Monroe was drafted seventh overall in the 2010 NBA draft out of Georgetown. Out of college, Monroe was thought to have a strong mind for the game and to be an above average passer. These skills contributed to the growth evident in Chart 6.3. Given that Monroe will be just 23 years old this year, his future is bright.

In 2012-13, Washington Wizards rookie shooting guard Bradley Beal had an abysmal .29 OE in the clutch. By clutch time, we mean in the last five minutes of a game when the score is within five. Of the 113 players that played at least 100 minutes of clutch time in 2012-13, Beal had the lowest OE. Beal, who was the third overall pick in the 2012 draft, shows a lot of promise. We will not be so foolish as to say he cannot develop into an efficient scorer in the clutch.

NBA players develop. This is particularly true for younger players. When Winston stated that he would not recommend the Mavs take Durant for free, he underestimated Durant's potential for growth. Once a player is a star, it can be very difficult to acquire his talents. Part of building a successful NBA franchise is finding those players that are poised for significant improvement in the near future. We will talk more about this as we transition from player evaluation to team evaluation and construction.

Chart 6.2: Tiago Splitter EOP

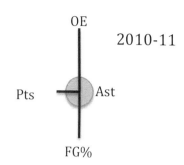

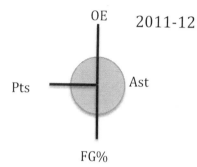

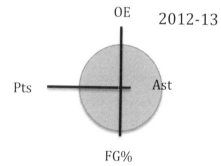

Chart 6.3: Greg Monroe EOP

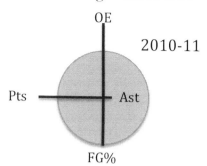

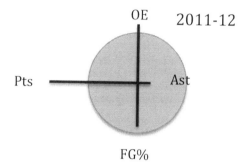

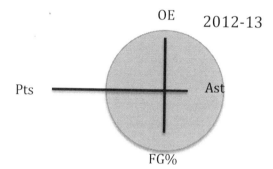

All for One:
Team Evaluation

"A basketball team is like the five fingers on your hand. If you can get them all together, you have a fist. That's how I want you to play."

-Mike Krzyzewski[1]

[1] Krzyzewski, M. Achievement.org. Retrieved August 15, 2013.
<http://www.achievement.org/autodoc/page/krz0int-3>.

7

Lineup Entropy

Miles plays basketball for the Predictables. In the first half of each game this season, the Predictables played Miles, Jimmy, Jason, Jacob, and Jordan. In the second half, the team played Michael, Marcus, Marvin, Mario and Mo. In the same season, Gavin played for the Unpredictables. At every stoppage of play, the coach of the Unpredictables randomly selected five players from the team of ten to play. If you were told at some time in the season, Miles was on the court, how difficult would it be to predict his teammates? Now, consider the same question for Gavin.

Teams in the NBA live between the predictable and unpredictable extremes described above. Exactly where each team stands on the spectrum of possibilities is important for our statistical analysis. Recall our classification of top down and bottom up metrics. A top down metric is one that measures a player's contributions by looking at the contributions of entire units on the court. For example, a player's plus-minus is the points scored by the player's team while he is on the court minus the points scored by the opponent in the same time frame. Top down metrics, and in particular plus-minus, have a major weakness. They are biased towards players that play with good teammates. The top 20 plus-minus totals for the 2012-13 season are in Table 7.1. The bias of plus-minus is overwhelming. Eight of the top nine players on the board are from Miami or Oklahoma City. Only six teams are represented in the top 20.

Table 7.1: Top 20 +/- for 2012-13 Regular Season

Rank	Player	+/-	Rank	Player	+/-
1	LeBron James (MIA)	720	11	Tony Parker (SA)	448
2	Kevin Durant (OKC)	717	12	Kevin Martin (OKC)	441
3	Russell Westbrook (OKC)	631	13	Marc Gasol (MEM)	432
4	Dwyane Wade (MIA)	571	14	Chris Paul (LAC)	431
5	Mario Chalmers (MIA)	569	15	George Hill (IND)	417
6	Thebo Sefolosha (OKC)	505	16	Kendrick Perkins (OKC)	403
6	Mike Conley (MEM)	505	17	Roy Hibbert (IND)	390
8	Serge Ibaka (OKC)	490	18	Blake Griffin (LAC)	387
9	Chris Bosh (MIA)	477	19	Tiago Splitter (SA)	378
10	Tim Duncan (SA)	457	20	Lance Stephenson (IND)	377

There are several ways to account for or attempt to correct the bias of top down metrics towards players that play with good teammates. When we consider plus-minus, one simple trick is to take the individual's plus-minus per 48 minutes and subtract his team's plus-minus per 48 minutes when he is off the court. This is the net plus-minus used in 82games.com's Simple Ratings, which we discussed in Chapter 2. We consider plus-minus per 48 minutes (as opposed to simply plus-minus) to find players that played well in limited time. Table 7.2 displays the top 20 in plus-minus per 48 minutes played. Here, we only considered players that played at least 400 minutes on the season. The bias is even more pronounced than in Table 7.1. Every player in the top 17 is from Miami, Oklahoma City or San Antonio.

Table 7.2: Top 20 +/- per 48 minutes for 2012-13 Regular Season

Rank	Player	+/-	Rank	Player	+/-
1	Mario Chalmers (MIA)	13.16	11	Kevin Martin (OKC)	9.84
2	LeBron James (MIA)	12.01	12	Serge Ibaka (OKC)	9.48
3	Dwyane Wade (MIA)	11.44	13	Kawhi Leonard (SAS)	9.44
4	Nick Collison (OKC)	11.10	14	Chris Bosh (MIA)	9.25
5	Kevin Durant (OKC)	11.10	15	Udonis Haslem (MIA)	9.23
6	Thabo Sefolosha (OKC)	10.77	16	Shane Battier (MIA)	9.14
7	Russell Westbrook (OKC)	10.64	17	Tiago Splitter (SAS)	9.09
8	Tim Duncan (SAS)	10.60	18	Chris Paul (LAC)	8.84
9	Kendrick Perkins (OKC)	9.95	19	Tayshaun Prince (MEM)	8.83
10	Tony Parker (SAS)	9.87	20	Mike Conley (MEM)	8.81

Table 7.3 presents the top 20 in net plus-minus per 48 minutes. Taking the net plus-minus goes a long way in eliminating the team bias. Amir Johnson who played for the not-so-great Toronto Raptors was third overall. There are also players from Sacramento, Portland, Washington and Dallas in the Top 20.

Table 7.3: Top 20 Net +/- per 48 minutes for 2012-13 Regular Season

Rank	Player	+/-	Rank	Player	+/-
1	Mike Conley (MEM)	15.43	11	Brook Lopez (BKN)	9.91
2	LeBron James (MIA)	15.29	12	Lance Stephenson (IND)	9.69
3	Amir Johnson (TOR)	14.04	13	John Salmons (SAC)	9.44
4	Vince Carter (DAL)	12.65	14	Dwyane Wade (MIA)	9.17
5	Marc Gasol (MEM)	11.32	15	Kevin Durant (OKC)	9.17
6	Mario Chalmers (MIA)	11.20	16	LaMarcus Aldridge (POR)	9.12
7	George Hill (IND)	11.06	17	Nene (WAS)	8.99
8	Damian Lillard (POR)	10.88	18	Tim Duncan (SAS)	8.93
9	Joe Johnson (BKN)	10.36	19	Kyle Korver (ATL)	8.83
10	Roy Hibbert (IND)	9.91	20	David West (IND)	8.61

The net plus-minus compares players to their typical team production. The statistic is saying, for example, that the Toronto Raptors were 14.04 points for 48 minutes better last season when Amir Johnson was on the court than when he was off. By comparison, the Miami Heat were 15.29 points per 48 minutes better last season when LeBron was on the court. The Heat without LeBron were much better than the Raptors without Johnson. In that respect, LeBron's net plus-minus is more impressive.

Net plus-minus does a good job in putting players from good and bad teams on a level playing field. It also can distinguish the talent among players on the same team. In plus-minus per 48 minutes, Nick Collison was better than Durant. However, in net plus-minus, Durant was better. In plus-minus per 48 minutes, seven players from the Thunder made the top 20. Durant is the only player from the Thunder in the top 20 for net plus-minus. Players like Nick Collison benefit from playing with Durant. Net plus-minus looks at production for each player on and off the court. The Thunder were about four times as good with Collison off the court than in the time with Durant off the court, showing that Durant was the more impactful presence.

Net plus-minus works in distinguishing players on the same team when these players do not always play at the same time. Suppose that we tried to run net plus-minus for the Predictables. Miles, Jimmy, Jason, Jacob and Jordan always play together. They would have the exact same plus-minus per 48 minutes and net plus-minus per 48 minutes. It is the most extreme team bias example. In contrast, Gavin can likely be distinguished from any of his teammates on the Unpredictables. The random selection of lineups means Gavin will play with a lot of different teammates and more than likely with each for approximately the same amount of time.

Statistically, the Unpredictables' mixing of lineups is ideal for trying to distinguish the contributions of the individual from that of his teammates. The Predictables' strategy is the worst possible statistically. While we do not see either extreme reached in the NBA, there are situations where players play a significant amount of time together. For example, Mario Chalmers played 1922 of his 2068 minutes with LeBron. In other words, Chalmers played 93% of his time with LeBron. Our metrics (and everyone else's) say LeBron is pretty good. There is an obvious opportunity for Chalmers' plus-minus numbers and net plus-minus numbers to be inflated. This is why Chalmers is sixth in net plus-minus when other Miami players such as Bosh and Battier drop out of the top 20.

If we want to consider top down metrics, we need to pay attention to the amount of time that players play with each of their teammates. For a specific player, we can look at their proportion of time with each teammate. However, to do this for all players would be tedious at best. It also does not give us a method to quickly identify players that might be particularly prone to team pull biases. This chapter is about taking all of the percentages of a player's playing time with each teammate and combining them into one number that well represents the degree to which that player mixes with different teammates. This will be called Lineup Entropy. Here, the more teammates the player plays with and the more evenly distributed the time with those teammates, the better.

To be clear, our new Lineup Entropy is not the sexy new metric everyone likes to read about. In this Chapter, we will not be producing top 20 lists with Jordan, Magic and LeBron. Instead, Lineup Entropy is about laying a proper foundation for and assigning confidence to top down metrics. It is about better understanding where stats such as adjusted plus-minus or net plus-minus might be misleading. Let us give an analogy that Boston sports fans will appreciate. Like stapling Curt Schilling's ankle before the famed bloody sock game in the 2004 ALCS, Lineup Entropy is ugly and essential.

What is Shannon's Entropy?

To quantify the diversity in lineups of an individual, we will use Shannon's entropy from information theory.[1] Our use of entropy here is motivated by its application as the measure of diversity in other settings. It has been used by entomologists (bug scientists) to study the variety of insects in a swamp[2] and economists to study concentration in industries[3]. We now explain

---

[1] Shannon, C. *Mathematical Theory of Communication.* Univ. of Illinois Press, Urbana, Ill, 1963.
[2] Houlihan, P.R., Harrison, M.E., and Cheyne, S.M, "Impacts of forest gaps on butterfly diversity in a Bornean peat-swamp forest." *Journal of Asia-Pacific Entomology* 16, pp. 67-73, 2013.

Shannon's entropy formula and how it can be used for these types of applications. This section will involve some of the most advanced mathematics in this book. For ease in comprehension, we will spend some time trying to explain the methodologies.

Let's flip a penny. You guess the outcome. Regardless of your guess, you have a 50% chance of getting the answer correct. It was heads by the way. Now, let's roll a six-sided die. Again, guess the outcome. It was a 2. It is less likely that you correctly guessed the outcome of the die. The die has more uncertainty. In this case, since all outcomes are equally likely, the die has more uncertainty simply because it has more outcomes.

Now, we visit the craps table in a casino. A gambler rolls two dice. If you are gambling, then you are trying to predict the number that will come up. If you have played craps, you know that seven is more likely to come up than the other numbers. That is why it has its special role as the out in the game. When rolling two dice, there are eleven possible numbers that can come up, but not all of them are equally likely to occur. Compare this to rolling an (imaginary) eight sided die where all possibilities are equally likely. How do we quantify the uncertainty of these types of events?

Let's consider a basketball example. Suppose you are the GM of the 1984 Portland Trail Blazers and (after a wise 1981 trade) are in the coin flip for the first overall pick in the draft. The fact that you should consider the guard out of the University of North Carolina is besides our point. Instead, compare the coin flip scenario to the following. Suppose there were six teams eligible for the first pick and the commissioner were going to roll a fair six-sided die to determine the first overall pick. The latter situation contains more uncertainty. It is harder to predict who will win the pick among the six teams than it was to predict the original Olajuwon sweepstakes of 1984. Simply having more teams in the mix does not imply more uncertainty, however. Consider a third scenario where one of the six teams eligible for the first pick is the New York Knicks and the commissioner would like to see this big market team land a high profile player. (This is simply a hypothetical and not meant to be an accusation of past practices.) In this scenario, the commissioner has fixed the six-sided die so that 99% of the time, it will come up Knicks. The other five teams can split the remaining percent. We can be fairly certain the Knicks will win. This six-team scenario has less uncertainty than the original two-team coin flip. What if the Knicks had a 70% chance of winning and the other five teams split the remaining 30%? It is not so easy to see how the uncertainty in this scenario compares to the coin flip.

Shannon's entropy measures the uncertainty in events like those described above. Suppose we have an event with three possible outcomes. Label the outcomes 1, 2 and 3. Now suppose the probability of each outcome i is p_i. For example, the probability of outcome 1 is p_1. The entropy of this scenario is $-p_1 \log p_1 - p_2 \log p_2 - p_3 \log p_3$. The choice of base in the logarithm is not important, as long as we are consistent in using whatever we choose. Sticking with Shannon's tradition, we take the base to be two.

Return to our example of the coin flip. It has two outcomes (heads and tails). The probability of each is ½. So, the entropy of the coin flip is $-½ \log ½ - ½ \log ½ = -\log ½$. Remembering our rules of logarithms, $-\log ½ = \log 2$. For the six-sided die, the entropy is 6 ($-1/6 \log 1/6$)= $\log 6$. Since log 6 is greater than log 2, the six-sided die has higher entropy. Note that the entropy formula accounts for the probability of all outcomes, not simply the most likely outcome.

---

[3] Ullah, A. "Entropy, Divergence and Distance Measures with Econometric Applications." *Journal of Statistical Planning and Inference* 49, pp. 137-162, 1996.

Now suppose more generally that we have n possible outcomes (where n is an integer). Label the outcomes 1, 2, ..., n. Let p_i be the probability of outcome i. The entropy of this situation is

$$-\sum_{i=1}^{n} p_i \log p_i$$

Informally, the more outcomes and the more equally spread the probability of each outcome, the higher the entropy. For those unfamiliar with this formula, it may seem a bit bizarre. Trust that it has been vetted many times over by the mathematics and statistics community.[4] Entropy has a number of nice mathematical properties that make it superior to other possible choices to aggregate the uncertainty, but we will spare the reader the details.

Defining Lineup Entropy

Fix a player B and a season that player B played. Let N={1,2,3,...,n} be the set of players that played with B at some point in the season. Let PT(B) be the total time played by B in the season. For each i in N, let PT(B,i) be the total time players i and B were on the court together in that season. Define p(i)=PT(B,i)/(4*PT(B)). At any point in the season, player B is playing with four teammates. So, there are a total of 4*PT(B) seconds of playing time with B that can be distributed among his teammates. Then, p(i) is the proportion of that time that i played. Think of the variation in linemates for B as the probability that at a random point in the season, we can guess the teammates on the court with B. Then, Shannon's entropy formula becomes a natural way to aggregate the variation. We define the Lineup Entropy of B, LE(B) to be

$$LE(B) = -\sum_{i=1}^{n} p(i) \log p(i).$$

Here (and always), we take the logarithm to be base 2. Recall our example of Miles and the Predictables. Miles always plays with the same four teammates. Thus, his LE is -4(1/4 log 1/4)=log 4=2. 2 represents the lowest LE a player in the NBA can have. It represents zero variation in linemates. A top down metric can be highly misleading for a player with a Lineup Entropy near 2. A purely top down statistic cannot differentiate between two players that always play together. In our example of the Predictables, Miles and his four linemates would all have identical plus-minus numbers.

We computed Lineup Entropy for each season for every player in the 2000-01 through 2012-13 seasons (5866 records in total). Table 7.4 displays the quartiles for this data. There are a number of players that only got on the court for a few minutes. These players had little opportunity to mix and are not particularly relevant for our analysis. For Table 7.5, we restricted the data to players that played at least 200 minutes on the season (4964 records in total). For the rest of this section, when we refer to percentiles in our data we are referring to the data restricted to players that played at least 200 minutes.

---

[4] A. Katok. "Fifty years of entropy in dynamics: 1958-2007." *Journal of Modern Dynamics*. vol 1, no. 4, 545-596. 2007.

Table 7.4: Quartiles for 2000-01 through 2012-13 Season LE

0%	25%	50%	75%	100%
2.00	3.19	3.37	3.55	5.11

Table 7.5: Quartiles for 2000-01 through 2012-13 Season LE (minimum of 200 minutes played)

0%	25%	50%	75%	100%
2.42	3.21	3.39	3.57	5.11

Note that for Tables 7.4 and 7.5, we are using full season lineup entropy for each player. In the Team-by-Team Advanced Metrics after Chapter 13, we provide the lineup entropy for each player restricted to the time the individual played for the given team. For example, Rudy Gay played for both Memphis and Toronto in 2012-13. He appears in the player stats for both Toronto and Memphis in the Team-by-Team Advanced Metrics. LE and other stats reported for Rudy Gay in the Memphis player stats section are his stats for Memphis. The same holds for Gay's stats under Toronto.

Players that are traded midseason have the opportunity to play with entirely new sets of teammates. Thus, their lineup entropy is typically high. The highest entropy in our study belonged to Bobby Jones in the 2007-08 season. His entropy that season was 5.11. Jones was drafted out of the University of Washington in the second round of the 2006 NBA draft by Minnesota. In the 2007-08 season, Jones played for a remarkable five clubs.

To put the numbers in Table 7.3 into perspective, let's consider some examples. We saw that if a player had no variation in linemates, he would have an LE of log 4=2. If a player played with two different sets of four linemates, and he played with each for exactly half his playing time, he would have an LE of $-8(1/8 \log 1/8)=\log 8=3$. Statistically, this hypothetical scenario is quite nice. We would be able to compare the player's production with one lineup as compared to the other. If his production (by whatever measure we are using) was approximately the same with the two, we can reasonably conclude that no one player is pulling his numbers (up or down).

Lineup Entropy as a Measure of Confidence in Top Down Metrics

Reconsider the Top 20 in plus-minus per 48 minutes for the 2012-13 regular season. Table 7.6 reprints that top 20 list. This time we include each player's LE. For Tayshaun Prince, the LE represents his LE for Memphis only. Our intuition told us that plus-minus per 48 was overrating players like Chalmers, Perkins, Sefolosha, and Haslem because these players played for excellent teams. These players also had very low LE. As a point of reference, Chalmers' LE of 2.97 is in the 5th percentile of our data. In other words, 95% of players mix at a higher rate than Chalmers did in 2012-13. We knew these players played for good teams. Low LE tells us that these players are playing almost all of their minutes with a select few players on that good team.

Perkins had the lowest LE among players that played at least 200 minutes in our study (which was over 13 seasons). We know Perkins plays with Durant and Westbrook. His LE of 2.42 tells us that he rarely plays without them. A check of his lineup statistics confirms this. Perkins played 1954 minutes in 2012-13. He played 1867 of those minutes with Durant and Westbrook. As a result, we should have very little confidence that Perkins is generally as good as his plus-minus numbers suggest. In other words, we are not confident that if Perkins were to be traded to another team, his plus-minus per 48 minutes would follow. Although not to the extreme demonstrated by Perkins, similar statements could be made for Sefolosha, Ibaka and other players in Table 7.6.

Table 7.6: Top 20 +/- per 48 minutes with LE for 2012-13 Regular Season

Rank	Player	+/-	LE	Rank	Player	+/-	LE
1	Mario Chalmers (MIA)	13.16	2.97	11	Kevin Martin (OKC)	9.84	3.29
2	LeBron James (MIA)	12.01	3.17	12	Serge Ibaka (OKC)	9.48	2.70
3	Dwyane Wade (MIA)	11.44	3.12	13	Kawhi Leonard (SAS)	9.44	3.28
4	Nick Collison (OKC)	11.10	3.30	14	Chris Bosh (MIA)	9.25	3.07
5	Kevin Durant (OKC)	11.10	2.98	15	Udonis Haslem (MIA)	9.23	2.96
6	Thabo Sefolosha (OKC)	10.77	2.80	16	Shane Battier (MIA)	9.14	3.23
7	Russell Westbrook (OKC)	10.64	2.79	17	Tiago Splitter (SAS)	9.09	3.45
8	Tim Duncan (SAS)	10.60	3.32	18	Chris Paul (LAC)	8.84	3.09
9	Kendrick Perkins (OKC)	9.95	2.42	19	Tayshaun Prince (MEM)	8.83	2.81
10	Tony Parker (SAS)	9.87	3.23	20	Mike Conley (MEM)	8.81	3.19

In contrast, Collison's LE of 3.30 makes his plus-minus per 48 minutes less suspect. Certainly, Collison's LE is not high. He is in the 37th percentile among our data, and so his numbers are more prone to being pulled by a particular individual or lineup than more than half the league. Also, he does still play for a good team and gets the opportunity to take the court with star teammates. With that said, his LE of 3.30 is much higher than that of Ibaka, Sefolosha, Chalmers and Perkins. Collison played 1582 minutes in 2012-13. 1016 of those minutes were with Durant. 791 minutes were played with Westbrook. A total of 591 minutes were played with both. Collison played 37% of his minutes with both Durant and Westbrook. Perkins played over 95% of his minutes with the elite twosome.

FUTURE DIRECTION

We only consider the LE of the individual. This reflects the individual's degree of mixing with his teammates. Quality and entropy of opposing lineups are another matter. For example, Collison may benefit from playing more minutes against second-string opponents, while Perkins generally defends the opposing teams' starters.

Lineup Entropy itself does not tell us who is doing the pulling in the plus-minus numbers and who is being pulled. We can use other metrics such as Approximate Value to do that. Our player evaluation metrics and general good sense tell us that Durant is a great player and that Sefolosha and Perkins are better defined as role players. If we want a purely top down approach to help confirm our instincts, we can consider again net plus-minus. Table 7.7 reposts the top 20 in net plus-minus for 2012-13. This time, we have included LE.

A low LE and high plus-minus per 48 minutes does not imply a high net plus-minus per 48 minutes. We know that Perkins played almost all of his minutes with Durant and Westbrook. So, his on court numbers are highly influenced by those two. Durant played over 1000 minutes more than Perkins, however. So, if Durant is largely the reason for the high plus-minus when Durant and Perkins play together, that production will follow Durant when Perkins is off the court, and Perkins' net plus-minus will not be so impressive. This is exactly what we see in the net numbers. Durant was 15th in net plus-minus per 48 minutes at 9.17. Perkins was 141st with a number of 1.60.

Looking at Table 7.7, we notice that four players from Indiana made the list and that all four had an LE below 3. We will talk more about each team's total lineup entropy in the next section. Indiana had one of the lowest team LEs in the league in 2012-13. The lineup of George, Hill, Hibbert, Stephenson and West played a large proportion of the team's minutes. All five of these players were in the top 26 in net plus-minus per 48 minutes. The high net plus-minus for these five and their low LE tell us that they played most of their minutes together and that they were particularly productive relative to the rest of the team's lineups.

Table 7.7: Top 20 Net +/- per 48 minutes and LE for 2012-13 Regular Season

Rank	Player	+/-	LE	Rank	Player	+/-	LE
1	Mike Conley (MEM)	15.43	3.19	11	Brook Lopez (BKN)	9.91	3.00
2	LeBron James (MIA)	15.29	3.17	12	Lance Stephenson (IND)	9.69	2.90
3	Amir Johnson (TOR)	14.04	3.66	13	John Salmons (SAC)	9.44	3.35
4	Vince Carter (DAL)	12.65	3.62	14	Dwyane Wade (MIA)	9.17	3.12
5	Marc Gasol (MEM)	11.32	3.27	15	Kevin Durant (OKC)	9.17	2.98
6	Mario Chalmers (MIA)	11.20	2.97	16	LaMarcus Aldridge (POR)	9.12	3.14
7	George Hill (IND)	11.06	2.91	17	Nene (WAS)	8.99	3.49
8	Damian Lillard (POR)	10.88	3.22	18	Tim Duncan (SAS)	8.93	3.32
9	Joe Johnson (BKN)	10.36	3.21	19	Kyle Korver (ATL)	8.83	3.21
10	Roy Hibbert (IND)	9.91	2.72	20	David West (IND)	8.61	2.91

Taking net plus-minus knocked role players like Collison, Perkins, Haslem and Battier out of the top 20, but Chalmers lingered. Perhaps he is more valuable than we suspected. A low LE is cause for concern with any top down statistic. Net plus-minus is better than plus-minus, but it is not an exception to this rule. Chalmers had a low LE. It was in the 5th percentile of our data. Like when a foul smell prompts a cop to search a car, Chalmers' LE reeks, and it's time to investigate. The Heat played 3976 minutes in 2012-13. James played 2877 of them. Chalmers played 2068. The Heat were +645 on the season. They were +720 with James on the court and -75 with him off. The Heat were +567 with Chalmers on and +78 with him off. Chalmers and LeBron played 1922 minutes together and were +571. Chalmers was -4 in the 146 minutes he played without LeBron. 40 of these minutes, Chalmers played with Wade. Here, there is a lot of evidence that James is a great player. There is no evidence that Chalmers can post high plus-minus numbers without James. The sample set with Chalmers on the court and James off is too small to say anything definitive about such a situation. Still, we were able to use LE to locate a situation where the top down statistic might be very misleading.

If we are concerned about a particular player's top down statistic, such as the case above with Chalmers, we can look into that player's playing time with each of his teammates. In this instance, we would look closely at Chalmers' playing time with James. The extreme overlap in playing time presents an obvious problem. If we were only worried about this one player, we would not need LE. Remember our goal is objective and efficient analytics. Simply perusing the lineup data of several players one at a time without some hard rule on whether or not the data presents a problem introduces subjectivity. LE provides a way to quantify the mixing in the lineups. We can fix a number, say 3.0, and declare a player whose LE is below 3.0 as being susceptible to misleading top down statistics. Once the bar is set, the outcome of the analysis is independent of the opinions and feelings of the individual running the test. Furthermore, there are objective means of establishing the bar. We chose 3.0 because it is equivalent to the case of a player playing exactly half his time each with two completely distinct lineups. As mentioned earlier, this is a good situation statistically. By quantifying the variation in linemates, we no longer have to go through the lineup data one player at a time. We can run a quick query and flag all players with an LE below 3.0. LE yields significant improvements in efficiency and objectivity.

In this chapter, we chose to look at the full season's LE for each player. This is because we often judge players based on full seasons of production. One can look at LE for any period of time.

Team Lineup Entropy

We can also define Lineup Entropy for the entire team. The team number allows an efficient and objective means of monitoring a team's situation. Allow us to give a somewhat depressing analogy. If an individual is not feeling well, he or a doctor might take his temperature. The temperature alone cannot determine the cause of the illness. However, it can be a means of classification, an indication that something is amiss. In a more serious scenario, a doctor might monitor a patient's respiratory or heart rate. The rates themselves do not give an answer, but abnormal numbers again can indicate malfunction of some sort. Team Lineup Entropy (TLE) is a measure of the degree of mixing of linemates for the entire team. Teams will have different baseline TLEs as TLE can be a reflection of coaching style and the make-up of the team. For example, the Spurs rely on second string units often as coach Gregg Popovich is excellent at resting his aging core of Duncan, Ginobili and Parker. Like monitoring a patient's heart rate, when TLE hits the extremes or varies a great deal from the team's baseline, it reflects a serious shift in the team and suggests that something has gone wrong. One possible cause is an injury to a star player.

Fix a team T and a time frame. Let's suppose we are interested in the full 2012-13 season. Let M={1,2,3…,100} be the 100 most common lineups that played for T in 2012-13. Any lineups after the top 100 were lineups that played ten or less minutes on the season. For each j in M, let q(j) be the time-on-court for lineup j . TLE is defined as follows.

$$TLE\ (T) = -\sum_{j=1}^{100} q(j) \log q(j)$$

In 2012-13, the Boston Celtics had the highest TLE at 6.09. This is not surprising. The Celtics lost two key players in Rajon Rondo and Jared Sullinger to season-ending injuries midway through the year. Oklahoma City had the lowest season TLE at 4.57. The players on the Thunder have well-defined roles and they stayed relatively healthy in 2012-13. The low TLE number tells us that there was very little turmoil in Oklahoma City last regular season. (However, the playoff injury to Russell Westbrook was tumultuous.)

It is more common for more successful teams to have a lower TLE and less successful teams to have a higher TLE. We have already mentioned that injuries drive up TLE. Of course, injuries also inhibit success. Also, when things are going well for a team, when they are winning, they are less likely to mix up their lineups. Coaches will stick with what worked. On the other hand, if a team is in the midst of a losing streak, they may shake things up. We want to emphasize that TLE is a reflection of the team's activities and not necessarily the source of the success or failures, in much the same way a high body temperature is an indication of illness more often than it is the cause.

Chart 7.8 presents TLE to win percentage for teams in the 2012-13 season. The trend is negative. That is, the higher TLE, the lower the win percentage (generally speaking). TLE is not a great predictor of team success. Teams can stick with a lineup even in tough times. Portland had the third lowest TLE on the season. They played the lineup of Aldridge, Lillard, Batum, Hickson and Matthews a remarkable 1073 minutes. The next most common lineup for the Trailblazers played 142 minutes. By comparison, the most common lineup in Minnesota played 376 minutes. Portland rode that lineup to a 33-49 season. As we can see in the chart, Portland stands alone as the only team with a TLE of less than 5.49 and a below .500 win percentage. On the other end, the Spurs had the 8th highest TLE while going 58-24. As mentioned above, the Spurs mix lineups often as a result of resting star players. We will see that San Antonio is also a bit of an anomaly in the data in the next chapter for the same reason.

Chart 7.8: TLE to W% for 2012-13

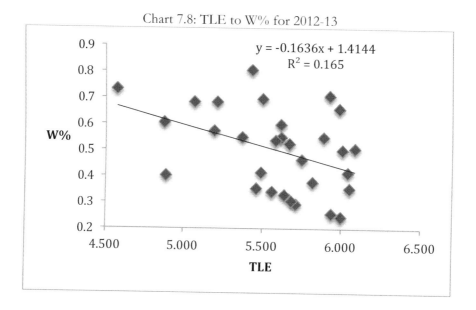

8

Introducing Player Involvement Metrics

In the NBA, there are players that we refer to as stars, and others that we refer to as role players. There are players that play near 40 minutes a game, and those that play 15 minutes. It is important to remember that almost all of the players in the NBA were once stars. A player who might be asked to be a defensive stopper off the bench may have been the star offensive player for his College, High School and AAU teams. Role players in the NBA were the main attraction at lower levels. As the premium talent on those previous teams, these players probably spent a lot of time with the ball in their hands. They played the most minutes, and they might have had the majority of plays drawn up specifically for them to take the shot. For an NBA team to function optimally, all of these former stars have to come together and succeed in their roles. The trouble here stems partly from player egos, but mostly from getting players to play in a way that they have never played before.

We explore three team statistics: Point Balance, Rebound Balance and Assist Balance. These stats measure the degree to which the players on the court for a particular team spread the production in the respective categories. Do the successful teams spread the responsibility or do they largely rely on the specialties of a few players? Is it better to have a balanced offense where all five players score or to have one or two elite scorers and other players that are largely responsible for facilitating the offense of the stars? Is it better to have several above average rebounders on the floor or one elite rebounder? How valuable is it to have five players that can pass effectively, or can one great passer drive an offense?

Star talents like LeBron James typically create unbalanced production. They carry a large proportion of the offensive load. We know that having LeBron James on the team is beneficial, but can a team be successful with a more balanced approach? Do players output a bit more energy or have an extra bounce in their step after making a few shots and having felt that they have contributed on the offensive end? Can getting all players involved in a serious manner outweigh the benefits of having an elite talent like a Jordan or Kobe take a majority of the shots? Should Carmelo and Durant be concerned with getting teammates involved?

Point Balance

The great coach Phil Jackson once said, "Good teams become great ones when the members trust each other enough to surrender the Me for the We."[1] This is an interesting quote from a man that coached Michael Jordan and Kobe Bryant. Perhaps he was talking to the other players. Or perhaps he understood that players trusting each other does not mean that they have to share the shots. Here, we explore the degree to which teams should try to balance the offense.

In basketball, offense is about getting high percentage shots. Ideally, every play would lead to an uncontested dunk. In reality, challenged shots are the norm. Some players are better shooters than others, and at times, getting higher percentage shots can mean letting the better players fire away (within reason).

Suppose you are watching a local high school basketball game. There are twelve seconds left on the clock and the home team is down by one. They are inbounding the ball at half court. We might expect them to run a few screens (at least some sort of play to open up a shooter or a cutter to the hoop for a good look). We would expect some movement on the court, and perhaps multiple options to take the final shot. This strategy is justified because the typical high school team struggles to defend screens or a well-executed play.

The NBA is quite different. Defenders are big, long, quick and athletic. They anticipate screens and are trained to switch or fight through them. Suppose you are watching the Miami Heat in the closing seconds of a playoff game. They are down by one with the ball at half court and twelve seconds on the clock. What will they do? It is likely they will give the ball to the best player in the world (at least by our metrics), a player with surprising agility and grace for his size. We expect the Heat to put their faith in LeBron James.

When the game is on the line, teams with great players put the ball in their stars' hands and let them work their magic. It is predictable and unbalanced. Is this the best NBA offense?

We will use Shannon's entropy formula again in the definition of our balance metrics. To see the similarities in the balance calculations to that of the Lineup Entropy calculations consider the following example. Table 8.1 presents the points and minutes played by each player on the 2012-13 Boston Celtics over the course of that season. Now let's pick a point in the season at random. Guess which Celtics player will score the next point. With no information besides what's in this chart, your best guess is Paul Pierce. Pierce made 1430 of the team's 7818 points. The probability that Pierce scores the next point is 1430/7818 or approximately .183. We want more than the probability associated to the most likely scorer. We want to aggregate all of the information in the event. To do this, we use Shannon's formula. Let PT_i be the points scored by player i. Let p_i denote $PT_i/7818$. The distribution of points scored by the Boston Celtics, denoted $h(PT)$, is

$$h(PT) = -\sum_{i=1}^{n} p_i \log p_i \,,$$

where the sum is over all players on the team. The more players to score points and the more evenly distributed the proportions of points scored, the higher $h(PT)$ will be.

[1] Jackson, P. Inspirational-Quotes-and-Quotations.com. Retrieved August 15, 2013. <http://www.inspirational-quotes-and-quotations.com/famous-phil-jackson-quotes.html>.

Table 8.1: 2012-13 Boston Celtics

Player	Min	Points
Paul Pierce	2575	1430
Jeff Green	2252	1036
Brandon Bass	2239	701
Jason Terry	2124	799
Kevin Garnett	2022	1004
Courtney Lee	1941	612
Avery Bradley	1435	461
Rajon Rondo	1423	522
Jared Sullinger	892	270
Chris Wilcox	830	259
Jordan Crawford	582	246
Leandro Barbosa	513	215
Jason Collins	330	37
Terrence Williams	318	110
Shavlik Randolph	198	67
D.J. White	86	29
Fab Melo	36	7
Kris Joseph	24	7
Jarvis Varnado	18	6
Darko Milicic	5	0
Total	19843	7818

A lot of factors besides the style of play can drive up h(PT). These include injuries, midseason trades, or players getting the occasional rest day. To accurately measure the balance in the offense, we want to account for these factors.

Define the distribution of minutes played, denoted h(Min), in the same way as h(PT) only replacing points with minutes. We define Point Balance (PB) to be

$$PB = h(PT)/h(Min).$$

By taking the ratio of the distribution of points scored to the distribution of minutes we are measuring the degree to which the five players on the court spread the offensive burden (in terms of points scored) regardless of how many players the team rotates in and how many minutes each player plays.

We calculated season h(PT) and h(Min) for all NBA teams from 2006-07 through 2012-13. Chart 8.2 indicates that h(PT) and h(Min) are highly correlated. In other words, the more the minutes played are spread the more the points scored will be spread. This is regular season data only.

Chart 8.2: h(PT) to h(Min) for 2006-07 through 2012-13 seasons

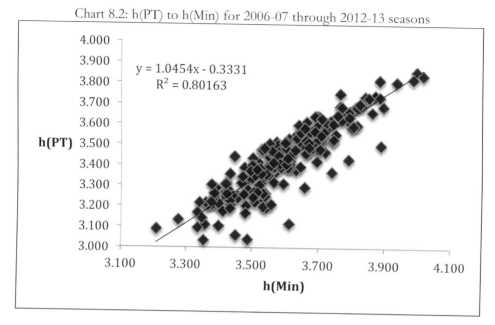

The most interesting information is revealed when we take the ratio of the distribution of points to the distribution of minutes. We begin by looking at the two extremes of the Point Balance spectrum. Table 8.3 presents the ten lowest season PB totals for our time frame. The group had a record of 496-276. Compare these totals to those in Table 8.4, which displays the ten highest season PB numbers. The high PB group had a record of 365-423, but the production was by no means consistent. The 2012 Chicago and 2013 Denver teams posted high PB numbers and had good regular season records.

Table 8.3: 10 Lowest PB Seasons

Season	Team	PB	W	L	W%
2011	MIA	0.862	58	24	0.707
2012	OKC	0.871	47	19	0.712
2013	OKC	0.886	60	22	0.732
2008	CLE	0.900	45	37	0.549
2009	MIA	0.900	43	39	0.524
2008	DAL	0.901	51	31	0.622
2012	MIA	0.901	46	20	0.697
2012	LAL	0.902	41	25	0.621
2010	OKC	0.904	50	32	0.610
2011	OKC	0.904	55	27	0.671
		TOTAL:	**496**	**276**	**0.642**

Let's now look at the whole landscape. Chart 8.5 displays win percentage (W%) to PB for all seasons in our study. We see that all of the least balanced teams have been successful. No team with a PB below .93 won less than 40% of their games. The balanced side of the chart covers the spectrum of win percentages. The chart mimics the trends we see at the extremes in Tables 8.3 and 8.4. We can sum up the picture by saying that there are many ways to win but only one way to lose.

Table 8.4: 10 Highest PB Seasons

Season	Team	PB	W	L	W%
2013	DEN	0.998	57	25	0.695
2011	PHO	0.996	40	42	0.488
2011	SAC	0.988	24	58	0.293
2010	PHI	0.986	27	55	0.329
2013	DET	0.986	29	53	0.354
2011	MIL	0.985	35	47	0.427
2008	TOR	0.984	41	41	0.5
2009	GSW	0.984	29	53	0.354
2012	PHO	0.984	33	33	0.5
2012	CHI	0.983	50	16	0.758
		TOTAL:	**365**	**423**	**0.463**

Chart 8.5: W% to PB for 2006-07 through 2012-13 Seasons

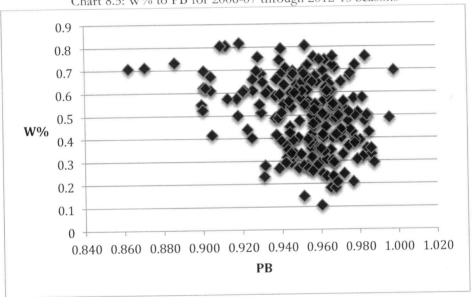

Theoretically, if one player scores all of the points for the team, PB can be 0. PB can exceed one, although it did not happen for any of the full seasons in our data. Table 8.6 has the quartiles for season PB from our data set.

Table 8.6: Quartiles for Season PB (2006-07 through 2012-13)

0%	25%	50%	75%	100%
0.862	0.944	0.956	0.967	0.998

It is a Star's League

Player involvement metrics were introduced with a study of offensive balance in NCAA Men's basketball.[2] There, offensive balance (OB) is defined as the distribution of field goals made divided by the distribution of minutes played. OB is PB with points replaced by field goals made. We chose to use points in this chapter because it accounts for free throws and the difference between a two-pointer and three-pointer. It provides a more robust measure of balance in the offense.

At the time of the NCAA study, an interesting trend was observed. There was a surprising correlation between offensive balance and the top 25 teams according to the Associated Press. See Chart 8.7. The better teams had less balance. The outlier in the group, marked by a square, is Virginia Commonwealth University (VCU). VCU is known for a unique havoc style full court defense. Thus, we should not be surprised that VCU is an outlier in this correlation. OB is a reflection of style of play.

The surprise here is that there is a strong correlation otherwise. Why should the less balanced teams be better? Aren't coaches from the pee-wee divisions through college preaching passing the ball, being selfless? At the time, we thought that the trend in Chart 8.7 was an anomaly. We were wrong.

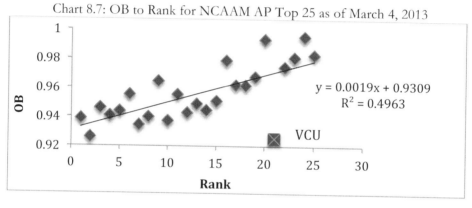

Chart 8.7: OB to Rank for NCAAM AP Top 25 as of March 4, 2013

$y = 0.0019x + 0.9309$
$R^2 = 0.4963$

In Table 8.3 we see that the most unbalanced teams are very good. We also notice that the most unbalanced teams typically feature a star offensive player. Every team in Table 8.3 had at least one of James, Durant, Bryant, Wade or Nowitzki. Putting the pieces together, we have the simple hypothesis that prolific scorers make both good and unbalanced teams.

In the course of our study, the game's leader in EOP, LeBron James, switched teams. This provides an opportunity to test the impact of a star scorer on a team's PB. In July 2010, James took his talents to South Beach. Unbalance and success followed. The transition is captured in Table 8.8.

In 2009-2010, Cleveland posted a PB higher than any of their previous three seasons. Yet they took a big leap again after LeBron. In the 2008-09 and 2009-10 seasons, Miami posted two of the seven lowest PB seasons for the entire league to that point in time in our study. Still, those seasons were *Hoosiers-four-passes-before-you-shoot* balanced compared to what followed. Miami posted

---

[2] Shea, S. "Measuring Offensive Balance in Basketball." TeamRankings.com. April 8, 2013. <http://www.TeamRankings.com/blog/ncaa-basketball/measuring-offensive-balance-stephen-shea>.

the lowest season PB in our study in 2011. Miami cleaned house so that they could sign LeBron, Wade and Bosh in the summer of 2010. As a result, the 2010-11 team was very thin around those big three. In the subsequent offseasons, Miami has been able to add key role players such as Shane Battier and Ray Allen. (We will discuss role players in more detail in the next chapter). Since the first season, Miami has added the right role players, become more balanced, and gotten better. We will look at this growth again after we have defined Assist and Rebound Balance.

Table 8.8: James Heads South

	2009-2010	2010-2011
	Cleveland	Cleveland
PB	.939	.966
Record	61-21	19-63
	Miami	Miami
PB	.918	.862
Record	47-35	58-24

Thus far, we have seen that the most unbalanced teams have been successful and that prolific scorers drive down PB. Digging deeper into this new metric, we next look at how teams balance scoring in the minutes that matter most.

PB in the Clutch

In the course of an NBA season, many minutes are not significant. This includes the ends of games in a blow out. It is possible that the season balance numbers do not accurately reflect how teams will play when the game is on the line. Here, we look at PB for teams during clutch minutes. Clutch minutes are defined to be five minutes or less left in the game with the difference in scoring no greater than five.

How a team performs in the clutch is of the utmost importance. Certainly, teams need to win close games to win championships, but production in the clutch is a reflection of more than just how a team performs in those tight situations. Chart 8.9 plots plus-minus in the clutch to win percentage in the 2012-13 season. Just about every team with a positive plus-minus in the clutch was above .500 on the season.

Table 8.10 presents the ten least balanced teams in the clutch from last season. (Every team's PB on the season and in the clutch is recorded in the Team-by-Team Advanced Metrics after Chapter 13.) It also presents the Point Balance and win percentage on the season and the plus-minus in the clutch for these teams. Every team in the table had a lower PB in the clutch than on the regular season. Not surprisingly, teams are turning to a select few from their roster to take the shots in the clutch. Most of the least balanced teams were successful. The biggest outlier is the Cleveland Cavaliers. First year player Dion Waiters and second year player Kyrie Irving combined for over 50% of Cleveland's clutch points. Individually, Irving was responsible for 35% of Cleveland's points in these pivotal moments. Recall that many players, and even future stars, have a low efficiency early in their careers. Irving and Waiters followed the trend with their production in the clutch. Of the 113 players that played 100 clutch minutes last season, Irving and Waiters were 86th and 82nd in terms of Offensive Efficiency (OE). Both had an OE of about .45. Cleveland was heavily reliant on inefficient scorers in the clutch. As a result, they were -205 in clutch minutes and had a win percentage of .293 on the season. Note that we do believe Irving and Waiters will continue to develop and are likely to improve their efficiency in the clutch in future seasons.

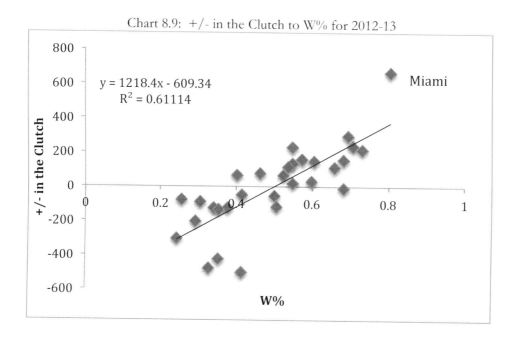

Chart 8.9: +/- in the Clutch to W% for 2012-13

$y = 1218.4x - 609.34$
$R^2 = 0.61114$

Table 8.10: 10 Lowest PB in the Clutch for 2012-13

Team	Seas.W%	+/- Clutch	PB Clutch	PB Seas.
OKC	0.732	215	0.735	0.886
LAC	0.683	-12	0.782	0.952
LAL	0.549	135	0.801	0.929
HOU	0.549	18	0.827	0.957
PHI	0.415	-51	0.861	0.961
CLE	0.293	-205	0.863	0.967
ATL	0.537	113	0.866	0.966
NYK	0.659	111	0.867	0.926
GSW	0.573	158	0.871	0.913
BOS	0.506	-120	0.874	0.961

We now have a single number that quantifies how teams spread the offense in the clutch. The example of the Cleveland Cavaliers demonstrates how this single number can direct us immediately to the sources of teams' failures (or successes.) Cleveland lost a number of close games last season. They rely a great deal on Irving and Waiters in the clutch. The continued maturity and development of its young and promising backcourt could swing a number of those close games in Cleveland's favor in the future.

PB in the clutch was lower than season PB for 27 of the 30 NBA teams. One of the largest differences came from the L.A. Lakers, a team that already had a low PB on the season. It is no secret that Kobe wants the ball at the end of games, but how does this sit with a cast of superstar teammates that includes Pau Gasol, Steve Nash and Dwight Howard? Could PB help explain the troubled union last season in Los Angeles?

The 2013 Lakers: a Recipe for Confusion

Earlier in this chapter, we discussed how certain players have to accept lesser roles for their NBA team than they were used to at lower levels. Sometimes, players have to relinquish touches and spotlight when they transition from one NBA team to another.

When the Lakers acquired Dwight Howard and Steve Nash in the 2012 offseason, some labeled this latest super team as the favorite to win the Western Conference. Instead, the Lakers just barely made the playoffs. In 2011-12, the Lakers were 41-25. This past season, they were 45-37. While injuries have likely contributed to the Lakers' inability to take off, it is hard to believe that they were the only factor. PB may shed more light on why Kobe, Gasol, Dwight and Nash are struggling to mesh.

We begin where the last section left off and look at L.A.'s numbers in clutch time. Table 8.11 displays the player stats for L.A. Although Howard played almost as many clutch minutes as Bryant, Bryant took over seven times as many shots. The question is whether or not the unbalance agrees with newcomers Nash and Howard.

Table 8.11: 2012-13 Los Angeles Lakers in the Clutch

Player	Min	FGM	FGA	Points
Jamison	44	8	12	18
Duhon	20	0	0	0
Morris	6	0	1	0
Howard	131	10	15	43
Clark	42	2	6	6
Meeks	71	4	14	15
Hill	2	1	1	2
Bryant	140	45	106	154
World Peace	114	9	24	26
Gasol	87	10	22	29
Blake	42	1	12	10
Nash	97	13	21	39

A Nash run Phoenix offense was one of the most balanced in the league in the last seven seasons (Table 8.12). Dwight Howard's Magic were also balanced, posting PB's between .941 and .978 in 2006-07 through 2011-12. While the Lakers have not been as unbalanced as the Heat in recent seasons, their .902 PB in 2011-12 was the 8th lowest in our study. Nash, Howard and Bryant were the stars of their respective teams. Three stars have come together with great success in the past. Garnett, Pierce and Allen won a championship their first season together in Boston. James, Wade and Bosh have been to three championships and won the last two since they joined forces in Miami. The union in L.A. was unlike the previous two, however. Nash and Howard facilitated offense and created space for their teammates. They found success in balance. Bryant and the other Lakers that remained from their previous seasons had found success at the other end of the balance spectrum. L.A. brought together stars that played the game in very different ways.

FUTURE DIRECTION

It is possible that the difference between the PB of a player's prior team and his new team contributes to the players' inability to acclimate quickly to the new system. As a future direction, one could run a large study of how quickly (or easily) players acclimate to a new system, and how this depends on the level of balance in the two systems. This study could include the effects of a team changing coaches, the transitions of offseason veteran signings and midseason acquisitions, and the impacts of PB on how college or international players transition to the NBA.

Table 8.12: Following Nash, Howard and Bryant

Season	Nash's Team PB	Bryant's Team PB	Howard's Team PB
2006-07	0.963	0.930	0.966
2007-08	0.957	0.946	0.952
2008-09	0.961	0.940	0.954
2009-10	0.963	0.951	0.978
2010-11	0.996	0.928	0.941
2011-12	0.984	0.902	0.944
2012-13	0.929	0.929	0.929

The Dwight Howard experiment failed in Los Angeles. Given the disparity in PB between Howard's Magic and Bryant's Lakers, it is not surprising that midway through the season, Howard was complaining about touches.[3] While we can never be sure how a group of stars will mesh, it is possible that PB can help us make better predictions.

Next up for Howard is the Houston Rockets. Houston had a PB of .957 last season. That is almost exactly the average PB for Howard's Magic from 2006-07 through 2011-12.

To Balance or Not to Balance?

Table 8.13 displays the 14 teams to make the NBA finals in the last seven seasons and their PB. Let us make two observations.

- Although there have been teams with high PB and a good regular season record (such as the 2012-13 Denver Nuggets), no team in the last seven seasons has made the finals with a PB above .967. A PB of .967 was in the 75th percentile in our study.
- With the exception of the 2013 San Antonio Spurs, there has recently been a significant drop in PB among finalists. The drop coincides with the formation of the Miami Heat and the dawn of what we call the "super team era." The game has changed since the league's top players started looking to join forces in the primes of their careers. This will be the focus of Chapter 13.

The 2013 Spurs are the anomaly to the trend down in PB in Table 8.13, so let us take some time to look specifically at how Coach Gregg Popovich manages his team. Chart 8.14 tracks the first half of the San Antonio season. We calculated PB for each game. At first glance, the ups and down of PB seem to be random and hard to predict. However, when we dig a little deeper into the box scores, it is easy to find factors driving up PB. The white circles denote games where Tim Duncan played less than 25 minutes. These games correlate with the high PB games on the season. When

---

[3] Zimmerman, K. "Dwight Howard regrets complaining about touches." SBNATION.com. January 13, 2013. <http://www.sbnation.com/nba/2013/1/23/3908388/dwight-howard-la-lakers-complain>.

the Spurs rest one of their stars, balance goes up. The lone black peak at game 30 was a blowout in Toronto. The Spurs won by 20 points and no starter played more than 29 minutes. Duncan played 27 minutes that night.

Table 8.13: NBA Finalists with PB

Season	Team	W	L	W%	PB
2007	CLE	50	32	0.610	0.933
2007	SAS	58	24	0.707	0.942
2008	BOS	66	16	0.805	0.952
2008	LAL	57	25	0.695	0.946
2009	LAL	65	17	0.793	0.940
2009	ORL	59	23	0.720	0.954
2010	BOS	50	32	0.610	0.966
2010	LAL	57	25	0.695	0.951
2011	DAL	57	25	0.695	0.961
2011	MIA	58	24	0.707	0.862
2012	MIA	46	20	0.697	0.901
2012	OKC	47	19	0.712	0.871
2013	MIA	66	16	0.805	0.912
2013	SAS	58	24	0.707	0.967

The Spurs' core players are older than the cores of most of the other premier teams in the NBA. Coach Popovich does an admirable job finding time to rest his aging stars. Chart 8.14 is showing that the Spurs are not truly the .967 PB team that their season number suggests. The team's PB is inflated because of the amount of rest the stars are given throughout the year. This coincides with San Antonio's PB in the clutch of .879.

Chart 8.14: Game PB for San Antonio's First 41 Games of 2012-13

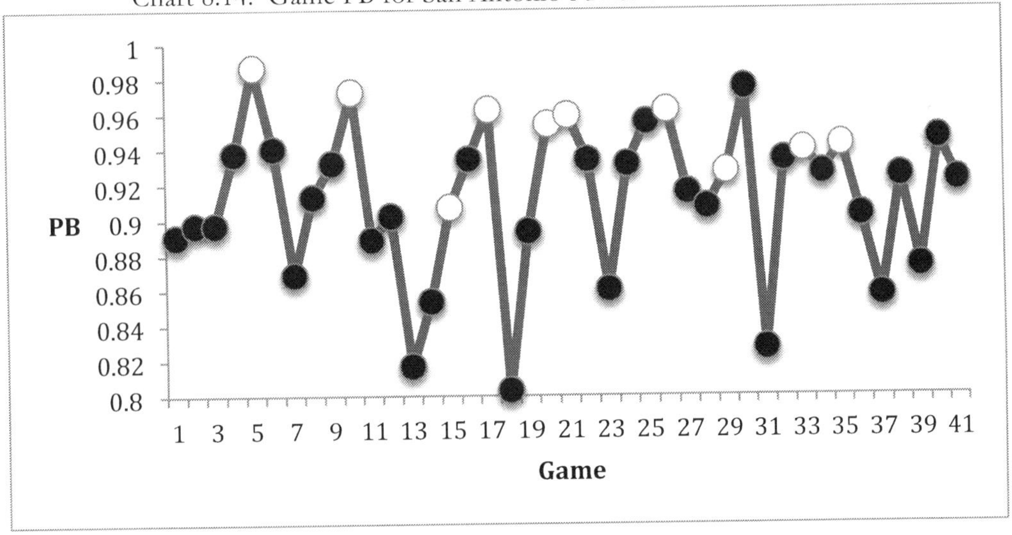

At this point, we are confident in the conclusion that low PB teams have fared better than high PB teams. We can also conclude that PB is highly dependent on the team's star players. We have seen the effect LeBron had on Cleveland and Miami. Chart 8.14 shows the effect of resting

Tim Duncan on San Antonio's PB. Constructing a team for a lower PB more or less equates to building around a star player or two. All of the data agree with our intuition that teams should look to acquire star players such as LeBron and Duncan. Teams just need to be sure that the rest of the roster is on-board with the stars' prevalence in the offense.

How should a team look to round out its roster? To what degree should the team and its star players try to involve teammates in the offense? The answer may be that teams should look for role players that have specialties besides scoring. Teams may round out their roster with good rebounders and passers for example. To get a sense of the value of rebound and assist specialists, we introduce Assist and Rebound Balance.

Assist and Rebound Balance

Assist Balance (AB) and Rebound Balance (RB) are defined analogously to PB, only we replace points with assists and rebounds, respectively. Table 8.15 displays the ten lowest AB seasons going back to 2006-07. The teams on this list featured premium passers such as Rajon Rondo, Steve Nash and Chris Paul. Overall the group won more than 60% of their games. In comparison, the 10 highest AB teams in Table 8.16 won 44% of their games. Similar to PB, the advantage at the extremes goes to the low end.

Table 8.15: 10 Lowest AB Seasons

Season	Team	AB	W	L	W%
2009	NO	0.721	49	33	0.598
2008	NO	0.732	56	26	0.683
2010	PHO	0.765	54	28	0.659
2011	NO	0.770	46	36	0.561
2012	BOS	0.775	39	27	0.591
2009	DAL	0.776	50	32	0.610
2012	WAS	0.777	20	46	0.303
2011	OKC	0.781	55	27	0.671
2012	LAC	0.788	40	26	0.606
2010	DAL	0.789	55	27	0.671
		TOTAL:	**464**	**308**	**0.601**

Table 8.16: 10 Highest AB Seasons

Season	Team	AB	W	L	W%
2009	WAS	0.979	19	63	0.232
2007	LAC	0.977	40	42	0.488
2009	HOU	0.971	53	29	0.646
2012	CHI	0.968	50	16	0.758
2010	IND	0.966	32	50	0.390
2013	CLE	0.963	24	58	0.293
2008	LAC	0.960	23	59	0.280
2008	IND	0.960	36	46	0.439
2010	NY	0.956	29	53	0.354
2012	LAL	0.955	41	25	0.621
		TOTAL:	**347**	**441**	**0.440**

Table 8.17 lists the 10 lowest RB seasons. Dwight Howard (ORL), Blake Griffin (LAC) and Kevin Love (MIN) led 9 of the 10 seasons on the list. A low RB is a reflection of having a top rebounder. The group had a win percentage of .521. Here, Minnesota is the anomaly. In our study, they were the only team to consistently post even remotely low RB numbers and poor win percentages. The collective winning percentage of the bottom 20 RB teams was .564. Table 8.18 displays the ten highest RB seasons. We see that among the most balanced rebounding seasons are some particularly abysmal records. The bottom ten had a win percentage of .394.

Table 8.17: 10 Lowest RB Seasons

Season	Team	RB	W	L	W%
2012	LAL	0.904	41	25	0.621
2007	ORL	0.905	40	42	0.488
2011	ORL	0.908	52	30	0.634
2011	MIN	0.908	17	65	0.207
2012	ORL	0.911	37	29	0.561
2011	LAC	0.913	32	50	0.390
2008	ORL	0.914	52	30	0.634
2009	ORL	0.918	59	23	0.720
2012	LAC	0.918	40	26	0.606
2007	MIN	0.920	32	50	0.390
		TOTAL:	**402**	**370**	**0.521**

Table 8.18: 10 Highest RB Seasons

Season	Team	RB	W	L	W%
2010	GS	1.019	26	56	0.317
2012	DEN	1.015	38	28	0.576
2011	CHA	1.010	34	48	0.415
2007	SAC	1.008	33	49	0.402
2010	POR	1.005	50	32	0.610
2012	POR	1.005	28	38	0.424
2012	PHI	1.002	35	31	0.530
2009	OKC	0.999	23	59	0.280
2008	MIA	0.999	15	67	0.183
2008	MEM	0.999	22	60	0.268
		TOTAL:	**304**	**468**	**0.394**

We presented the extremes of AB and RB in this section. Most teams do not have a Dwight Howard that can be relied upon for 14 rebounds a night or Rajon Rondo who can so deftly set up his teammates. For the teams without the super specialists, AB and RB are not great predictors of success. Still, the information at the extremes provides evidence that employing specialists is a reasonable strategy. Like the data on PB, the data on RB and AB suggest being unbalanced is favorable.

Every team would love to have a roster full of players that are excellent at everything (assuming each is comfortable with sharing the ball). In reality, teams are lucky to have one or two players that qualify as all-around superstars. Beyond the stars, teams have to decide what their role players will look like. Should the team stack its bench with players that are average at everything but not exceptional anywhere? Our data suggest that teams should go the other direction and find players that specialize in one aspect of the game.

The 1995-96 Chicago Bulls were arguably the greatest team of the modern NBA. Led by Michael Jordan, the Bulls won 72 games that season. That Bulls team had a PB of .907. There were only 11 seasons from 2006-07 through 2012-13 that were lower. The Bulls had a rebounding and defensive specialist in Dennis Rodman. Rodman led the league with 14.9 rebounds per game. The Bulls had an RB of .938. That would put them in the 17th percentile among the seasons in our study. The Bulls did not rely on a single individual for assists. Instead, they employed the triangle offense, which helped to spread the assists. The Bulls also had specialists in other categories. Steve Kerr played over 1900 minutes for the Bulls that season. His role was to knock down perimeter shots. Half of Kerr's field goals came from behind the arc (where he shot 51.5%).

Our data strongly suggest that unbalance is preferable to balance, and that teams should surround their stars with specialists. In Chapter 9, we look specifically at the type of role players or specialists that are currently helping NBA teams succeed.

Balance Metrics and Lineup Entropy as Predictors of Win Percentage

In Chapter 3, we saw that a linear regression from a team's Offensive Efficiency (OE) to win percentage for 2012-13 provided an R-squared of .57, which was already superior to points scored. When we considered a multiple regression to win percentage with the components of EOP and Defensive Stops Gained (DSG), we found a remarkable R^2 of .81. Can balance metrics and Lineup Entropy (LE) at all improve our accuracy in predicting team wins? When we add PB, RB, AB, and LE to the previous regression, the R^2 improves to .87.

Imagine trying to predict the outcome of several upcoming NBA games. You might try to look at past performance as indicators of future success. If you are a statistics nut like we are, you might run regressions based on past performance. We see Lineup Entropy and balance metrics as great ways to identify games where teams implemented anomalous strategies (perhaps due to resting a star player). When filling the database with past games upon which to build the regression, you can flag and disregard games where balance or entropy were out of whack in comparison to the team's baseline numbers. In other words, we can disregard the games where teams had a high temperature and weren't feeling so well.

Conclusions and Future Directions

Player involvement and balance are not synonymous. Teams can be unbalanced in their rebounding, assists, three point shooting and scoring, but still get many players significantly involved, provided their roster features specialists in each category. Our numbers suggest that this is a better strategy than attempting to build a team for balance in each aspect.

FUTURE DIRECTION

In this chapter, we have only scratched the surface of what we believe can be accomplished with balance and player involvement metrics. To get a more complete measure of player involvement, a study could be conducted on how teams balance touches and possession among the individuals on the roster. In other words, players can be involved in a play even if they did not score the bucket or get the assist. This data would be available through SportVU. It is possible that players will play with more energy on the defensive side if they feel they are getting their deserved touches on offense. A thorough study with SportVU technology could shed some light on the impact of offensive balance on defensive energy.

In the modern super team era, the Heat and Thunder have taken unbalance to new lows. When Miami cleared its roster to bring together James, Wade and Bosh, they went off the charts and probably beyond the ideal unbalance in scoring. In the last couple offseasons, the Heat have been able to supplement their roster with role players such as Ray Allen and Shane Battier. As a result, the Heat have become more balanced, and arguably better. Chart 8.19 displays the team's progression in RB, PB and AB over the last three seasons.

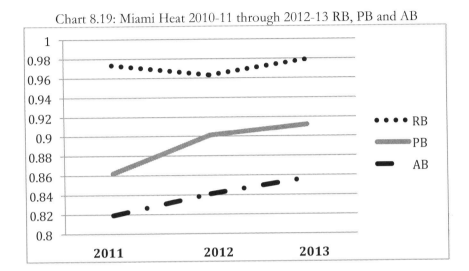

Chart 8.19: Miami Heat 2010-11 through 2012-13 RB, PB and AB

9

New Positions?

Basketball teams need players that can pass, shoot, defend, and rebound to be successful. Height, length, leaping ability, and weight can be advantageous when trying to defend the interior and pull down rebounds. Speed and agility are useful when defending the perimeter and moving the ball in transition. Teams need players to handle the ball and pass efficiently so that the offense can run smoothly. Teams need players that knock down perimeter shots to keep the defense from collapsing into the paint. The ideal basketball player would have all of these attributes. He would able to shoot like Bird, pass like Stockton, and block shots like Mutombo. He would have the body of Shaq, the speed of Parker, and the athleticism of Jordan. There has never been a player that matches that idealistic description. The ability to defend the interior and rebound rarely comes with the ability to handle the ball and knock down threes. So, teams have evolved to typically play five guys of various heights, weights, speeds and specialties. Teams will play bigger players called power forwards and centers that are good rebounders and can guard the post. They will play a shorter player that can handle the ball, pass, and generally run an offense. This player is labeled a point guard. The team will field a couple of midsized players that can do a little of everything while maybe specializing in one area such as perimeter defense or three point shooting. We call these players shooting guards or small forwards. The distinction between the two is often determined by the height of the player.

Basketball has five traditional positions, the point and shooting guards, small and power forwards, and center. There are five positions because a basketball team plays five players at one time. It is convenient to have labels for the five players on the court that reasonably approximate the different roles that the players will play. A coach can refer to the positions when drawing up plays in the huddle or practice, for example. The play might call for whoever is the center to be on the block, while the shooting guard is stationed on the weak side three-point line. The players know which positions they will likely be called upon to play and so they can visualize their role specifically in that play.

Basketball teams often field what they refer to as the traditional five positions on the court, but there is nothing forcing teams to label all players as specifically one of the five positions. The most extreme example of a player that could play multiple positions was Magic Johnson. We discussed earlier how Magic played all five positions for the Lakers at one point or another. Positions also do not require that players play them in a specific manner. Rajon Rondo and Stephen Curry play point guard in very different ways. Curry is an elite 3-point shooter and will look for his shot whenever possible. Rondo is a below average jump shooter for a guard and will always look to create scoring chances for his teammates first. Neither is necessarily more effective than the other. In fact, both are typically considered all-stars for their position.

A coach that tries to pigeonhole a player into one position, or even worse, identifies a position with a particular skill set, is foolish. The Atlanta Hawks' offense has a certain feel and style when 3-point specialist Kyle Korver is on the court. Korver typically plays what we would label as a small forward. I am certain that if the Hawks were to acquire LeBron, head coach Mike Budenholzer would not run the same offense for LeBron at the small forward as he has designed for Korver.

A start-up company called Ayasdi has created software that allows for cutting edge topological data analysis.[1] This type of analysis is typically used to study the "shape" of data and can be used to find sets of comparable data points in a large data set. Here, the data would be comparable on some subset of the variables entered into the analysis. Muthu Alagappan has used this software to understand and organize the skill sets of NBA players.[2] In his presentation at the 2012 MIT Sloan Sports Analytics Conference, Alagappan revealed that according to his analysis, NBA players could largely be grouped into 13 types. For his TEDx Spokane talk, he reduced that number to ten.[3]

Alagappan refers to the ten types of players as new positions—a more advanced categorization that should replace the old positions. As long as a basketball lineup consists of five players, we have no objection to coaches using the traditional terms to refer to the positions in the lineup. When the coach is drawing up the last second shot, he can refer to a particular role in the play by the point guard, the one, or the Shirley Temple (for all we care). Relabeling the positions is not so important. The great value in Alagappan's work is that he has categorized player skill sets and shown that most players fall into one of ten classes.

For basketball analytics, a sound classification of abilities is important. Consider the many times we have discussed our statistics according to a particular position. For example, we looked at Approximate Value relative to position. Or recall that Berri, et al. used adjustments relative to position in the construction of Wins Produced. In these situations, the position is not an assignment on the court. It is being used to classify the skills of the individual athlete. In this context, Alagappan's classification would be an improvement. Advanced analytics constructed in the context of a more advanced classification of player skill sets could be of great value to NBA teams. If the Atlanta Hawks had lost Kyle Korver to free agency, they might have wanted a similar skill set to replace him in their offense. Instead of fishing through a list of small forwards, the Hawks would have benefited from an analysis of small forwards that can shoot the three.

Alagappan also talks about how his more refined classification scheme can be used to study what skill sets fit best in which offenses. Here, we can envision a large study of the many plays NBA offenses run. We pick a particular offensive play, call it A. Play A has five roles (or positions) on the floor, but the players chosen to play those positions have varying skills. We could see if particular combinations of certain skill sets are more effective than others. Is the play more successful when the small forward is a 3-point shooter than when that player is better at slashing to the hoop? Alagappan has found a better classification of NBA players' skills. This opens up a

---

[1] http://www.ayasdi.com/.

[2] Alagappan, M. "From 5 to 13: Redefining the Positions in Basketball." 2012. <http://www.sloansportsconference.com/?p=5431>.

[3] Alagappan, M. "The new positions of basketball." 2013. <http://tedxtalks.ted.com/video/The-new-positions-of-basketball, 2013>.

number of possibilities for analyzing how teams play and studying why certain lineups are more effective than others.

The new positions have descriptive names such as "scoring rebounder," "3-point specialist" and "paint protector." There is also a type called "two-way all-star" which includes Kobe Bryant and Kevin Durant. If there is a particular group of players on which Alagappan's classification is not so helpful, or even a bit silly, it is where the analysis groups some of the game's superstars. There is no one in the NBA comparable to LeBron James, Dwight Howard, Kobe Bryant or Kevin Durant. These players are elite anomalies. They come with a multitude of skills, the specifics of which will be the focus of their team's offensive and defensive design.

We believe that a more refined classification of traditional positions is particularly useful when looking at a team's role players. In this chapter, we present three roles that we believe have become particularly important in today's NBA, and rank according to our new metrics the current NBA players capable of playing these roles. We present the defensive wing that can shoot threes, the super stretch big man, and the defensive big man. Our new positions overlap somewhat with Alagappan's classification. For example, the defensive big men will include what Alagappan calls a "paint protector." However, we will not restrict players to one role. If a center is both a defensive presence and is able to knock down perimeter shots, he will be in the super stretch and defensive big man categories. After all, a team that needs a defensive big man would probably not refuse a defensive big man that came with a little offense.

The Defensive Wing that can Knock Down Threes (3DW)

The shots closest to the rim are the highest percentage shots. Defenses are designed to prevent players from getting to the rim. There are very few players in the NBA that can consistently prevent great offensive players like LeBron and Wade from getting to the hoop without a little help from teammates. Defenses prefer when defenders off the ball can shade off of their man and put a foot in the paint. Teams also like to double-team certain players at times. If Oklahoma City's center Kendrick Perkins strolls out to the three-point line, his defender will have no trouble dropping back into the paint or doubling the ball. Perkins is no threat to knock down that shot. However, if the Heat's Ray Allen were on the weak side and positioned to knock down a jump shot, the defender would be wise to stay close. Allen is the NBA's all-time leader in three-point field goals. Good perimeter shooters keep defenses honest. They prevent help defense on LeBron's drives. This is why the Heat play shooters like Mike Miller, Ray Allen and Shane Battier. In fact, anyone who watched the 2013 NBA finals between the Heat and Spurs saw that Miami needed to keep shooters on the floor if they were going to be successful on offense.

It is important to note that the ability for defenders to help was more limited prior to 2001-02. That year the NBA eliminated the illegal defense guidelines that prevented players from playing a "zone" or drifting into the center of the half-court without guarding a man specifically. Illegal defense was replaced with a rule preventing defenders from staying in the paint for three seconds consecutively when they are not guarding a man. This is a far milder restriction on help defense. Then Miami coach Pat Riley said of the rule, "There's not going to be anybody able to drive."[4] Riley is now the team president for Miami. He has found a few players that can drive and the role

---

[4] Wise, M. "PRO BASKETBALL; N.B.A.'s Illegal-Defense Rule Will Most Likely Be Eliminated." NY Times. April 12, 2001. <http://www.nytimes.com/2001/04/12/sports/pro-basketball-nba-s-illegal-defense-rule-will-most-likely-be-eliminated.html>.

players that can keep the defenses out of a zone. The weak side three-point shooter is more important now than it was before the rule change.

Three-point shooters are great offensive role players, but there are two sides to the game of basketball. If a player cannot defend, it will be difficult for him to have much overall value to his team. Teams want shooters that can also defend on the perimeter. Thus, the modern game has born the defensive wing that can knock down threes (3DW).

The 3DW is today's ideal role player at the shooting guard or small forward position. His 3-point ability keeps defenses from helping on or double-teaming his team's first option on offense. On the defensive side, he can shoulder the burden of guarding the opposing team's best perimeter player, often saving the energy of his team's star players. To arrive at a list of players fulfilling this role in the NBA currently, we started with the players currently classified as shooting guards or small forwards. We then cut out any players that played less than 200 minutes in the 2012-13 season (so that our per minute statistics have meaning). We then restricted this list to players that made at least 30 field goals from behind the arc. Finally, to ensure that they meet a certain defensive standard, we cut out any remaining players that did not have positive Defensive Stops Gained (DSG). In this final list, there will be players that are better defensively, and those that are better shooters. We rank by both. Table 9.1 presents the top 20 3DWs in DSG per minute played (DSG/M). Table 9.2 ranks the group by Efficient Offensive Production per minute played (EOP/M). Note that DSG is a team specific number. So, if a player changed teams midseason, such as Rudy Gay, we consider the play for each team as a separate entry.

Table 9.1: 3DWs ranked by DSG/M

Rank	Player	Team	Min	DSG/M	3P%	OE	EOP/M
1	Devin Harris	ATL	1421	0.074	0.335	0.54	0.420
2	Vince Carter	DAL	2093	0.070	0.406	0.52	0.462
3	Metta World Peace	LAL	2530	0.059	0.342	0.48	0.289
4	Alec Burks	UTA	1137	0.055	0.359	0.49	0.343
5	Kawhi Leonard	SAS	1810	0.054	0.374	0.57	0.364
6	Matt Barnes	LAC	2058	0.052	0.342	0.56	0.378
7	Andre Iguodala	DEN	2779	0.051	0.317	0.58	0.431
8	Rudy Gay	TOR	1146	0.050	0.336	0.47	0.445
9	Royal Ivey	PHI	698	0.043	0.420	0.52	0.220
10	Jae Crowder	DAL	1353	0.041	0.328	0.49	0.257
11	Jamal Crawford	LAC	2230	0.038	0.376	0.48	0.456
12	Gordon Hayward	UTA	2104	0.037	0.415	0.52	0.442
13	Danilo Gallinari	DEN	2309	0.035	0.373	0.49	0.416
14	J.R. Smith	NYK	2678	0.032	0.356	0.48	0.442
15	Kyle Singler	DET	2293	0.029	0.350	0.50	0.256
16	Anthony Tolliver	ATL	963	0.029	0.338	0.45	0.197
17	Jared Dudley	PHO	2170	0.028	0.391	0.58	0.409
18	Paul George	IND	2972	0.026	0.362	0.50	0.413
19	Jeff Taylor	CHA	1507	0.025	0.344	0.51	0.268
20	Jason Richardson	PHI	936	0.023	0.341	0.47	0.295

Table 9.2: 3DWs ranked by EOP/M

Rank	Player	Team	Min	DSG/M	3P%	OE	EOP/M
1	Manu Ginobili	SAS	1393	0.013	0.353	0.55	0.546
2	Paul Pierce	BOS	2575	0.015	0.380	0.52	0.523
3	Monta Ellis	MIL	3076	0.000	0.287	0.51	0.492
4	Tyreke Evans	SAC	2016	0.009	0.338	0.56	0.487
5	Vince Carter	DAL	2093	0.070	0.406	0.52	0.462
6	Jamal Crawford	LAC	2230	0.038	0.376	0.48	0.456
7	Rudy Gay	TOR	1146	0.050	0.336	0.47	0.445
8	J.R. Smith	NYK	2678	0.032	0.356	0.48	0.442
9	Gordon Hayward	UTA	2104	0.037	0.415	0.52	0.442
10	Chandler Parsons	HOU	2758	0.019	0.385	0.57	0.432
11	Andre Iguodala	DEN	2779	0.051	0.317	0.58	0.431
12	Devin Harris	ATL	1421	0.074	0.335	0.54	0.420
13	Danilo Gallinari	DEN	2309	0.035	0.373	0.49	0.416
14	Paul George	IND	2972	0.026	0.362	0.50	0.413
15	Jared Dudley	PHO	2170	0.028	0.391	0.58	0.409
16	DeMar DeRozan	TOR	3013	0.014	0.283	0.49	0.404
17	Luol Deng	CHI	2903	0.001	0.322	0.53	0.389
18	C.J. Miles	CLE	1364	0.015	0.384	0.44	0.380
19	Matt Barnes	LAC	2058	0.052	0.342	0.56	0.378
20	Rudy Gay	MEM	1541	0.004	0.310	0.46	0.365

We see some players in both tables that we would consider as more than role players. We did not want to exclude any player capable of playing the role simply because they had more skills. After a recent trade to Brooklyn, Paul Pierce, who was the go-to-guy in Boston, may be more of a role player next to Deron Williams, Joe Johnson and Brook Lopez. Among the players making both lists were Gordon Hayward, Andre Iguodala, Vince Carter and Paul George. Kawhi Leonard (who ranks 5th in DSG/M among 3DWs) drew the tough assignment of LeBron James in the 2013 NBA finals and did an admirable job. Leonard also showed some of his offensive ability in the series. Leonard was largely a role player for San Antonio this year. He is still a young player and will likely develop into something more in the near future. A few notable 3DWs just missed our top lists. These were Jimmy Butler in Chicago, Thabo Sefolosha in Oklahoma City, and Lance Stephenson in Indiana. There were 44 players in total that qualified as a 3DW.

Super Stretch Big Man (SSB)

Centers and power forwards typically spend a lot of time near the hoop on both offense and defense. However, certain big men have the ability to knock down shots from the perimeter. This provides an added dimension to the offense. Like the 3DW, this big man's ability to shoot keeps his defender from helping on defense. Centers and power forwards are typically the best interior defenders and rebounders on the floor. So, there is added value to an offense when the opposing team's big men are out guarding the perimeter.

We look specifically at the near seven footers that can shoot jump shots. In our ideal stretch big man, we want more than a mid-range jump shooter like Glen Davis in Orlando. We want a super stretch big man (SSB) that can sink 3-pointers.

To arrive at our list of SSBs, we started with all players classified as power forwards or centers. We cut out players that played less than 200 minutes last season or made less than 20 three-point field goals. The bar for three-point field goals is below that for the 3DWs since wingmen typically have more opportunities to shoot three-pointers. Table 9.3 presents the top 20 SSBs in EOP/M.

The top of Table 9.3 contains star names. The more interesting players are those after the 5th position. Kevin Love (who is ranked 15th) had an injury-shortened season, but is known to be a star big that can shoot threes. Boris Diaw, Rasheed Wallace, Andrea Bargnani and Matt Bonner are among the SSBs to just miss the top 20. There were 33 players in total that qualified as SSBs.

Table 9.3: SSBs ranked by EOP/M

Rank	Player	Team	Min	DSG/M	3P%	OE	EOP/M
1	LeBron James	MIA	2877	0.065	0.406	0.65	0.837
2	Carmelo Anthony	NYK	2482	-0.026	0.379	0.49	0.618
3	Dirk Nowitzki	DAL	1661	-0.002	0.414	0.53	0.494
4	Chris Bosh	MIA	2454	-0.038	0.284	0.59	0.485
5	Josh Smith	ATL	2683	0.011	0.303	0.55	0.485
6	Ersan Ilyasova	MIL	2012	-0.005	0.444	0.58	0.460
7	Shawn Marion	DAL	2010	-0.025	0.315	0.64	0.451
8	Serge Ibaka	OKC	2486	-0.019	0.351	0.68	0.448
9	Chris Copeland	NYK	862	-0.020	0.421	0.49	0.440
10	Patrick Patterson	HOU	1219	-0.037	0.365	0.60	0.438
11	Wilson Chandler	DEN	1079	0.028	0.413	0.51	0.431
12	Ryan Anderson	NOH	2503	-0.067	0.382	0.51	0.426
13	Tobias Harris	ORL	974	0.024	0.31	0.53	0.421
14	Spencer Hawes	PHI	2233	-0.010	0.356	0.59	0.416
15	Kevin Love	MIN	618	-0.022	0.217	0.47	0.414
16	Donatas Motiejunas	HOU	538	-0.012	0.289	0.52	0.403
17	Antawn Jamison	LAL	1636	-0.020	0.361	0.56	0.387
18	Jonas Jerebko	DET	892	0.002	0.301	0.56	0.387
19	Jeff Green	BOS	2252	-0.019	0.385	0.50	0.380
20	Derrick Williams	MIN	1916	-0.029	0.332	0.46	0.351

Defensive Big Man (DB)

Note that of the 20 SSBs in Table 9.3, 15 had negative DSG/M totals. This is telling us that most of the big men in the NBA that can knock down the perimeter three are not particularly good defenders. Big men that are above average on both sides of the ball are hard to come by. So, teams round out their rosters with centers and power forwards that specialize in one or the other. The previous section focused on bigs with a special offensive skill. In this section, we look at the bigs that earn playing time for their defense.

To create our list of defensive big men, we started with all players classified as centers or power forwards. We cut out the players that played less than 200 minutes. We then restricted to players with positive DSG/M. Recall the Goldsberry study discussed in Chapter 2. There, two new measures of interior defense were presented. One looked at how rarely players attacked the rim when a particular big was near the hoop. The other looked at opponents' field goal percentage when they did challenge the big. Both are more sophisticated metrics than blocks alone, and both aim to see which big men decrease the opponents' field goal percentage. We also believe this is an important trait for a defensive big. The final restriction for our DBs is that their opponent's effective field goal percentage is at least 1% lower when they are on the court than when they are off.

Table 9.4: DBs ranked by DSG/M

Rank	Player	Team	Min	DSG/M	BK/M	OE	EOP/M
1	Kevin Garnett	BOS	2022	0.111	0.031	0.56	0.469
2	Lamar Odom	LAC	1616	0.105	0.036	0.60	0.248
3	Enes Kanter	UTA	1078	0.096	0.030	0.63	0.469
4	Kevin Jones	CLE	334	0.081	0.015	0.61	0.284
5	Amir Johnson	TOR	2325	0.078	0.047	0.74	0.438
6	Quincy Acy	TOR	342	0.076	0.044	0.73	0.400
7	Hamed Haddadi	PHO	235	0.075	0.089	0.57	0.277
8	Marc Gasol	MEM	2796	0.075	0.050	0.64	0.478
9	Hasheem Thabeet	OKC	770	0.074	0.078	0.84	0.279
10	Jared Jeffries	POR	350	0.068	0.017	0.51	0.120
11	Chuck Hayes	SAC	1209	0.068	0.015	0.84	0.299
12	Dwight Howard	LAL	2722	0.066	0.068	0.65	0.496
13	Tiago Splitter	SAS	1997	0.064	0.032	0.69	0.488
14	Ronny Turiaf	LAC	701	0.061	0.050	0.72	0.231
15	Larry Sanders	MIL	1937	0.059	0.104	0.71	0.420
16	Brendan Haywood	CHA	1162	0.058	0.042	0.72	0.223
17	Andrew Nicholson	ORL	1249	0.057	0.026	0.56	0.418
18	Glen Davis	ORL	1064	0.056	0.020	0.51	0.411
19	Taj Gibson	CHI	1459	0.048	0.062	0.61	0.355
20	Rasheed Wallace	NYK	296	0.041	0.051	0.41	0.320

Table 9.5: DBs ranked by BK/M

Rank	Player	Team	Min	DSG/M	BK/M	OE	EOP/M
1	Larry Sanders	MIL	1937	0.059	0.104	0.71	0.420
2	Roy Hibbert	IND	2269	0.003	0.091	0.59	0.406
3	Hamed Haddadi	PHO	235	0.075	0.089	0.57	0.277
4	Tim Duncan	SAS	2078	0.009	0.088	0.57	0.568
5	Ed Davis	MEM	544	0.022	0.086	0.73	0.390
6	Hasheem Thabeet	OKC	770	0.074	0.078	0.84	0.279
7	Andre Drummond	DET	1243	0.006	0.076	0.92	0.557
8	Jermaine O'Neal	PHO	1029	0.035	0.076	0.55	0.392
9	Derrick Favors	UTA	1787	0.025	0.073	0.59	0.395
10	DeSagana Diop	CHA	226	0.026	0.071	0.55	0.096
11	Chris Andersen	MIA	624	0.034	0.071	0.82	0.439
12	Dwight Howard	LAL	2722	0.066	0.068	0.65	0.496
13	Taj Gibson	CHI	1459	0.048	0.062	0.61	0.355
14	Jeremy Evans	UTA	215	0.026	0.060	1.03	0.604
15	Joakim Noah	CHI	2426	0.033	0.058	0.70	0.430
16	Marcus Camby	NYK	250	0.037	0.056	0.53	0.171
17	Jason Smith	NOH	876	0.034	0.051	0.55	0.424
18	Ryan Hollins	LAC	663	0.013	0.051	0.68	0.334
19	Rasheed Wallace	NYK	296	0.041	0.051	0.41	0.320
20	Ronny Turiaf	LAC	701	0.061	0.050	0.72	0.231

Table 9.4 presents the top 20 DBs according to DSG/M. Table 9.5 presents the top 20 according to blocks per minute (BK/M). Overall, 40 players were DBs in 2012-13. Kevin Garnett was the top DB in terms of DSG/M, but he was not in the top 20 in BK/M. This shows how important it is to look beyond blocks when assessing the interior defense of a player. The two young bigs in Utah, Enes Kanter and Derrick Favors, were DBs while Utah's starting bigs, Jefferson and Millsap, were not. Both Jefferson and Millsap moved on to other teams in the 2013 offseason. Some of the more competitive NBA teams carry DBs. The backup centers in Miami and Oklahoma City, Chris Anderson and Hasheem Thabeet, are both DBs. Both starters in San Antonio made the cut. We continue the discussion of the types of players comprising the NBA's elite teams in the next section.

The Make-up of the Eastern and Western Conference Champs

The Heat and Spurs met for an epic seven game NBA finals this past season. Let's take a moment to see whether or not either team makes use of 3DWs, SSBs, or DBs.

Table 9.6 presents all players that played at least 200 minutes for the Heat. In the last column we identify the players that qualify in the roles described in this section. Miami had three players qualify as SSBs and had one player qualify as a DB. LeBron James would qualify as a 3DW if he were classified initially as a small forward. Chalmers also could have qualified if he were listed as a shooting guard. Miami has a number of other players that can shoot the three. Miller, Allen and Battier all play this role, but all fell short last season in DSG/M to qualify as a 3DW. Certainly, the Heat are utilizing players that stretch the defense. Recall that DSG is computed by looking at production while the individual is on the court as compared to his team's production otherwise. Given the defensive abilities of the Heat's star players LeBron and Wade, DSG likely under appreciates the defense of Miami's role players such as Battier.

Table 9.6: 2012-13 Miami Heat

Player	Min	DSG	EOP	AV	3PM	Roles
LeBron James	2877	186	2408	2781	103	SSB
Chris Bosh	2454	-92	1190	1005	21	SSB
Dwyane Wade	2391	164	1556	1884	17	
Mario Chalmers	2068	108	734	949	123	
Ray Allen	2035	-110	736	516	139	
Shane Battier	1786	-20	415	375	136	
Norris Cole	1590	-79	439	281	35	
Udonis Haslem	1414	89	341	520	0	
Mike Miller	900	-48	310	213	73	
Rashard Lewis	792	-21	212	171	51	SSB
Chris Andersen	624	21	274	316	2	DB
Joel Anthony	566	-17	122	87	0	
James Jones	221	0	47	46	16	

Table 9.7 presents those that played at least 200 minutes for the Spurs last season. The Spurs utilized at least two players that qualified in each of our defined categories (DB, 3DW and SSB). The Spurs have done a masterful job finding role players that complement their core talent. Splitter was a defensive stopper in the middle, while Diaw and Bonner came off the bench to help stretch opponents' defenses. Danny Green was a proficient three-point shooter. He broke the

NBA finals record for three-point field goals. He just missed the DSG cutoff last season to be considered a 3DW though.

Table 9.7: 2012-13 San Antonio Spurs

Player	Min	DSG	EOP	AV	3PM	Roles
Danny Green	2201	-2	728	725	177	
Tony Parker	2174	53	1613	1719	24	
Tim Duncan	2078	19	1181	1219	2	DB
Tiago Splitter	1997	127	974	1229	0	DB
Kawhi Leonard	1810	97	658	852	65	3DW
Boris Diaw	1709	-40	587	507	30	SSB
Gary Neal	1484	-70	540	399	89	
Manu Ginobili	1393	18	761	798	83	3DW
Stephen Jackson	1075	5	266	275	46	3DW
Nando De Colo	920	-28	321	265	31	
Matt Bonner	909	-18	275	240	53	SSB
DeJuan Blair	851	-27	343	290	0	
Patrick Mills	656	-35	272	202	52	
Cory Joseph	388	-14	152	124	6	

Conclusions

In the last chapter, we showed that great players make great teams. Teams constructed for unbalance on offense were the most successful. This does not mean that the team's other players are not important. Here, we see that both the Spurs and Heat make use of particular types of role players. Specifically, both feature wings and bigs that can shoot from the perimeter.

All of our work to this point sets a straightforward strategy for team construction. Teams need to identify and acquire the true superstars, those players that bring the most overall value to their teams. The first portion of our book discussed how to properly assess the contributions of the individual. The next step is to complement those players with appropriate role players. This chapter identified particularly important types of complementary players and those currently in the NBA that are the best in these roles. The final portion of our book will be about where to find these players and how to acquire them—the strategies for and options in team construction.

10

A Commentary on the Unpredictability of Outcomes

In Game 6 of the 2012-13 NBA Finals, the Spurs were winning by five with 28 seconds to go. The Spurs were winning three games to two in the series, and some Heat fans were already leaving the stadium, believing their Heat's season had ended. Then, LeBron knocks down a three. Kawhi Leonard goes one for two at the line on the other end. After a James miss from three, Bosh pulls down the offensive board and kicks to Ray Allen. Allen drains the three to send Game 6 into overtime. Deservedly so, the Heat fans that gave up and left were locked out and unable to return for the overtime session. The Heat went on to win game 6 and then game 7.

The Spurs were winning by five with 28 seconds to go. What were the chances the Heat were going to come back? Certainly the fans that left weren't betting on it. In those last 28 seconds, so many things had to go right for the Heat and wrong for the Spurs. If Allen misses that three, the game is over. If Bosh does not pull down the rebound on LeBron's miss, the game is over. If Kawhi Leonard's first three throw falls in instead of dipping in and then sliding out, the game is likely over. In all cases, San Antonio is celebrating. If we cannot predict the Spurs to win that game when they were up by five with 28 seconds to go, what can we predict?

The NBA can seem so unpredictable. A season can be derailed by an injury. The Thunder probably believe it would have been them in the finals and not the Spurs had Westbrook not gotten injured. For that matter, the Bulls are probably still wondering what would have been had Rose not been lost for the season. Sometimes, a season never really takes off because the players that you thought could not miss (and were relying on to develop) end up busting before your eyes. The Los Angeles Clippers drafted in the top eight for seven consecutive years between 1998 and 2004. They probably expected more from Darius Miles (3rd overall in 2000), Shaun Livingston (4th overall in 2004), and Michael Olowakandi (1st overall in 1998). It is hard to predict who the best players will be. It is perhaps more difficult to predict injuries. Even when the players pan out and the team stays healthy, it can feel like the stars need to align for your team to win a championship.

The Heat were a Ray Allen miss from losing the NBA finals. In a sense, they were a coin flip from defeat. The Heat's championship was anything but random, however. The Heat were the favorites to win it all out of the gate. They were the returning champs. They feature the greatest player in the world. They went 66 and 16 on the season, including a 27 game win streak. As for that moment, Ray Allen is not just another shooter. He is the NBA's all-time leader in three-point field goals. He has a reputation for being clutch. Allen was a priority addition to the already elite Heat team in the 2012 offseason because of his three-point shooting ability and NBA championship experience. Ray Allen chose to leave Boston and join the Heat because he believed the Heat had a great chance at winning a title. In one sense, game 6 came down to a coin flip. In another sense, it went just as Miami and Allen planned it. Over the course of the season, the ball bounces this way and that, shots fall and shots miss, knees bend one way and then the wrong way. In the end, the best team won.

Basketball is not inherently random. That would imply that all the hours Ray Allen spent perfecting his jump shot didn't matter. If the game were random, there would be no hope in improving predictions. The game is not random. Instead, it is unpredictable. The difference is that unpredictable can become predictable (at least in part). The game is unpredictable because it is complex, with far too many variables to account for. The unpredictability stems from a lack of information. We do not mean to imply that the game will ever be predictable. Rather, we suggest that we can improve predictions with more information.

When assessing a team's performance, we must account for the unpredictable events that contributed to any lack of success the team endured. Unpredictable catastrophes like major injuries can derail a player's season, but unpredictability is not all negative. For one, it makes the season exciting. In the case of a star player getting injured, it gives another player a chance to perform where they may never have had the opportunity otherwise. More relevant to the activities here, teams can use unpredictability to acquire talent and rebuild a roster. In this chapter, we suggest how our team metrics can help reduce the noise in seemingly random team production. We then discuss how the Houston Rockets used a high variance strategy to rebuild their roster.

Factoring Unpredictability into Team Evaluation

In the next section, we will discuss the recent moves of the Houston Rockets. These moves have seemingly turned around the organization in a short period of time. Now that the Rockets have acquired Dwight Howard, it is easy to look back and say that all of the moves they made to position themselves for this acquisition were the right ones. Dwight Howard's choice of where to sign this year was not easily predicted. Had he chosen to go elsewhere, it would not have meant that Houston's strategy was wrong. It is important to remember that teams can be employing the right strategy even if it is not immediately translating to wins. A sound approach can only shift the odds of success. A good strategy cannot guarantee wins.

> A sound approach can only shift the odds of success. A good strategy cannot guarantee wins.

This chapter is about team evaluation. However, it is not about a team's win percentage, or even how many points they score. It is not as much about what teams have accomplished (or failed to accomplish), but rather how they go about the attempt. The outcome of a game, whether a team wins or loses can come down to a single shot at the buzzer. Player involvement metrics and Lineup Entropy are not nearly as fickle. However, these "how" metrics are subject to unpredictability. An injury to a star player can change a team's rotation significantly, and thus alter player involvement and Lineup Entropy. The beauty and utility of these metrics is that they help identify the unpredictability in metrics measuring production. For example, suppose we ran a large study looking at teams' performance in the second of back-to-back road games. In this study, we might find that teams play worse in these games than they would typically. However, the trend is not universal. If you also run Lineup Entropy and scoring balance in these games, you might find that many of the anomalies in the study correspond with the home team in that second game having an unusual entropy or balance figure. An unusually high entropy or balance number could reflect that the home team was resting or had an injured star. This is a hypothetical scenario, but the point is that balance and entropy might help explain away part of what appears to be random noise in the game.

Basketball is a complex system. The outcome of games and seasons can be unpredictable. The unpredictability comes from a lack of knowledge of the many variables at play. If we can grow our understanding of how teams win and lose, we can increase our predictive power.

High Variance Team Construction

In the 2013 offseason, the Miami Heat added veteran Ray Allen. The previous season, they added Shane Battier. Neither of these players was added because the Heat thought he would take a giant leap forward from his production of past seasons. Instead, Allen and Battier were added because their production was predictable and a good fit for Miami. With a core of LeBron, Wade and Bosh, the Heat were (and still are) championship contenders. The three also meant the Heat had little financial flexibility to add players. In the few moves the Heat could make, they looked to add that role player that will make the difference between runner-up and champion. Allen made that difference with his game tying shot in game 6 of the NBA finals. Battier made six three-pointers in game 7. With few resources, good teams often do not have the luxury to take chances on their offseason acquisitions.

Teams looking to rebuild have an opportunity to take chances. At the 2013 MIT Sloan Sports Analytics Conference, there was a panel on "True Performance and Science of Randomness." The moderator of the panel was Houston Rockets General Manager Daryl Morey. Towards the end of the panel, a question came up about whether or not the format of having one winner among about 30 teams (in various sports) motivates teams to take bigger risks. Speaking about the Rockets' 2012 offseason, Morey said, "We didn't really have someone to build around, so we were searching for variance anywhere."[1] To win in the NBA, teams need great players. Coming into the 2012 offseason, the Rockets did not really have the core of great talent around which to build a championship. They also did not have the opportunity to grab proven great players. So, they chose to go after players that had high potential, the possibility of being great. They also chose other high risk strategies that have now paid off.

In the 2012 offseason, the Houston Rockets made five high variance choices. First, they acquired Jeremy Lin. Lin was undrafted out of Harvard University, which is not your typical basketball powerhouse. After being waived by a few NBA teams, he finally stuck with the New York Knicks in 2011-12. Midseason, he went wild, scoring at least 20 points in nine of ten games. In total, Lin played 35 games for New York, scoring 14.6 points per game. After that season, Lin was far from proven. He had flashed moments of brilliance, however. The Rockets offered Lin a fairly sizable contract given his experience.

In this same time frame, the Rockets made a large offer to Omer Asik. Asik was the backup center in Chicago in 2011-12 and averaged only 14.7 minutes per game. However, Asik had NBA size and had shown he could be a solid defender. Rather than going after a proven but mediocre center, the Rockets signed Asik, a player that could be very good, but also came with more risk.

With the 16th pick in the 2012 NBA draft, the Houston Rockets selected Royce White out of Iowa State. White had a lot of potential, but came with an acknowledged anxiety disorder. If not

---

[1] http://www.sloansportsconference.com/?p=9841. The quote can be heard at 54:45.

for the disorder, White would have likely gone a lot higher in the draft. White was a high variance acquisition of a different type. Here, the risk was that the anxiety would prevent him from playing, not so much that if he played, he would not be valuable. There were plenty of safe picks to be made when the Rockets selected White. The Rockets took the chance on him because they thought he had the most talent of the players still on the board. While the acquisitions of Lin and Asik have worked out for the Rockets, White did not. He never played a minute for Houston, and now has been traded to the 76ers.

The highest upside, lowest risk acquisition of the offseason for Houston was the trade for James Harden. Harden was the third man behind Durant and Westbrook on a very talented Thunder team. With several other key pieces on large contracts, the Thunder decided Harden could not be in their long term plans. With one year left on his contract, the Thunder dealt Harden to the Rockets. As was mostly expected, Harden became the go-to-guy the Rockets desperately needed. He averaged just under 26 points per game in 2012-13.

The last high variance move by the Rockets in the 2012 offseason was not a player acquisition. Instead, it was the choice to keep the financial flexibility necessary to land a top free agent in the 2013 offseason. This was a high variance move; there was no guarantee that they would land such a player. The Rockets could have used that cap space to sign or trade for veterans on long-term contracts. Had the Rockets believed they already had the core talent to win a championship, they might have gone the veteran route. Instead, the Rockets kept the flexibility, and in 2013 reaped the rewards. The Rockets signed Dwight Howard, making them an instant contender in the Western Conference.

The Rockets used the unpredictability of the NBA to their advantage. As a team far from a championship, they chose the path of high variance. They did not need every high-risk decision to pan out. It appears that enough of them have worked out, and in a short period of time, Morey has quickly turned the Rockets into one of the best teams in the NBA. The next third of our book is about team construction. We will keep in mind that there is unpredictability in any strategy. For example, we will look at the probability of landing a premium offensive player at each draft pick. The degree of risk a team should take at any given time is largely dependent on the team's circumstances. As we examine the bottom feeders of the NBA, we will keep in mind the success of Houston's high variance strategy.

If You Build It:
Team Construction

"He was a tremendous athlete with a strong body that looked like it was going to get better. He was competitive, and a fair shooter. Good ball handler, though not a great one at that time, but a good one, and a good defensive player. His shooting was what we were concerned with. We didn't know what kind of shooter he was going to turn out to be."

-Rod Thorn on Michael Jordan's Scouting Report[1]

[1] Thorn, R. NBA.com. Retrieved August 15, 2012.
<http://www.nba.com/bulls/news/jordanhof_thorn_090908.html>.

11

Draft Pick Value Chart

Each year, only one team can be crowned the champion of the world's most elite basketball league. For everyone else, it's nice try, good effort, and maybe next year. For the particularly destitute, the NBA draft can bring hope for a brighter future. But how much value does each draft pick bring? What is the difference between the first, second or tenth overall pick? What can teams reasonably expect from the protected future first rounder acquired via trade? What is at stake when the NBA conducts its annual draft lottery?

The crop of talent available in each draft class varies. Rightfully, there was a lot of hype around LeBron's class of 2003. By comparison, there was far less talent in the 2001 class where Kwame Brown was drafted first overall. Any team looking to acquire a pick in an upcoming draft will likely pay attention to the projected value of the draft. Still, some picks are obtained years in advance when the draft's pool of talent is unpredictable. On these occasions, understanding the typical production by pick can help teams in their decision-making.

To get a sense of the typical production by pick we need to study a large number of drafts. Looking at only the last five or ten years would be susceptible to anomalies—players drafted low that performed particularly well or players drafted high that busted. Also, it is the recent drafts where we have the least amount of information. For players drafted in 2011, we have at most two seasons of production on which to base our assessment. That is hardly enough to make any judgment.

To conduct our analysis, we need a statistic that measures the production or value of a player. In Chapter 4, we introduced player Approximate Value (AV). By combining Defensive Stops Gained (DSG) and Efficient Offensive Production (EOP), AV accounts for both offensive and defensive production. We would like to use AV in this chapter's analysis. Unfortunately, we can only calculate DSG back to 2001. Since we must consider prior draft years for a thorough study, AV is not an option.

In general, there are not publicly available statistics on which we can measure accurately individual defense in the last thirty or so years. The best available statistics are steals and blocks, and these are incomplete if not misleading. Rather than soil our study with weak defensive numbers, we resign to looking only at offensive production.

In Chapter 3, we introduced EOP+, an era independent EOP. EOP+ was designed to account for the differences in scoring rates in the different decades and to eliminate any biases towards the higher scoring eras. EOP (and thus, EOP+) can be calculated back to the 1977-78 season (when turnovers were first officially recorded by the NBA). We will use EOP+ as our measure of production and start our study with the 1977 draft. We end our study with the 2010 draft so that all of the draftees in our study have had the possibility of playing at least three seasons.

We will present the value by pick based on the average career EOP$^+$ and average EOP$^+$ per game (EOP$^+$/G). Our player involvement metrics support our intuition that the NBA is a star's game. Consequently, we will look at the likelihood of landing a star with each pick. In previous chapters, we discussed the importance of quality role players, and so, we will also calculate the likelihood of landing a quality offensive role player with each pick. We also find the best value picks outside of the top ten, identify the greatest draft blunders in the top 15, and rank teams based on the quality of their drafts. Finally, we rank the draft classes.

EOP$^+$ Again

Offensive Efficiency (OE) is positive offensive outcomes (baskets) divided by net possessions used. More specifically, the numerator is the sum of the player's assists and field goals made. The denominator is field goals attempted plus assists plus turnovers minus offensive rebounds. EOP adjusts a player's combined production in points and assists according to their OE. EOP$^+$ adjusts EOP so that the output is on a points scored scale consistent with the 2013 season's production. A high career EOP$^+$ reflects tremendous ability and value.

Table 11.1 presents the top 20 in career EOP$^+$ (among players drafted in the top 60 in the 1977 through 2010 drafts). There are six first overal picks in the top 20. No players drafted after the 16th overall pick made the board. The Utah pair of Malone and Stockton tops the list. Notables to just miss the top 20 included Larry Bird, Dominique Wilkins, David Robinson, Scottie Pippen, and Isiah Thomas.

Table 11.1: Career EOP$^+$ Leaders

Rank	First Name	Last Name	Draft	Pick	EOP$^+$	EOP$^+$/G
1	Karl	Malone	1985	13	33930	22.99
2	John	Stockton	1984	16	31240	20.77
3	Shaquille	O'Neal	1992	1	31115	25.78
4	Kobe	Bryant	1996	13	28932	23.35
5	Michael	Jordan	1984	3	28657	26.73
6	Kevin	Garnett	1995	5	27231	20.58
7	Gary	Payton	1990	2	25996	19.47
8	Jason	Kidd	1994	2	25107	18.05
9	Charles	Barkley	1984	5	24721	23.04
10	Steve	Nash	1996	15	24647	20.50
11	Tim	Duncan	1997	1	24590	20.84
12	Hakeem	Olajuwon	1984	1	23667	19.12
13	Magic	Johnson	1979	1	22542	24.88
14	Allen	Iverson	1996	1	22283	24.38
15	LeBron	James	2003	1	22127	28.92
16	Dirk	Nowitzki	1998	9	22121	19.96
17	Reggie	Miller	1987	11	22014	15.85
18	Ray	Allen	1996	5	21759	17.73
19	Clyde	Drexler	1983	14	21695	19.98
20	Paul	Pierce	1998	10	21303	19.33

Career EOP favors those that have long healthy careers. Of course, this is important when considering the complete value the player provided. However, it disadvantages the players whose careers are not yet complete. To get a more complete picture of the value provided, we also consider the rate statistic EOP⁺/G. Table 11.2 presents the top 20 in EOP⁺/G. We see current players such as Paul, Griffin, Rose, Durant, Westbrook and Anthony in Table 11.2 when they were not in Table 11.1. When ranking by per game statistics, current players have the benefit of not yet hitting the twilight of their career, when their numbers will likely diminish. Even though EOP⁺/G will have a slight bias to recent players, it is a better representation of a player's star quality than career EOP. It is not always how long the player plays as much as it is how good they were when they played.

Table 11.2: Career EOP⁺/G Leaders

Rank	First Name	Last Name	Draft	Pick	EOP⁺	EOP⁺/G
1	LeBron	James	2003	1	22127	28.92
2	Michael	Jordan	1984	3	28657	26.73
3	Shaquille	O'Neal	1992	1	31115	25.78
4	Chris	Paul	2005	4	14088	25.38
5	Dwyane	Wade	2003	5	16859	25.35
6	Magic	Johnson	1979	1	22542	24.88
7	Allen	Iverson	1996	1	22283	24.38
8	Kobe	Bryant	1996	13	28932	23.35
9	Charles	Barkley	1984	5	24721	23.04
10	Karl	Malone	1985	13	33930	22.99
11	Blake	Griffin	2009	1	5119	22.45
12	Larry	Bird	1978	6	20135	22.45
13	Derrick	Rose	2008	1	6250	22.40
14	Deron	Williams	2005	3	12985	22.23
15	Stephon	Marbury	1996	4	18642	22.04
16	Kevin	Durant	2007	2	10033	21.76
17	Kevin	Johnson	1987	7	15981	21.74
18	Chris	Webber	1993	1	17623	21.21
19	Russell	Westbrook	2008	4	8339	21.16
20	Carmelo	Anthony	2003	3	15052	21.11

Table 11.3 presents the quartiles for EOP⁺ and EOP⁺/G. Again, these are among players drafted in the top 60 in their respective drafts from 1977 through 2010. Note that 25% of players drafted have provided virtually no value.

Table 11.3: Quartiles for Career EOP⁺ and EOP⁺/G

Quartile	EOP⁺	EOP⁺/G
0	0	0.00
25	30	1.61
50	893	4.66
75	4501	8.72
100	33930	28.92

Offensive Draft Pick Value Charts

Now that we have an understanding of EOP$^+$ and EOP$^+$/G at the career level, we can use that as a framework for understanding the historical averages for offensive production per draft position. Table 11.4 presents the average career EOP$^+$ and average EOP$^+$/G for each draft position for the 1977 through 2010 drafts. For a visual representation, Charts 11.5 and 11.6 present average career EOP$^+$ and average EOP$^+$/G by pick, respectively.

Table 11.4: Draft Pick Value Chart

Picks	Avg EOP$^+$	AVG EOP$^+$/G	Picks	Avg EOP$^+$	AVG EOP$^+$/G
1	12285	16.45	31	1725	4.26
2	9204	12.21	32	1034	3.45
3	10247	13.76	33	1318	3.99
4	8808	12.52	34	948	3.52
5	9677	12.27	35	1262	3.88
6	5271	9.27	36	1778	4.07
7	7356	11.56	37	1857	4.56
8	6347	9.67	38	870	2.62
9	7391	10.09	39	1137	3.41
10	6573	10.33	40	1581	4.23
11	5738	8.33	41	1366	3.43
12	4524	7.73	42	894	2.62
13	6105	8.79	43	1631	4.07
14	4656	8.08	44	591	1.72
15	4082	6.93	45	1685	3.98
16	4218	6.91	46	1566	3.33
17	3428	6.59	47	1768	4.56
18	4391	7.39	48	1201	3.26
19	3018	6.61	49	953	2.65
20	3174	6.47	50	640	2.31
21	3793	7.02	51	465	1.48
22	2550	6.20	52	621	2.33
23	3210	6.01	53	644	2.09
24	4209	7.49	54	694	1.60
25	2066	5.59	55	614	2.34
26	2167	5.06	56	437	1.70
27	2227	5.33	57	831	2.08
28	2320	5.24	58	442	1.44
29	2865	4.77	59	303	0.88
30	2094	4.75	60	726	2.02

Random fluctuations aside, the table and charts have a near continuous decline as the pick positions increase. Possible exceptions occur near the top of the draft. The first pick has been a fair margin more valuable on average than the second pick. After the top five picks, there appears to be another drop. In the next chapter, we discuss the strategy of rebuilding through the draft. Since the best delineations between value at the top of the draft occur after the first and fifth picks, we will focus in the next chapter on teams that have had the opportunity to draft first overall and those that have drafted in the top five.

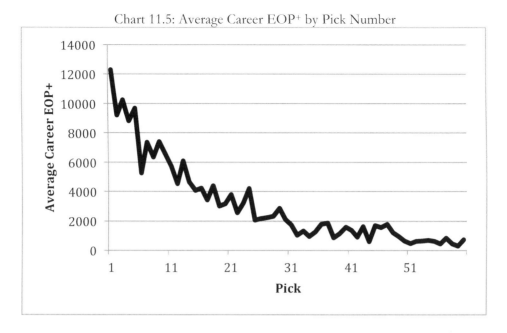

Chart 11.5: Average Career EOP+ by Pick Number

Chart 11.6: Average EOP+/G by Pick Number

One of the best draft classes in our study was the 2003 group. That year, LeBron went first overall, Carmelo was drafted third, Bosh went fourth, and Wade was drafted fifth. With the second overall selection, the Detroit Pistons drafted Darko Milicic. By comparison to those drafted around him, Darko was a complete bust. The Pistons passing on Carmelo and Wade for Milicic was reminiscent of when Portland passed on Jordan to take Sam Bowie second overall in 1984. There have been some famous blunders with the second overall pick and our average numbers seem to reflect this. In EOP+/G, the second overall selection ranks below the third, fourth and fifth overall picks.

Table 11.4 might suggest that the first overall selection is equivalent to the sum of the 10th and 11th selection if we look at career EOP+ or the 12th and 13th if we look at EOP+/G. We believe it would be a rare draft when a team might be willing to swap its first overall pick for two picks in the early teens. The reason is that the first overall pick produces stars, those rare talents that lead teams to championships. Experience tells us that picks in the early teens are less likely to do this. Our analysis on Point Balance in the NBA tells us that teams with elite scorers are more successful than their more balanced counterparts. It is better to have a team with a few great players than a team with a lot of good players. To understand the trade value of a pick, we need to use the Draft Pick Value Chart in conjunction with the probability that the pick produces a star or a role player.

To understand the trade value of a pick, we need to use the Draft Pick Value Chart in conjunction with the probability that the pick produces a star or a role player.

The Likelihood of Landing a Star

Of the 1982 draftees in our study, 119 or about 6% had an EOP+/G of 15 or better. The 15+ club is exclusive and it is asking a lot to expect to land such a rare talent. Still, it seems that in order to be successful in recent NBA seasons, teams need these types of players. Table 11.7 lists the NBA Conference Champions since 2008.

Table 11.7: Recent Conf. Champions and Star EOP+/G

Year	Team	Star Players	Career EOP+/G
2013	MIA	James	28.92
		Wade	25.35
	SAS	Parker	19.48
		Duncan	20.84
2012	MIA	James	28.92
		Wade	25.35
	OKC	Durant	21.76
		Westbrook	21.16
2011	DAL	Nowitzki	19.96
		Kidd	18.05
	MIA	James	28.92
		Wade	25.35
2010	LAL	Bryant	23.35
		Gasol	20.19
	BOS	Pierce	19.33
		Garnett	20.58
2009	LAL	Bryant	23.35
		Gasol	20.19
	ORL	Howard	19.21
		Nelson	14.25
2008	BOS	Pierce	19.33
		Garnett	20.58
	LAL	Bryant	23.35
		Gasol	20.19

With the exception of the 2009 Orlando Magic, every team has had at least two players from our exclusive club. The Magic were close. Their point guard Jameer Nelson had an EOP+/G of 14.25. If anything, the standards seem to be on the rise with no team in the last two years making the finals without two players having an EOP+/G above 19.4. In last year's finals, each team relied heavily on at least three players from the 15+ club. In addition to the players in the chart, the Heat also feature Chris Bosh who has a career average EOP+/G of 18.32. Manu Ginobili of the Spurs has a career EOP+/G of 15.02.

Given that teams like Miami, Oklahoma City and San Antonio all feature multiple players with an EOP+/G above 19, why set the bar as low as 15 for our elite group? The reason is that certain players who are elite for the prime of their careers, will play long beyond their best years, bringing their career average to a deceivingly low level. Examples include Scottie Pippen (16.92 EOP+/G) and Patrick Ewing (16.70 EOP+/G).

All evidence supports the necessity of star offensive players in order for teams to be champions or even to play for championships. If we are to properly assess the value of a draft position we need to know the likelihood that the pick will result in a superstar. We will consider those that have had a career EOP+/G of at least 15 as one of these franchise talents.

Table 11.8: Number of 15+ EOP+/G Players by Pick Number

Number	#15+	%	Number	#15+	%
1	20	59	28	1	3
2	9	26	29	0	0
3	13	38	30	2	6
4	8	24	31	0	0
5	11	32	32	0	0
6	3	9	33	0	0
7	8	24	34	1	3
8	2	6	35	0	0
9	6	18	36	0	0
10	5	15	37	1	3
11	4	12	38	0	0
12	1	3	39	0	0
13	2	6	40	1	3
14	2	6	41	0	0
15	2	6	42	0	0
16	1	3	43	1	3
17	1	3	44	0	0
18	2	6	45	0	0
19	2	6	46	1	3
20	1	3	47	0	0
21	1	3	48	1	3
22	1	3	49	0	0
23	0	0	50	0	0
24	2	6	51	0	0
25	2	6	52	0	0
26	0	0	53	0	0
27	0	0	54	0	0

Table 11.8 tallies the number of picks in the 34 drafts in our study that resulted in a player that has a career EOP$^+$/G at or above 15. Not all of the drafts had the full 60 picks, but all had at least 54 picks. We present the tallies through 54 picks. Only one player drafted 55th through 60th had an EOP$^+$/G above 15. That was Manu Ginobili, who was drafted by San Antonio 57th overall in 1999.

The first overall pick produces a star in six drafts out of ten. By comparison, picks two through five produce a top offensive player between 24 and 38 percent of the time. If the goal is to land a star with one of these top picks, then the first overall pick is (on the average) about twice as valuable as a 2nd through 5th overall pick.

Table 11.8 shows it is highly unlikely to land a premier player outside of the top 11 or so picks. In fact, for each pick position, it happens about once every 34 drafts. This does not mean that these picks yield nothing the rest of the time. Late in the first round and into the second round, often a solid role player is the best a team can reasonably hope for.

Out of the 1982 draftees in our study, 564 or about 28% have a career EOP$^+$/G at or above 8.0. Players producing at just above 8.0 are solid offensive role players. They are the type of player that functions well as the 4th or 5th option on offense in the starting lineup or one of the first options off the bench. Current players in this category include Nick Collison in Oklahoma City, Courtney Lee in Boston, Shane Battier in Miami, and Jared Dudley who was recently traded from Phoenix to the Clippers. Our numbers show that late first round picks are not likely to turn into superior offensive weapons. At the same time, teams drafting in the late first round typically already have a core in place that led them to the playoffs. The end of this round and the second round can be a place for teams to add depth and possibly target the ideal role players to round out their roster.

Table 11.9 displays the number of times each pick has produced a player with a career EOP$^+$/G of at least eight. All of the picks in the top ten produce one of these players more often than not. This is not the case for any pick outside of the top ten. Notice that there is not much of a difference in the likelihood of a team landing an 8+ player between picks 11 and 24. Chart 11.10 is a line graph representing the probabilities in Tables 11.8 and 11.9.

In the next chapter, we will look at the strategy of rebuilding a roster through the draft. Take a moment to dwell on the probabilities in these charts. A team could land picks in the top five in three consecutive seasons and still only expect to acquire one 15+ EOP$^+$/G player, the type of player that championship teams typically require. Perhaps more discouraging is that even lottery picks are not a guarantee for the 8+ club.

Table 11.9: Number of 8+ EOP+/G Players by Pick Number

Number	#8+	%	Number	#8+	%
1	32	94	28	7	21
2	28	82	29	8	24
3	30	88	30	6	18
4	30	88	31	5	15
5	23	68	32	2	6
6	17	50	33	2	6
7	27	79	34	2	6
8	21	62	35	5	15
9	19	56	36	4	12
10	23	68	37	5	15
11	16	47	38	3	9
12	16	47	39	5	15
13	16	47	40	6	18
14	17	50	41	5	15
15	11	32	42	2	6
16	14	41	43	6	18
17	11	32	44	0	0
18	12	35	45	5	15
19	12	35	46	5	15
20	10	29	47	8	24
21	15	44	48	4	12
22	10	29	49	2	6
23	9	26	50	2	6
24	16	47	51	1	3
25	5	15	52	0	0
26	9	26	53	1	3
27	6	18	54	0	0

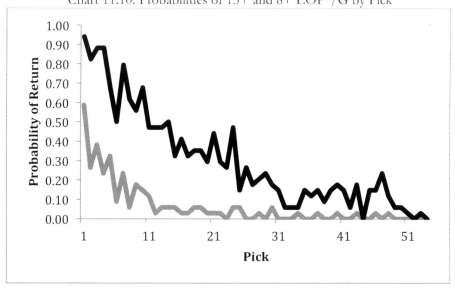

Chart 11.10: Probabilities of 15+ and 8+ EOP+/G by Pick

Best Picks Outside of the Top 10

In the last section, we showed that picks outside of the lottery rarely produce a star player. Still, it has happened. Who were these steals? What were the best picks? To measure how good or bad a pick was, we take the career EOP$^+$/G of the pick and subtract the average career EOP$^+$/G of all picks taken at the same pick number. This way, we measure how much better or worse the pick performed compared to what a team typically gets for the same position in the draft. Table 11.11 lists the top 20 picks outside of the top 10 according to this metric. Again, we are accounting for offensive production only, and this rate statistic is ignorant of the player's longevity in the league.

Utah's selection of John Stockton at 16th overall in 1984 was 7th on the board. Stockton is the NBA's all-time leader in assists (by the impressive margin of more than 3700 over number two Jason Kidd). Utah followed up its steal of Stockton with the selection of Karl Malone 13th overall in 1985. Malone is number two in points scored in the NBA, behind only the great Kareem Abdul-Jabbar. The selection of Malone was the fourth best draft steal in our list. Malone is one of the few big men in our top 20. Power forwards and centers with offensive ability or upside do not typically last long in NBA drafts. Sometimes, fans forget that the Charlotte Hornets drafted Kobe Bryant. Bryant was drafted 13th overall in 1996. He is the second best draft day steal according to our chart. He was then traded for Vlade Divac in what may be the worst draft day trade of all-time. Gilbert Arenas holds the top spot in our chart. This is a clear reminder that we are dealing with a rate statistic. Arenas did not have near the longevity in the league that Stockton, Malone or some of the others on this list had.

Table 11.11: All-time Best Draft Day Steals

Rank	Team	Pick	First Name	Last Name	Year
1	GSW	30	Gilbert	Arenas	2001
2	CHH	13	Kobe	Bryant	1996
3	SAS	28	Tony	Parker	2001
4	UTA	13	Karl	Malone	1985
5	CLE	34	Carlos	Boozer	2002
6	GSW	40	Monta	Ellis	2005
7	UTA	16	John	Stockton	1984
8	PHO	15	Steve	Nash	1996
9	SAS	57	Manu	Ginobili	1999
10	PHO	46	Jeff	Hornacek	1986
11	NYK	30	David	Lee	2005
12	MIL	43	Michael	Redd	2000
13	LAL	37	Nick	Van Exel	1993
14	POR	14	Clyde	Drexler	1983
15	GSW	14	Tim	Hardaway	1989
16	LAL	48	Marc	Gasol	2007
17	POR	53	Anthony	Mason	1988
18	MIL	56	Ramon	Sessions	2007
19	SAS	55	Luis	Scola	2002
20	ATL	49	Eddie	Johnson	1977

The top 40 picks according to EOP$^+$/G minus the average EOP$^+$/G for that draft position can be found in Table A10 in the Appendix. This list does not exclude picks in the top 10.

Biggest Draft Blunders

We have highlighted the best draft selections. We now cover the worst draft selections. (Portland fans may want to skip to the next section.) In 2003, Detroit selected Darko Milicic second overall. Darko was selected just after LeBron and just before Carmelo. In 2007, Portland selected Greg Oden over Kevin Durant. Oden has struggled to stay healthy while Durant has developed into one of the game's elite. The situation is eerily reminiscent of the 1984 draft where Portland drafted Sam Bowie just before the Bulls drafted Michael Jordan. The picks of Bowie, Milicic, and Oden did not work out well for their respective clubs, but how do they rank among the biggest draft blunders since 1977?

As we did with Table 11.11 for draft steals, we consider each player's EOP$^+$/G minus the average EOP$^+$/G of players drafted at the same position. Table 11.12 provides the 20 worst picks in terms of value relative to the average for that draft position.

Len Bias tops the list. He was selected second overall in 1986 by the Boston Celtics. Bias was a draft bust in the sense that he provided no value on the court for the Celtics. This lack of value was not due to a lack of talent. Tragically, Bias died less than two days after the draft. He was found with cocaine in his system.[1]

Table 11.12: Picks that Provided the Least Relative Value

Rank	Team	Pick	First Name	Last Name	Year	EOP$^+$/G
1	BOS	2	Len	Bias	1986	0.00
2	GSW	3	Chris	Washburn	1986	2.08
3	DEN	5	Nikoloz	Tskitishvili	2002	2.21
4	DEN	5	James	Ray	1980	2.49
5	LAC	1	Michael	Olowokandi	1998	6.67
6	WAS	1	Kwame	Brown	2001	7.18
7	MEM	2	Hasheem	Thabeet	2009	2.95
8	SEA	10	Mouhamed	Sene	2006	1.82
9	ORL	11	Fran	Vasquez	2005	0.00
10	GSW	9	Patrick	O'Bryant	2006	1.84
11	MIL	1	Kent	Benson	1977	8.20
12	CHA	3	Adam	Morrison	2006	5.65
13	TOR	5	Jonathan	Bender	1999	4.34
14	ATL	5	Jon	Koncak	1985	4.61
15	ATL	5	Shelden	Williams	2006	4.62
16	CLE	10	Luke	Jackson	2004	2.78
17	DET	24	Fred	Banks	1987	0.00
18	TOR	8	Rafael	Araujo	2004	2.24
19	SAC	1	Pervis	Ellison	1989	9.26
20	IND	3	Rick	Robey	1978	6.63

Certainly, the players in Table 11.12 were not the franchise saviors that teams hope for with high picks. Still, they do not all have the same stigma of an ultimate draft blunder that has followed Bowie and Milicic. In fact, neither Bowie nor Milicic is on the list. What makes the Bowie and

[1] Harriston, K. and Jenkins, S. "Maryland Basketball Star Len Bias is Dead at 22." *Washington Post.* June 20, 1986.

Milicic picks so memorable and heart wrenching is that they were taken just before premier players. These are the ultimate mistakes.

In 2003, the Detroit Pistons were already a good team. They were 50-32 the previous season and reached the Eastern Conference Finals. The Pistons acquired the 2nd overall pick from the Memphis Grizzlies as part of a 1997 deal that sent Otis Thorpe to the (then) Vancouver Grizzlies.

In the season following their selection of Darko Milicic, the Pistons were NBA Champions. They were a good team and two of their better young players were wing players similar to Carmelo Anthony. Those wing players, Tayshaun Prince and Richard Hamilton, were going to be 23 and 25 respectively in the 2003-04 season. The Pistons did not have a glaring need at small forward. Still, Carmelo was highly touted, and he had to be part of the draft discussion. The Pistons looked at both players seriously (or should have), and made the specific choice for Milicic over Anthony. This is a true draft mistake. In contrast, we cannot fault Cleveland for drafting Trajon Langdon 11th overall in 1999 when Manu Ginobili was still on the board. No team had Ginobili rated that high. If they did, they would have found a way to draft him before the 57th overall selection. In 2003, Detroit had to consider Carmelo; his name had to be tossed around the table with the coaches, scouts and front office. Taking Milicic over Anthony is the type of decision that can haunt teams for decades.

We looked at all players drafted in the top 15 overall. We then took the individual's EOP+/G and subtracted the EOP+/G of the player selected just after him. Table 11.13 presents the 20 lowest scores with respect to this measure. These are the greatest "just misses" of the NBA draft.

Table 11.13: The Top 20 "Just Misses" of the NBA Draft

Rank	Team	Pick	First Name	Last Name	Year	Next Pick
1	WSB	12	Kenny	Green	1985	Karl Malone
2	POR	2	Sam	Bowie	1984	Michael Jordann
3	CLE	12	Vitaly	Potapenko	1996	Kobe Bryant
4	BOS	13	Michael	Smith	1989	Tim Hardaway
5	DET	2	Darko	Milicic	2003	Carmelo Anthony
6	DAL	15	Terence	Stansbury	1984	John Stockton
7	ATL	5	Shelden	Williams	2006	Brandon Roy
8	GSW	8	Adonal	Foyle	1997	Tracy McGrady
9	TOR	8	Rafael	Araujo	2004	Andre Iguodala
10	DAL	4	Sam	Perkins	1984	Charles Barkley
11	ATL	2	Marvin	Williams	2005	Deron Williams
12	NYK	15	Frederic	Weis	1999	Metta World Peace
13	KCK	13	Ennis	Whatley	1983	Clyde Drexler
14	TOR	12	Aleksandar	Radojevic	1999	Corey Maggette
15	SAC	6	Joe	Kleine	1985	Chris Mullin
16	MEM	2	Hasheem	Thabeet	2009	James Harden
17	DET	9	Rodney	White	2001	Joe Johnson
18	LAC	8	Chris	Wilcox	2002	Amar'e Stoudemire
19	ATL	10	Keith	Edmonson	1982	Fat Lever
20	MIN	6	Jonny	Flynn	2009	Stephen Curry

For those of you who may not remember, there is a funny story related to line 10 in Table 11.13. In 1978, the San Diego (pre-Los Angeles) Clippers traded a future first round pick to the

Philadelphia 76ers for World B. Free. Six years later, the Clippers were still their usual basement-dweller selves, and the Philadelphia 76ers used that pick from the Clippers to select Charles Barkley 5th overall.

As for the rest of these just misses, there is something of a theme in the chart. We see post players like Bowie, Potapenko, Milicic, Foyle, Araujo, Klein and Thabeet were taken over perimeter players like Jordan, Bryant, Anthony, McGrady, Iguodala, Mullin and Harden. We talked about the advantage of high variance strategies. It is very difficult to find premier big men. The limited supply of big men increases the demand. Honestly, we would have drafted Greg Oden over Kevin Durant. As a big man that could influence the game on both ends of the court, Oden had the potential for a much greater impact than a scoring small forward. The selection of Oden did not work out, but it was not necessarily the wrong strategy. Perhaps the strategy needs to be tweaked to diminish the probability of landing a bust.

Players bust for a number of reasons. Most often, we can categorize the lack of production as due to injuries or a general lack of development. For Oden, it was injuries that prevented the production in his first few seasons. For Bowie, it was the same. Oden did have an injury late in his high school career. He had wrist surgery in 2006, and had to sit out part of his freshman season at Ohio State.[2] However, it was Oden's knees that derailed the early part of his career. Bowie's injuries were more predictable. He was sidelined with leg injuries for two consecutive seasons while at Kentucky. In a 2012 ESPN documentary titled "Going Big," Bowie admitted to lying to Portland team doctors about pain in his leg.[3] Identifying the potential for future injuries is largely out of the scope of current basketball analytics. Sure, past injuries of certain types do increase the likelihood of similar future injuries. Today's analytics would have strongly cautioned against selecting Bowie. However, today's analytics would not have provided much reason not to select Oden. Teams must rely heavily on the reports from their doctors when evaluating the health of individuals. The Oden versus Durant decision would likely have differed based on which team had the pick, the current needs of that team, and that team management's risk aversion.

Darko Milicic simply never developed into the premier player he was drafted to be. Recently, Joe Dumars was asked to comment on his selection of Milicic, and his response is telling. He said, "After I drafted Darko, from that point on, the amount of background we do on every player that you see us draft is ridiculous… The background on [Milicic] was about 20 percent of what we do now. I look back on it now and realize you didn't know half of the stuff you needed to know."[4] When trying to project if a player will continue to develop, teams need to look at the individual they are drafting. Does he appear to have the work ethic necessary to improve? What do his former coaches, teachers and others familiar with him say about his personality? Teams also

---

[2] Lamb, K. "Oden Facing Wrist Surgery; OSU Hosts Camp." Ohiostate.scout.com. June 15, 2006. <http://ohiostate.scout.com/2/540039.html>.

[3] Dwyer, K. "Sam Bowie reveals that he lied to Portland about feeling leg pain before the infamous 1984 draft. Sports.yahoo.com. December 11, 2012. <http://sports.yahoo.com/blogs/nba-ball-dont-lie/sam-bowie-reveals-lied-portland-feeling-leg-pain-212349458--nba.html>.

[4] Dwyer, K. "Joe Dumars on drafting Darko Milicic: 'I look back on it now and realize you didn't know half of the stuff you needed to know.'" Sports.yahoo.com. June 29, 2012. <http://sports.yahoo.com/blogs/nba-ball-dont-lie/joe-dumars-drafting-darko-milicic-look-back-now-203845303--nba.html>

need to look at their current roster and coaches and assess to what extent those individuals can help this prospective pick's development. Analytics can assess a coach's track record when developing players, but much of this aspect of scouting is handled well by more traditional methods.

We do not think that rebuilding a roster solely through the draft is the best strategy for current NBA teams. We will analyze this strategy specifically in the next chapter. Still, drafts can be a part of the rebuilding equation, and on a rare occasion can provide a cornerstone talent. Teams need star players to compete for championships, and so, we support high variance strategies for acquiring talent. In other words, we often support drafting unproven players that have the potential to be great. To reduce the likelihood of landing on one of our future draft blunders chart, teams need to gather as much information as they can about each potential pick and how he fits into their current and future plans. At this time, much of this work is beyond simply measuring on-the-court production.

Which Teams Have Drafted the Best?

We now have a measure of production relative to the expected production for each pick. We take the player's EOP^+/G and subtract the average EOP^+/G for all players drafted at the same number pick. This is how we generated our rankings for Table 11.11. We can use this new metric to measure how well franchises have drafted over the years. To rate the team we begin by taking each of their picks and computing the pick's EOP^+/G relative to the average for the pick. We then average all of these differences. We will call this the average draft yield (ADY) for the team. We cannot simply take the average EOP^+/G of all picks, because it would be biased towards teams that regularly pick in the lottery. We want to see which teams draft the best given their drafting position.

Table 11.14 ranks the teams based on their average return over the average EOP^+/G for the pick. This is based on the 1977 through 2010 drafts (if the franchise has existed so long). Note that several franchises moved in this time frame. For example, the New Orleans Jazz became the Utah Jazz. Those franchises that moved will have additional abbreviations beyond the current one in the team column.

Table 11.14: Ranking Franchises' Draft History

Rank	Team	ADY	Rank	Team	ADY
1	CLE	1.05	16	MIA	-0.12
2	MIL	0.85	17	HOU	-0.16
3	LAL	0.81	18	CHA	-0.24
4	DET	0.74	19	TOR	-0.26
5	PHO	0.73	20	CHI	-0.26
6	SAS	0.62	21	IND	-0.31
7	NOH, CHH, NOK	0.49	22	PHI	-0.32
8	OKC, SEA	0.45	23	ORL	-0.41
9	MEM, VAN	0.41	24	POR	-0.41
10	UTA, NOJ	0.18	25	DAL	-0.43
11	SAC, KCK	0.15	26	WAS	-0.45
12	GSW	0.12	27	DEN	-0.58
13	BOS	0.10	28	NJN	-0.64
14	NYK	-0.04	29	ATL	-0.73
15	MIN	-0.06	30	LAC, SDC, BUF	-1.01

Cleveland ranks the highest. They benefited from winning the LeBron sweepstakes. The Bucks are number two. Milwaukee had two very good second round picks in Michael Redd (2000) and Ramon Sessions (2007). They are also credited with drafting Dirk Nowitzki, even though he was subsequently traded. The Los Angeles Clippers rank last. We will focus a bit on this franchise in the next section when we consider the idea of rebuilding a team through the draft. The Clippers have had a lot of busts among their many lottery selections. Some may be surprised that Chicago is not ranked higher. They did draft Michael Jordan. In the next chapter, we will also look specifically at Chicago's string of high draft picks since Jordan left. There were several misses before the selection of Derrick Rose, prolonging Chicago's rebuilding efforts.

The rating system uses team's draft picks only, and does not look at whether or not the team kept the player. For example, the Charlotte Hornets (and now New Orleans Pelicans) get credit for drafting Kobe Bryant, even though he was subsequently traded in a blundersome exchange. In a similar way, Milwaukee earns points for drafting Nowitzki even though they immediately traded him to Dallas in a deal for Robert Traylor. We only looked at the draft pick. Any subsequent foolish moves are another matter.

Ranking the Draft Classes

The talent pool in drafts varies from year to year. For example, the talent at the top of the 2013 draft has not created much excitement. Instead, many teams are already salivating over the 2014 class, headlined by future Kansas Jayhawk Andrew Wiggins. Historically, which drafts have born the best players? Here, we rank the draft classes in our study.

Table 11.15 displays the 34 draft classes in our study ranked by the average EOP^+/G among the top 54 selections (column three). We chose 54 because it is the largest number of picks that all of our drafts contained. The fourth column, labeled Top 10, is the average EOP^+/G of the top 10 picks in that draft class. The fifth column, labeled #15+ is the number of players in the class that have a career EOP^+/G above 15. The last column lists the top two in EOP^+/G for the class.

According to average EOP^+/G, first place goes to the 1998 draft class. In addition to Pierce and Nowitzki, the class contained Vince Carter, Antawn Jamison, and Mike Bibby. Second on the board is the 2008 class. This was perhaps the deepest class among the 34. Deandre Jordan, Mario Chalmers, Nikola Pekovic, Goran Dragic and Omer Asik all went in the 2nd round of the 2008 draft. The 2009 class ranks third. This class was not particularly great offensively at the top. Look at the average EOP^+/G of the top 10 compared to 2003 or 1999. It was a great draft for point guards, producing Stephen Curry, Brandon Jennings, Ty Lawson, Jrue Holliday, Darren Collison, Ricky Rubio and Jeff Teague. You could say seven of the 30 starting floor generals in the NBA today came from the 2009 draft class. Other notables in the class were Blake Griffin, Tyreke Evans and James Harden.

Last place in average EOP^+/G was the 2010 class. The 2010 class was not particularly strong, however its number could improve as many of the picks in the class continue to mature.

As for the best average EOP^+/G among the top 10 picks, 1999 is the winner. That top 10 didn't feature a Jordan, Magic or LeBron. Its high average is not a result of a few exceptional talents. Instead, it is a result of having only one real bust. Other than the fifth overall selection, Jonathan Bender, every pick in the top 10 had an EOP^+/G above 13.7. Second prize in this category goes to the famous 2003 class.

Table 11.15: Ranking the Draft Classes by Average EOP$^+$/G

Rank	Year	Top 54	Top 10	#15+	Top Performers
1	1998	7.29	13.87	5	Dirk Nowitzki, Paul Pierce
2	2008	7.25	14.24	5	Derrick Rose, Russell Westbrook
3	2009	7.24	13.61	6	Blake Griffin, Stephen Curry
4	2005	7.17	12.98	5	Chris Paul, Deron Williams
5	2003	6.78	15.03	5	LeBron James, Dwyane Wade
6	1996	6.75	14.39	7	Allen Iverson, Kobe Bryant
7	1988	6.66	11.77	2	Mitch Richmond, Rod Strickland
8	1992	6.46	12.58	3	Shaquille O'Neal, Latrell Sprewell
9	2001	6.43	10.79	6	Pau Gasol, Tony Parker
10	1977	6.40	13.07	5	Marques Johnson, Bernard King
11	1990	6.26	10.46	1	Gary Payton, Derrick Coleman
12	2007	6.21	11.75	3	Kevin Durant, Al Horford
13	1999	6.19	15.48	8	Steve Francis, Baron Davis
14	2004	6.13	11.42	3	Dwight Howard, Andre Iguodala
15	1989	6.13	8.65	2	Tim Hardaway, Mookie Blaylock
16	1997	6.10	12.16	3	Tim Duncan, Tracy McGrady
17	1984	5.94	13.41	4	Michael Jordan, Charles Barkley
18	1986	5.93	8.19	3	Brad Daugherty, Mark Price
19	1981	5.89	12.31	3	Isiah Thomas, Larry Nance
20	2002	5.82	11.60	3	Amar'e Stoudemire, Yao Ming
21	1995	5.81	11.41	2	Kevin Garnett, Damon Stoudemire
22	1994	5.78	12.13	3	Jason Kidd, Glenn Robinson
23	1983	5.77	10.05	1	Clyde Drexler, Jeff Malone
24	1991	5.64	10.49	2	Larry Johnson, Terrel Brandon
25	1985	5.60	10.81	3	Karl Malone, Patrick Ewing
26	1987	5.59	13.43	4	Kevin Johnson, David Robinson
27	1978	5.59	12.67	3	Larry Bird, Reggie Theus
28	2000	5.49	8.80	1	Michael Redd, Jamal Crawford
29	1982	5.47	10.55	4	Dominique Wilkins, Clark Kellogg
30	1980	5.43	10.43	3	Jeff Ruland, Kevin McHale
31	1993	5.40	12.23	5	Chris Webber, Sam Cassell
32	2006	5.37	9.29	3	Brandon Roy, LaMarcus Aldridge
33	1979	5.11	10.88	1	Magic Johnson, Calvin Natt
34	2010	4.72	10.66	2	John Wall, Greg Monroe

Last in average EOP$^+$/G among the top 10 was the 1986 draft class. This class included 2nd overall selection Len Bias who died of a drug overdose shortly after his draft night. Third to last in EOP$^+$/G among the top 10 was the 2000 draft class. This class also only produced one player that has a career EOP$^+$/G above 15. That was Michael Redd, who was drafted 43rd overall. The average EOP$^+$/G of the top 10 was 8.80, about equivalent to a good offensive role player. This is fitting considering the 2nd best EOP$^+$/G producer of the class, the 8th overall selection Jamal Crawford, is best used as a complimentary piece in an offense.

Conclusions

FUTURE DIRECTION

In this study, we are looking at the offensive production of the players. Defense is only indirectly measured. A player that plays particularly poor defense would struggle to earn enough playing time to generate high EOP$^+$ numbers. Also, strong defensive plays can lead to break away points and assists. Still, we would like to run a similar study with a more complete measure of player value, such as Approximate Value (AV). Right now, we can compute AV back to the 2001-02 season. In time, we will have a large enough data set to run a reasonable draft pick value study using AV instead of EOP.

Looking only at offensive production, we have learned quite a bit. We can now quantify the difference in offensive quality in different draft years, and there has been significant variation. We also now understand just how likely a pick is to turn into a premier offensive player. Learning how often a pick yields a premier offensive player and a reasonable offensive role player can help shape draft strategy. Teams are now better informed to decide if they should be chasing a possible star with the 15th overall selection (6% odds on average) or settling for a more known commodity that will be a decent role player (32% odds on average). Together the draft pick value chart and likelihood of landing various levels of quality provide a good baseline on which teams can determine the value of a pick. Teams can adjust the baseline depending on their projections of the quality of the draft.

We have quantified the best steals of the draft and how effectively teams have drafted in general. We can now quantify why the Clippers have been so unsuccessful despite having so many high draft picks. They have been the least effective franchise when it comes to drafting for offense. On the other hand, we see great draft steals such as San Antonio's selections of Parker and Ginobili coinciding with a good overall draft ranking for the franchise. This partially explains why San Antonio has sustained success despite rarely drafting high since their selection of Tim Duncan.

We bet that the likelihood of landing a quality player high in the draft is a bit lower than many realize. The numbers tell us that rebuilding a roster through the draft has pitfalls and can be highly unpredictable. In the next chapter, we dig deeper into this strategy.

12

Rebuilding Through the Draft (or Not)

Each summer, as the league's best teams battle for the championship, the league's worst teams pray the bouncing Ping-Pong balls of the NBA Draft Lottery land them a high pick. The teams hope the high pick will turn into a franchise player, one that can turn around their fortunes.

There are three ways a team can acquire new talent—trades, free agency and the draft. The draft is often the path of least resistance. The NBA lottery system does not guarantee the worst team the best pick, but the non-playoff teams will draft first. It is a gift for mediocrity. Unlike Major League Baseball, where the futures of top draft picks are hard to project, the top of the NBA draft sometimes offers can't miss types like Shaquille O'Neal, LeBron James, and Tim Duncan. The NBA collective bargaining agreement guarantees that the first round draft picks won't be too costly. To consummate a trade for talent, a struggling team would have to surrender assets. Given their low place in the standings, they are probably short on tradable pieces. To sign a premier free agent, teams need to surrender large amounts of cash and cap space. They also need to convince the free agent that their team is where he wants to play. For a team on the bottom of the standings, this can be a tough sell. Accordingly, teams short on wins turn to the draft and pray their pick is the next Ewing or Magic and not the next Greg Oden or Michael Olowokandi.

The 2014 NBA draft class, which is headlined by Kansas recruit Andrew Wiggins, projects to be one of the best in years. Teams like Orlando and Phoenix are already drooling over the prospects. There are even rumors that proud franchises like the Boston Celtics are prepared to "tank" the 2013-14 season in hopes of adding a key building block for their future. The Celtics deny these rumors.[1]

We look at why a strategy of building through the draft might work and why it might not. We determine exactly how successful teams have been when using this strategy. We compare recent trends with those in the '70s and '80s. Our results show that the NBA landscape is changing, and the draft is not delivering the rewards it once did.

---

[1] Washburn, G. "Tanking for lottery won't help the Celtics." *Boston Globe.* July 1, 2013. <http://www.bostonglobe.com/sports/2013/07/01/danny-ainge-says-celtics-won-tank-next-season-and-that-right-decision/c4845EXC8paWShTcvWxVPP/story.html>.

Why Rebuilding Through the Draft Might Work

There are several reasons why high draft picks can turn around a franchise. In the last chapter, we saw the value provided by players picked at the top of the draft. We did not need the formal analysis to tell us that many high draft picks have turned out to be great players. Top picks in the NBA draft have included Magic Johnson, Hakeem Olajuwon, Patrick Ewing, David Robinson, Shaquille O'Neal, Tim Duncan, LeBron James, Dwight Howard, and Derrick Rose. These are the types of talents around which a franchise can build a dynasty.

Being bad should not require a lot of high priced talent. A team with a high pick should have cap space. Cap space is very valuable. We will touch on this a bit more in the next chapter. For now, we present the Detroit Pistons as an example. The Pistons have drafted high in the last few drafts. As a result they have some young players like Greg Monroe and Andre Drummond to build around. They also entered the 2013 offseason with a good amount of financial flexibility. They used cap space to land a big free agent in Josh Smith. The Pistons are hoping that their young core will continue to develop, and their growth along with the addition of Josh Smith will be the right recipe for several consecutive playoff appearances.

A team that is willing to endure a few miserable seasons can have the opportunity to accrue inexpensive talent through the draft and clear cap space. Then when the timing is right, when the team's youth has progressed to a certain point, and the team can determine where their strengths and weaknesses lie, the team can use the room under the salary cap and add veterans to fill the last remaining holes.

Why It Might Not Work

To land high draft picks, teams generally need to be very bad. To land several high picks, teams need to be bad for a few years. After a few 20 win seasons, it can be difficult to convince any free agents to join your roster. We would also be concerned that during that time, the team is getting accustomed to losing. This mentality can be demoralizing, making it difficult to put in the work needed for the young players acquired through the draft to continue to improve. Sometimes the bad required to land high picks can linger. Young players can benefit from solid role models in the locker room. A bad team probably lacks these players that lead by example. Also, coaches can use playing time as a motivation for young players. To be particularly bad, a team probably lacks suitable veterans to play over the young players. As a result, the team may be more pressured to let these young kids get their minutes, compromising some of the coach's leverage.

Even the first pick in the draft is not a guarantee. See the last chapter for the numbers. The 2005-07 drafts yielded top picks of Andrew Bogut, Andrea Bargnani and Greg Oden. Oden's career was derailed by injuries. Bogut and Bargnani are decent players, but not exactly the type of talent a team would choose to suffer for. In return for several losing seasons, a team might be left with only a few busts and a poor reputation.

From First Pick to First Place

Every team is trying to win a championship (we think). Let us start by assessing how often teams with high draft picks go on to win the NBA title. In the last 25 years (going back to 1989), only one team has drafted first overall and then subsequently won a title. The San Antonio Spurs drafted Tim Duncan in the 1997 draft, and then went on to win titles in 1999, 2003, 2005, and 2007. The Spurs were no ordinary first overall pick type of team. In 1995-96, the Spurs went 59-23 and were the 2nd seed in the Western Conference Playoffs. The 1996-97 season fell apart when the Spurs star, David Robinson, went down to an injury, and the Spurs suffered through a record of 20-62. Robinson only played six games that year. Tim Duncan was really joining a playoff caliber team after an off year.

Only one team in the last 25 years has drafted first overall and then gone on to win the NBA championship, and that Spurs team was quite the anomaly for a team drafting first overall. Has it always been so difficult to find a first overall pick that can lead a team to a championship? In 1969, Milwaukee drafted Kareem Abdul-Jabbar. They won the title in 1971. In 1974, Portland drafted Bill Walton. They won the title in 1977. In 1979, the Lakers drafted Magic Johnson. They also drafted James Worthy first overall in 1982. The Lakers won championships in 1980, 1982, 1985, 1987, and 1988. Of course, the Lakers had those picks thanks to some clever trades, not because they were one of the league's worst teams. The Lakers were 47-35 and lost in the Western Conference Semi-finals the year before they drafted Magic. The Lakers were 57-25 and, as we covered, won the championship in the 1982, just before drafting Worthy. In 1984, the Rockets drafted Hakeem Olajuwon. Olajuwon would later lead the Rockets to titles in 1994 and 1995.

It is not that the first overall picks in the last twenty-five years have been so terrible in comparison to those in the 20 years prior. Plenty of first overall picks have now gone on to win championships. Most notably, Shaq, who was drafted by Orlando in 1992, went on to win four titles. These titles just were not for the team that drafted him. Shaq won three titles for the Lakers and one for the Heat. More recently, LeBron has won two titles after leaving the Cavaliers.

The results of Shaq and James make for nice anecdotal evidence. We now formally review the production of first overall picks to see if there has been a drop-off in return rate on these picks. For the same reasons as the previous chapter, we use EOP+ as our measure of offensive production, and we will not attempt a measure of defensive production. We looked at EOP+ for the first overall pick in the 1977 through 2010 drafts. Chart 12.1 presents the EOP+/G for each first overall pick as a function of his season drafted.

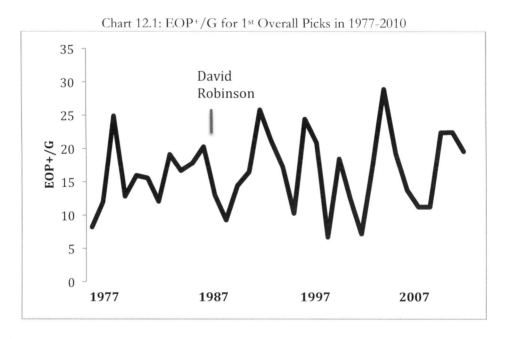

Chart 12.1: EOP+/G for 1st Overall Picks in 1977-2010

If there is an interesting and pertinent trend, it is that the frequency of complete busts has increased post 1987. In 1987, the Spurs drafted David Robinson. Recall that the Spurs are the only team since 1987 to draft first overall and then win a championship. A first pick that busts like Kwame Brown will do nothing to help his team escape the lottery.

Chart 12.2 presents the career EOP+ for each of the first overall picks. The trend down in career EOP+ is due to the obvious fact that the recent picks have yet to complete their careers. Career EOP+ is important for our discussion because to turn a franchise around, a pick must have a lasting impact.

Chart 12.2: Career EOP+ for 1st Overall Picks in 1977-2010

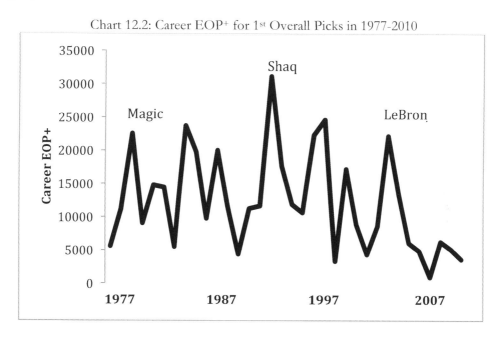

In addition to the increased frequency of busts, we can think of two reasons why recent high picks have not led teams to championships. First, there are simply more teams. When Magic went first overall, there were 22 teams in the league. While more teams may water down the talent pool in the league, increasing the value of a single great player, it also increases the number of teams with a chance at winning the championship.

Secondly, it seems that today's star players are less likely to stick around with the team that drafted them, especially if the team is in a small market. Players like Shaquille O'Neal, LeBron James, and Dwight Howard were and are concerned with marketing their brand. Miami and L.A. are bigger markets than Orlando and Cleveland. Players are also bolting to form "super teams." Shaquille left Orlando to join Kobe in L.A. Dwight made the same move, only to move again to join James Harden in Houston. LeBron famously left Cleveland to join Wade and Bosh in Miami. Before we continue this discussion of the NBA's current super team culture, let us expand our analysis on rebuilding through the draft beyond the first overall pick.

From Nearly the First Pick to First Place

For a team to rebuild through the draft, they do not need the first overall pick. The Bulls stole Michael Jordan with the third overall pick. Jordan then led the Bulls to six NBA championships.

To give the strategy of rebuilding through the draft a fair chance, we consider teams that drafted in the top three overall and then teams that drafted in the top five.

Recall that after 1997, no team that had the first overall pick has gone on to win the championship. After 1997, only two teams that have drafted in the top three overall have gone on to win the championship. The Pistons used the second overall pick in 2003 to select Darko Milicic and then won a title in 2004. As discussed previously, Milicic was not a significant contributor to that or any other Detroit team. The Heat used the second overall pick in 2008 to take Michael Beasley. Beasley was essentially given away prior to the Heat's recent championships. To make room under the cap to sign James, Wade and Bosh, the Heat had to clear the roster. Beasley was traded to Minnesota in the wholesale.

Of all the teams that drafted in the top five after 1997, only three have gone on to win NBA championships. The Boston Celtics drafted Jeff Green fifth overall in 2007. The Celtics then traded Green in the deal for Ray Allen. Allen helped the Celtics win the title that following season. Certainly, the high draft pick helped the Celtics to a title, but not in the traditional build through the draft sense. Obviously, the Pistons and Heat were the other two teams in this group. The Heat had two picks in the top 5 in that time frame. In addition to Beasley, the Heat also drafted Dwyane Wade (5th overall). Finally, we have found an example of a draft pick since 1997 that has through his own performance and production helped his team win a championship. Wade alone was not enough to win the championship. The first title came after the Heat completed a blockbuster deal for Shaq. The second and third titles came with a lot of help from LeBron.

From Nearly First Pick to Nearly First Pick Again

If the high picks have not lead to championships, what have they brought their teams? Well, the sad truth is that many of the teams drafting in the lottery return to the lottery. Of the teams that were fortunate (or unfortunate) enough to land a top five pick (between 1998 and 2012), 39% ended up drafting in the top five in the following season. Over 67% (of those drafting between 1998 and 2008) returned to the top five in the draft within five seasons. Let's take a look at some of the lottery's most loyal customers.

We are using the pick position for two purposes in this analysis. First, the high pick represents the opportunity to rebuild through the draft. We are interested in whether or not these picks lead to future success. So, we are not interested in high pick positions when those picks were previously dealt. We are also loosely using the pick as a representation of the quality of the team. This is not perfect as teams can trade picks, and the lottery somewhat jumbles order of finish. To help with the second role of the pick position, we also include the team's win percentage from that season. Note also that if a team had multiple picks in the first round, we are only listing the team's top first round pick. Again, we are interested in the team's opportunity to add talent early in the draft, and if enduring some poor seasons to rebuild through the draft has been or could be a successful strategy.

The Los Angeles Clippers may have finally turned a corner with the trade for Chris Paul in the 2011 offseason. However, prior to that trade, the Clippers were almost a guarantee each season to make the lottery. The four consecutive top four picks from 1998 to 2001 did little to rebuild the franchise (see Table 12.3). In the 2013 offseason, the Clippers have lured championship coach Doc Rivers from the Celtics and traded for role players Josh Reddick and Jared Dudley. Both Reddick and Dudley shoot efficiently from behind the three-point arc. The Clippers are hoping that these two can keep defenses honest and prevent too much help defense on their stars Chris Paul and

Blake Griffin. As we saw in Chapter 9, the Miami Heat and San Antonio Spurs have successfully used role players in this way.

Table 12.3: Los Angeles Clippers' 1st Round Picks

Year	W%	Pk	Player
1998	.207	1	Michael Olowokandi
1999	.180	4	Lamar Odom
2000	.183	3	Darius Miles
2001	.378	2	Tyson Chandler
2002	.476	8	Chris Wilcox
2003	.329	6	Chris Kaman
2004	.341	4	Shaun Livingston
2005	.451	12	Yaroslave Korolev
2006	.573	-	-
2007	.488	14	Al Thornton
2008	.280	7	Eric Gordon
2009	.232	1	Blake Griffin
2010	.354	8	Al-Farouq Aminu
			Average: 5.83

The Jordan led Bulls were great, and the team has been competitive of late, but Chicago fans have not forgotten the down years in between. Between 1999 and 2008, the Bulls drafted in the top five a remarkable seven times. See Table 12.4. Bulls' fans are hoping Rose can return healthy in 2013 after a torn ACL sidelined him for all of the 2012-13 season. The Bulls had consistently high draft picks for about a decade. A healthy Rose, along with Noah, might finally bring the Bulls back to the NBA finals in 2014, and yield some returns for Chicago's long run rebuilding project.

Table 12.4: Chicago Bulls' 1st Round Picks

Year	W%	Pk	Player
1999	.260	1	Elton Brand
2000	.207	4	Marcus Fizer
2001	.183	4	Eddy Curry
2002	.256	2	Jay Williams
2003	.366	7	Kirk Hinrich
2004	.280	3	Ben Gordon
2005	.573	-	-
2006	.500	2	LaMarcus Aldridge
2007	.598	9	Joakim Noah
2008	.402	1	Derrick Rose
			Average: 3.67

From Nearly First Pick to Nearly First Place

Several teams have gone from near the bottom of the draft to nearly a title. The Knicks drafted Ewing first overall in 1985. They made it to the finals in 1994 and 1999. The Magic made the finals three years after drafting Shaq. First overall pick Allen Iverson led Philadelphia to an Eastern Conference title in 2001. LeBron took the Cavs to the finals in 2007. A Dwight Howard led Magic lost to the Lakers in the 2009 finals. Given the unpredictability in the game, making the NBA finals and playing for a championship cannot be considered a failure. Still, Cleveland owner Dan Gilbert probably had visions of far greater glory with LeBron on his roster.

The campaigns of the above teams as they were constructed have come to an end short of the ultimate prize. There is still, however, one team that has turned high picks into nearly a championship and whose story is still not over. The now Oklahoma City Thunder (and former Seattle Supersonics) drafted Kevin Durant 2nd overall in 2007, Russell Westbrook 4th overall in 2008 and James Harden 3rd overall in 2009. The Thunder hit big in three consecutive drafts. The trio brought the team to the finals in 2011-12, only to lose to LeBron and the Heat. Given the difficulty of fitting Harden into the salary construction of the team, the Thunder dealt their excellent third scoring option to the Rockets prior to the 2012-13 season. Now the Rockets also have Dwight Howard and will be a formidable obstacle on the Thunder's route to another finals appearance. Still, there is a possibility that Durant and company can get over the last hurdle and win a championship. It would be the first top three pick since Duncan to lead the team that drafted him to a championship.

Conclusions

The NBA draft provides value, and teams have used their picks to acquire talent and become competitive or maintain production. We are not suggesting that the NBA draft is worthless or that teams cannot rebuild a roster largely through draft picks. The purpose of this chapter is to show that a high pick in the lottery is not a springboard. Only in the most unusual circumstances do teams sink to the depths of the standings for one year only to resurface the next year as a serious contender for a title. Instead, many teams bottom feed for a number of years before they come close to the light of the surface again. We have shown that high picks in the draft are no guarantee for talent. When teams do land a premier player, it is often not enough to get them out of the lottery immediately. They often return to find a second star or at least a complementary piece. Even when a team has been so lucky as to draft a star like Shaq, LeBron or Dwight and find some reasonable complementary pieces, they have still fallen just short of a title. When we put it all together, a strategy of "tanking for picks," or put more lightly, rebuilding through the draft, is like enduring a grueling hike up a mountain only to realize that you just climbed a landfill. It stinks and all you can see is the league's trash.

13

The Super Team Era

In 1996, the Houston Rockets traded for Charles Barkley. Barkley, Olajuwon and Drexler gave Houston three future Hall of Famers. They were all at least 33 years old that following season. Gary Payton and Karl Malone joined Kobe Bryant and Shaq in L.A. for the 2003-04 season. At the time, Payton was 35, and Malone was 40. It was Malone's final season. Before the 2007-08 season, Boston acquired Kevin Garnett and Ray Allen. That season Garnett was 31, Allen was 32, and Paul Pierce was 30. Unlike the previously mentioned unions, this one did lead to a title. Boston's big three won a title in their first season together. The NBA has seen great players come together in the past, but it has never seen anything quite like Miami's 2010 offseason.

In 2010, Miami gutted what remained of its roster to be able to sign LeBron James, Dwayne Wade and Chris Bosh. This union of great talents was different from the ones mentioned above. Wade was 29 that 2010-11 season. James and Bosh were each 26. James, Bosh and Wade were three of the game's elite, and they came together in the primes of their careers. Since they joined forces, they have been to three straight NBA finals and have won the last two championships.

When Miami formed this super team, it raised the standard for excellence in the NBA. At a pep rally of sorts, LeBron gleefully predicted a bevy of championships for him and his new teammates, "Not 2, not 3, not 4, not 5, not 6, not 7." Miami has been successful, but we won't compare LeBron to Nostradamus. With the talent Miami had assembled, it would have been hard to imagine them not winning.

In 2013, Dwight joined Harden in Houston, hoping to form a new super team of his own. There are already rumors that the Lakers will keep the financial flexibility necessary to go after LeBron and Carmelo in 2014. The super aggregation of talent in Miami is just the beginning of a new era in the NBA.

We may be mistaken, but we do not remember whispers of Bird wanting to play with Magic, or Malone looking to join Jordan and Pippen in Chicago. What has changed? Players jumping teams in free agency seems to be more acceptable in recent years. Once one super team is assembled, it is understandable why other players might try to do the same to compete. Perhaps one variable that is not being discussed here is that today's superstars have had more of an opportunity to play together on the national team. Until the Dream Team assembled in 1992, the U.S. Men's Basketball team was all amateurs. In 2008, LeBron, Wade and Bosh played together in the Olympics. Perhaps this experience brought the trio closer together and made them realize that they could coexist on the court. Maybe the plan to come together at the end of their contracts was tossed around (if not seriously) half-heartedly at the time. Whatever the reasons, the landscape of the NBA changed in 2010.

All of our metrics tell us that the NBA's elite teams are changing. The current NBA champions are less balanced offensively than previous winners and contenders. The EOP[+]/G of Miami's star players far exceeds what was necessary to win just five years ago. The way teams win has changed and teams need to adjust.

In the previous chapter we talked about the lack of success teams have had trying to rebuild their roster through the draft. With the standard to win now greater, it will only become more difficult. Oklahoma City was able to find three superstars in three consecutive drafts, but teams banking on the same success are likely to be disappointed. Teams must find other ways to acquire talent, and the two options are trades and free agency.

The Heat were able to bring together their trio of stars because they made the necessary moves to clear enough room under the NBA's salary cap. Houston was able to sign Dwight Howard because they had enough room under the cap. When the Memphis Grizzlies dealt Marreese Speights, Wayne Ellington, Josh Selby and a future first round pick to Cleveland for Jon Leuer this past season, it was far more about cutting salary than improving the talent on the roster. "It's a trade that had to be made from a business decision, so we have a chance to keep our core together and we move forward," Memphis coach Lionel Hollins said.[1] Financial flexibility has value and is a tradeable commodity in the NBA. The role of the general manager in today's NBA is as much about managing the short and long-term cap flexibility of the team as it is about assessing talent.

Next, we analyze two NBA teams, the Boston Celtics and the Miami Heat. An era ended in Boston when the Celtics shipped Pierce and Garnett to the Brooklyn Nets. Now, the team hopes to reload quickly with younger talent. Boston assembled an incredible trio of players in Garnett, Pierce and Allen. Miami outdid the Celtics a few years later. The age and declining skills of Boston's core forced the team to turn over the roster. Age will not be a factor for Miami any time soon as their trio of James, Wade and Bosh are still in their primes. However, Miami does have to worry that free agency will overthrow their kingdom, as James may look to take his talents to L.A. or Cleveland next summer. We take a look at how these teams built their championship rosters, where they are now, and how they are set up for the future.

A Case Study: The Boston Celtics

The Boston Celtics have 17 NBA titles. Danny Ainge was on the roster for two of the championship seasons, 1983-84 and 1985-86; however, when he became the Executive Director of Basketball Operations for the Celtics in 2003, the organization had not won a title since that same 1985-86 season. The 2007 offseason came on the heels of the Celtics' second consecutive losing season. The team was built on its own draft picks. Pierce was in the prime of his career; he was the type of talent that could lead a team to a championship. The rest of the roster was not quite ready though. The team had potential in Rajon Rondo, Al Jefferson, Tony Allen, Kendrick Perkins and Delonte West, but little in the way of proven talents. The Celtics were at a crossroads, and Danny Ainge had some big decisions to make. The Celtics had drafted well and had young talents that could develop into solid NBA players. They also owned the fifth pick in the upcoming draft (where

---

[1] Windhorst, B. "Memphis trade sheds $6M in payroll." ESPN.com. January 23, 2013. <http://espn.go.com/nba/story/_/id/8868058/memphis-grizzlies-cleveland-cavaliers-agree-multiplayer-trade>.

they would draft Jeff Green). The Celtics could have chosen to continue to let their young players develop, kept Green, and maybe even traded Pierce to acquire more young talent and picks. If the Celtics had a higher pick that year and could have gotten Oden or Durant, they may have gone that route.

Instead of waiting on their youth and continuing their rebuilding through the draft, the Celtics went in a completely different direction. The Celtics acquired Kevin Garnett and Ray Allen. The deal for Garnett was built around Al Jefferson and an expiring contract. The Timberwolves were after the young talent and financial flexibility. The Allen deal was built around Jeff Green.

Our analysis of the success of teams building through the draft would have strongly suggested that the Celtics make these moves. The subsequent success of the team confirmed Ainge's brilliance.

The Celtics were champions in 2008. The construction of every great team begins with a core of exceptionally talented players. We have already covered how the Celtics got theirs. Next, the team has to have the right role players. In Chapter 8, we talked about player involvement and how this does not necessarily imply everyone needs to share in the scoring. Instead, balance metrics suggest that specialists in other categories have great value. In Chapter 9, we discussed the types of role players that have been utilized with great success recently in the NBA. These are the wing player that can both defend and knock down threes (3DW), the super stretch big man (SSB), and the defensive big man (DB). The Celtics surrounded their core with a (still developing) pass first point guard in Rondo, a solid defensive center in Kendrick Perkins, and a power forward in Posey that knocked down 106 3-pointers that season.

An injury to Garnett derailed the 2008-09 season, but the Celtics returned to the finals in 2009-10, only to lose a fiercely contested game seven to the Lakers. The next two seasons, the Celtics were competitive, but never made it back to the finals.

In 2012, for the first time since the 2007 offseason, Ainge and the Celtics organization had to make difficult decisions about the direction of the team. There were reasons to believe the Celtics could still compete. After all, they had pushed Miami to a game seven in the playoffs that year. Pierce and Garnett are exceptional talents, and it may be a long time before the Celtics can build a comparable core. Also, the 2013 draft class did not project well, so a high draft pick was not so enticing. Finally, we now know that coach Doc Rivers was not thrilled with the idea of sticking around Boston during the rebuilding process, given his "trade" to the Clippers in 2013.

There were also reasons to believe the time had come to move on. The Celtics core was getting older, while other teams like the Heat and Thunder seemed to be getting better. Perhaps, most importantly, the finances lined up for Boston to largely blow up the roster in 2012. Details on this will follow shortly.

Instead of starting the rebuilding process in 2012, the Celtics decided to retool their bench and role players in hopes of building a roster that could better support the aging core. They signed Jeff Green and Jason Terry. They re-signed Brandon Bass, and worked a sign and trade for guard Courtney Lee. They also drafted Jared Sullinger in the first round of the draft, a player that could come in and contribute in his rookie season. The biggest loss in the 2012 offseason was Ray Allen's decision to join the Miami Heat.

On paper, the Celtics looked significantly improved. They had more depth, a second unit that could play more minutes and give more rest to Pierce and Garnett. However, the season's production did not match the paper projections. For the first half of the year, the team hovered around .500 and looked like a non-contender. Then, Rajon Rondo suffered a partially torn ACL in January. He was done for the year. The Celtics rallied in his absence, but could not escape the first round of the playoffs.

We acknowledge the unpredictability of the game. Had the Celtics stayed healthy, the outcome may have been different. They lost not only Rondo, but also Jared Sullinger to season-ending injuries. The Celtics did not get as far as they hoped with the rebuilt roster, but that does not mean it was the wrong strategy.

In the 2012 playoffs, it became apparent that while Garnett and Pierce can still contribute to a competitive team, they cannot carry a team through the playoffs. The Celtics again had to seriously consider the option of starting the rebuilding process.

The finances and salaries on the Boston roster in the 2013 offseason were not as amenable to a rebuild as the 2012 offseason. We will avoid the gory details of the NBA's salary cap rules and regulations, and stick to what is relevant to our discussion. The NBA's salary cap for 2013 is just under 59 million. Teams can exceed the cap in certain circumstances, like resigning their own players. However, to sign a big free agent outright, they must be under the roughly 59 million mark and in fact, enough under the cap to fit the contract. While building the supporting cast in Boston, the Celtics went far over the cap, so far that even if Garnett had retired and the Celtics could have moved Pierce's contract (without taking much salary in return), they would not have been enough under the cap to land a big ticket free agent.

According to hoopshype.com, the Celtics entered the offseason with seven players owed at least five million in 2013-14. They were Pierce, Garnett, Rondo, Green, Terry, Bass, and Lee. Garnett, Green, Terry, Bass and Lee were all re-signed or acquired in the 2012 offseason. Had the Celtics opted to go a different direction in 2012, they could have entered the 2013 offseason with considerable financial flexibility. What is worse is that role players like Terry, Bass and Lee were under contract for at least 2014-15 as well. The Celtics have since traded Terry, but in a deal where they took Gerald Wallace's large contract in return.

Time will tell how costly the Celtics' gamble in 2012 will be. Green looks like a promising talent and may be a big part of the reloading in Boston. Rondo and Green, along with recent draft picks of Avery Bradley, Sullinger, and Olynyk may be enough for the Celtics to compete in future years. We do not fault the Celtics for wanting to make one last push with Garnett and Pierce. We also realize that to obtain or keep Lee, Terry and Bass, the Celtics probably had to commit to longer deals.

The Celtics moved Garnett, Pierce and Terry in a blockbuster deal with the Brooklyn Nets. They have acquired a number of future picks with their deals as well as a large expiring contract in Kris Humphries. The Celtics have some tradeable assets, and so it is unlikely that Ainge is done. It will be interesting to follow their rebuilding project and eventually assess the series of moves they have made.

We tell the story of the Celtics because they have seen much of their core depart while they still have a number of role players filling the cap. We have shown how difficult it is to rebuild through the draft, and discussed how the Rockets retooled their roster through trades and free agency. We also know that the Heat were able to build their super team by creating enough cap space to sign all three stars in the same summer. If possible, teams should look to line up their contracts so that when the stars exit, they will have a virtually clean slate. This provides the fastest way to, and the best odds for, a rebuild.

A Case Study: The Miami Heat

We are all aware that the Heat brought together James, Wade and Bosh in 2010, and that this union has been incredibly successful. Over the last three seasons, the Heat have seemingly gotten stronger as a unit. Much of this improvement can be traced to the additions of players that well complement the skills of the big three. In recent offseasons, the Heat have added Shane Battier and Ray Allen, for example. Like the Celtics, building this supporting cast has put the Heat well over the NBA's salary cap. The Heat also must contend with the possibility that all three of Bosh, Wade and James can opt out of their contracts in 2014. If the big three all decide to walk, it would be the largest exodus of talent from a roster in one offseason that the NBA has ever seen. As a result of the Heat's recent success, the team has not had high draft picks, and thus they have not had a reasonable opportunity to draft young talent that could eventually lead their team. We saw in Chapter 12 the string of mediocrity that followed the Bulls after Jordan retired. Are the Heat destined for the same fate? How will they rebuild, and how long might it take?

Suppose that all goes wrong for the Heat, and the big three all take their talents out of South Beach. If Miami was left with multiple years owed to Mike Miller, Ray Allen, Mario Chalmers, Shane Battier, and other role players, it could be a long rebuilding process. They would have too much money tied up in these players to sign multiple or even one premium free agent. Even if they had the room for one big free agent, having so much cap space tied to complimentary players may dissuade a premium talent from joining the Heat. Fortunately for Miami fans, the Heat are prepared to make the best of what could be a bad situation. If James, Wade and Bosh opt out, the Heat could possibly clear its roster just as it did when it acquired the big three. According to Hoopshype.com, Udonis Haslem and Joel Anthony have player options that could cost the Heat a combined 8.4 million. This offseason, the Heat have added Greg Oden. The Heat will pay Oden 1.03 million in 2013-14. Oden then has a player option for 1.14 million the following season.[2] Otherwise, the Heat can completely clean house. (This may change as the Heat continue to look to improve their team for 2013 and beyond.)

The 2014 free agent class will be loaded. It could include James, Wade, Bosh, Carmelo Anthony, Kobe Bryant, Luol Deng, Eric Bledsoe, and others. The Heat have prepared well for the 2014 offseason. They have set up the contracts of their role players to expire when their stars may exit. Doing so provides the opportunity for an immediate rebuild. It is possible that even if the big three split, the Heat could have two to three of the better available free agents, and an extremely competitive roster for 2014-15 and beyond.

---

[2] ESPN.com. "Greg Oden finalizes deal with Heat." August 7, 2013. <http://espn.go.com/nba/truehoop/miamiheat/story/_/id/9547501/greg-oden-former-no-1-overall-pick-finalizes-signing-miami-heat>.

Conclusions

We introduced original ways to evaluate individual players. These included Offensive Efficiency (OE) and Efficient Offensive Production (EOP). We saw how these stats can differentiate two of the best players in the game in LeBron and Carmelo. LeBron has always been more efficient than Carmelo, and the gap has only widened over the years. Improved OE likely reflects maturation and work ethic. We also introduced Defensive Stops Gained (DSG), a defensive metric that accounts for defensive contributions beyond blocks or steals. EOP, DSG and their combination in Approximate Value yield far more information about a player than typical box score statistics alone.

An NBA roster can take many forms, and there are many ways to win. Our player involvement metrics support a strategy of obtaining a few stars and complimenting those stars with specialty role players, over trying to build a team with all-around depth, but with no individual superiority in a particular stat. We saw that certain types of role players have been used with great success by some of the NBA's top teams. Our player evaluation metrics help distinguish the abilities and overall value of the league's star and role players. With this added information, teams can better assess which types of players (and which players among those types) are most appropriate for their organization.

Knowing what you want is important, but obtaining it is another matter. We saw that the NBA draft is littered with busts, perhaps typically providing less value than most realize.

When the Miami Heat turned into the super team they are now, it changed the landscape of the NBA. The bar to greatness was raised. The league's most elite teams are now more elite than ever. Other players are now looking to join forces to compete with the talent in Miami. Finding a star player in the draft is challenging enough; having to find two or three to compete with a team like Miami is near impossible. Rebuilding through the draft alone is far from the best strategy in today's NBA. Free agent acquisitions and opportunistic trades form today's best teams. Thus, cap flexibility is of the utmost importance.

Every summer, only a handful of teams have enough flexibility to make serious runs at signing free agents such as Dwight Howard. So long as this trend continues, the odds of landing a premier player in free agency should remain high. As long as the likelihood for success is high, the strategy will remain viable. It is possible that things will change in the future. The NBA's next collective bargaining agreement may make super team assembly more difficult. Players may just become more reluctant to join forces with other top players. More teams may put a higher priority on cap flexibility and increase the number of options for high priced free agents each summer. New strategies would have to be developed in each of these scenarios. What we now know is that super teams exist, and we are comfortable with our prediction that they will be part of the NBA for some time. Even if LeBron leaves Miami, we have a hard time believing he will bolt for a roster with significantly less talent.

This book could not have been written several years ago. For one, much of the work is inspired by or depends directly on very recent advances in basketball analytics. Also, the NBA today is different from what it was several years ago. The game is changing and the methods for analyzing the game are evolving. Much like our current state of knowledge exceeds past states, we expect our future abilities to exceed the present ones. We will continue to work with the metrics developed here and to design and test new theories. We will report on our progress through our website, BasketballAnalyticsBook.com. Our site will also provide a forum for reader feedback on the book and suggestions for improved metrics. We welcome your comments and questions, and we look forward to future exciting years for the NBA and basketball analytics.

Team-by-Team Advanced Metrics

Here, we organize by team some of the advanced statistics covered in the book. The teams are presented in alphabetical order of location. For each player, we present the following statistics introduced in Chapters 3, 4 and 7:

- Offensive Efficiency   (OE)
- Efficient Offensive Production   (EOP)
- Efficient Offensive Production per minute   (EOP/M)
- Defensive Stops Gained   (DSG)
- Defensive Stops Gained per minute   (DSG/M)
- Approximate Value   (AV)
- Approximate Value per minute   (AV/M)
- Lineup Entropy   (LE)

We list if the player qualified for one of the three "new positions" from Chapter 9. Those were the following:

- Defensive and three-point shooting wing   (3DW)
- Super stretch big   (SSB)
- Defensive big   (DB)

We also present the following team stats (largely from Chapters 7 and 8):

- Team Offensive Efficiency   (TOE)
- Point Balance   (PB)
- Point Balance in the clutch   (PBC)
- Assist Balance   (AB)
- Rebound Balance   (RB)
- Team Lineup Entropy   (TLE)

We provide each team's rank in the above statistics in 2012-13. Higher TOE means a higher rank. For the other statistics, the lower value is given the higher rank. So, for example, Oklahoma City is ranked first in PB since they had the lowest PB. We then spotlight a specific player or group of players from the team for a visualization of his or their statistics. These visualizations were introduced in Chapter 5.

Finally, we present the team's last ten draft picks leading into the 2010 NBA draft. For each pick we present the player's games played (GP), EOP^+/G and what we label yield. Yield is the player's EOP^+/G minus the average EOP^+/G of all players drafted at the same pick from 1977 to 2010. We end at the 2010 draft so that all draft picks have had the opportunity to play at least three seasons.

Atlanta Hawks

Record: 44-38

Team Stats

	Stat	Rank
Offensive Efficiency	.559	6
Point Balance	.966	19
Point Balance in the clutch	.866	7
Assist Balance	.880	14
Rebound Balance	.932	4
Lineup Entropy	5.582	13

EOP Player Spotlight: Jeff Teague

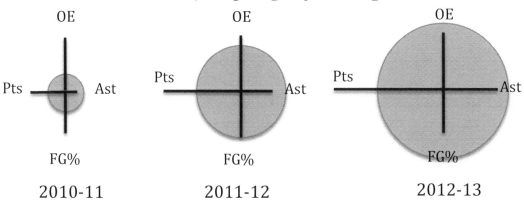

2010-11   2011-12   2012-13

Draft Pick Success

Year	Pick	First Name	Last Name	GP	EOP$^+$/G	Yield
2005	31	Salim	Stoudamire	157	5.87	1.61
2005	59	Cenk	Akyol	0	0.00	-0.88
2006	5	Shelden	Williams	361	4.62	-7.65
2006	33	Solomon	Jones	270	3.20	-0.79
2007	3	Al	Horford	391	15.90	2.14
2007	11	Acie	Law	188	4.11	-4.22
2009	19	Jeff	Teague	287	10.55	3.94
2009	49	Sergiy	Gladyr	0	0.00	-2.65
2010	24	Damion	James	32	3.61	-3.88
2010	53	Pape	Sy	3	1.89	-0.20

Player Stats

Player	Age	Pos	Min	OE	EOP	EOP/M
Al Horford	26	C	2756	0.65	1454	0.528
Josh Smith	27	PF	2683	0.55	1300	0.485
Jeff Teague	24	PG	2628	0.58	1410	0.537
Kyle Korver	31	SF	2259	0.53	744	0.329
Devin Harris	29	SG	1421	0.54	597	0.420
DeShawn Stevenson	31	SG	1158	0.47	231	0.199
Zaza Pachulia	28	C	1134	0.75	415	0.366
Louis Williams	26	SG	1119	0.50	501	0.448
Ivan Johnson	28	PF	1035	0.58	430	0.415
Anthony Tolliver	27	SF	963	0.45	189	0.197
John Jenkins	21	SG	902	0.50	317	0.351
Dahntay Jones	32	SG	381	0.49	76	0.200
Mike Scott	24	PF	376	0.58	169	0.451
Johan Petro	27	C	352	0.55	100	0.283
Anthony Morrow	27	SF	301	0.49	98	0.326
Shelvin Mack	23	PG	268	0.56	117	0.435
Jannero Pargo	33	PG	113	0.52	39	0.348
Jeremy Tyler	21	C	5	0.00	0	0.000

Player	DSG	DSG/M	AV	AV/M	LE	Roles
Al Horford	-63	-0.023	1329	0.482	3.310	
Josh Smith	28	0.011	1357	0.506	3.289	SSB
Jeff Teague	-36	-0.014	1338	0.509	3.276	
Kyle Korver	-2	-0.001	739	0.327	3.210	
Devin Harris	105	0.074	806	0.567	3.423	3DW
DeShawn Stevenson	-32	-0.027	167	0.145	3.324	
Zaza Pachulia	24	0.021	463	0.408	3.397	
Louis Williams	-1	-0.001	498	0.445	3.359	
Ivan Johnson	48	0.046	526	0.508	3.807	
Anthony Tolliver	28	0.029	245	0.254	3.794	3DW
John Jenkins	-61	-0.068	194	0.216	3.823	
Dahntay Jones	-15	-0.040	46	0.120	3.489	
Mike Scott	-13	-0.034	144	0.382	3.664	
Johan Petro	-28	-0.079	44	0.125	3.662	
Anthony Morrow	2	0.008	103	0.342	3.333	
Shelvin Mack	0	0.000	116	0.435	3.334	
Jannero Pargo	6	0.052	51	0.451	3.405	
Jeremy Tyler	-3	-0.627	-6	-1.255	2.235	

Boston Celtics

Record: 41-40

Team Stats

	Stat	Rank
Offensive Efficiency	.549	17
Point Balance	.961	16
Point Balance in the clutch	.874	10
Assist Balance	.902	18
Rebound Balance	.975	23
Lineup Entropy	6.085	30

EOP Player Spotlight: Jeff Green

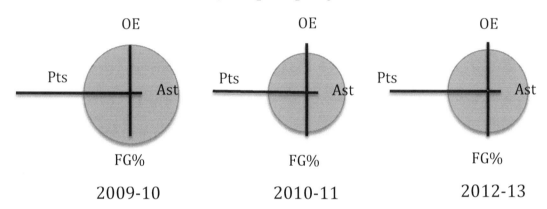

2009-10   2010-11   2012-13

Draft Pick Success

Year	Pick	First Name	Last Name	GP	EOP$^+$/G	Yield
2005	50	Ryan	Gomes	482	9.11	6.80
2005	53	Orien	Greene	131	2.57	0.48
2006	7	Randy	Foye	471	10.33	-1.23
2007	5	Jeff	Green	396	11.01	-1.26
2007	32	Gabe	Pruitt	62	1.86	-1.59
2008	30	J.R.	Giddens	38	1.87	-2.88
2008	60	Semih	Erden	69	3.94	1.92
2009	58	Lester	Hudson	52	4.01	2.57
2010	19	Avery	Bradley	145	6.15	-0.46
2010	52	Luke	Harangody	70	3.13	0.80

Player Stats

Player	Age	Pos	Min	OE	EOP	EOP/M
Paul Pierce	35	SF	2575	0.52	1346	0.523
Jeff Green	26	PF	2252	0.50	857	0.380
Brandon Bass	27	PF	2239	0.59	688	0.307
Jason Terry	35	SG	2124	0.52	742	0.349
Kevin Garnett	36	C	2022	0.56	949	0.469
Courtney Lee	27	SG	1941	0.54	586	0.302
Avery Bradley	22	PG	1435	0.47	388	0.271
Rajon Rondo	26	PG	1423	0.65	831	0.584
Jared Sullinger	20	PF	892	0.74	333	0.374
Chris Wilcox	30	C	830	0.86	358	0.432
Jordan Crawford	24	SG	582	0.50	226	0.388
Leandro Barbosa	30	PG	513	0.53	210	0.409
Jason Collins	34	C	330	0.58	37	0.111
Terrence Williams	25	SF	318	0.56	118	0.372
Shavlik Randolph	29	PF	198	0.94	100	0.505
D.J. White	26	PF	86	0.64	31	0.362
Fab Melo	22	C	36	0.43	5	0.126
Kris Joseph	24	SF	24	0.23	3	0.113
Jarvis Varnado	24	PF	18	0.60	6	0.342
Darko Milicic	27	C	5	0.00	0	0.000

Player	DSG	DSG/M	AV	AV/M	LE	Roles
Paul Pierce	38	0.015	1423	0.552	3.352	3DW
Jeff Green	-43	-0.019	771	0.342	3.586	SSB
Brandon Bass	-142	-0.063	404	0.181	3.361	
Jason Terry	2	0.001	745	0.351	3.529	3DW
Kevin Garnett	225	0.111	1400	0.692	3.256	DB
Courtney Lee	-64	-0.033	458	0.236	3.571	
Avery Bradley	5	0.003	398	0.277	3.241	
Rajon Rondo	25	0.017	880	0.619	3.161	
Jared Sullinger	37	0.041	407	0.456	3.265	DB
Chris Wilcox	-49	-0.059	261	0.315	3.459	
Jordan Crawford	-22	-0.037	182	0.313	3.368	
Leandro Barbosa	3	0.006	216	0.422	3.237	
Jason Collins	9	0.027	54	0.165	3.286	
Terrence Williams	-9	-0.028	100	0.316	3.331	
Shavlik Randolph	-9	-0.045	82	0.415	3.211	
D.J. White	3	0.031	36	0.424	2.974	
Fab Melo	-5	-0.133	-5	-0.140	2.922	
Kris Joseph	-2	-0.085	-1	-0.056	3.149	
Jarvis Varnado	4	0.197	13	0.736	2.798	
Darko Milicic	1	0.212	2	0.425	2.311	

Brooklyn Nets

Record: 49-33

Team Stats

	Stat	Rank
Offensive Efficiency	.551	14
Point Balance	.947	7
Point Balance in the clutch	.913	18
Assist Balance	.847	4
Rebound Balance	.925	1
Lineup Entropy	5.615	14

AV Player Spotlight: 2012-13

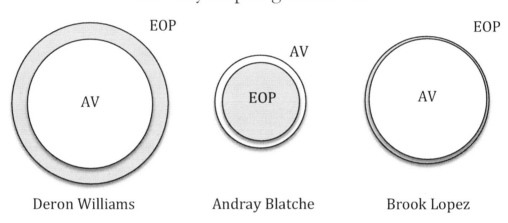

Deron Williams   Andray Blatche   Brook Lopez

Draft Pick Success

Year	Pick	First Name	Last Name	GP	EOP+/G	Yield
2006	23	Josh	Boone	256	6.77	0.76
2006	54	Hassan	Adams	73	2.56	0.96
2007	17	Sean	Williams	137	4.34	-2.25
2008	10	Brook	Lopez	325	16.70	6.37
2008	21	Ryan	Anderson	335	10.19	3.17
2008	40	Chris	Douglas-Roberts	161	6.23	2.00
2009	11	Terrence	Williams	153	6.82	-1.51
2010	3	Derrick	Favors	220	8.53	-5.23
2010	27	Jordan	Crawford	176	11.03	5.70
2010	31	Tibor	Pleiss	0	0.00	-4.26

Player Stats

Player	Age	Pos	Min	OE	EOP	EOP/M
Deron Williams	28	PG	2842	0.57	1682	0.592
Joe Johnson	31	SG	2642	0.51	1049	0.397
Brook Lopez	24	C	2253	0.59	1330	0.590
Gerald Wallace	30	SF	2076	0.53	541	0.261
Reggie Evans	32	PF	1967	1.08	650	0.331
Andray Blatche	26	C	1555	0.60	820	0.528
C.J. Watson	28	PG	1521	0.54	547	0.360
Keith Bogans	32	SG	1408	0.47	262	0.186
Kris Humphries	27	PF	1191	0.63	379	0.318
MarShon Brooks	24	SG	912	0.52	353	0.387
Jerry Stackhouse	38	SF	544	0.45	141	0.260
Mirza Teletovic	27	PF	499	0.48	150	0.301
Tyshawn Taylor	22	PG	221	0.40	62	0.280
Josh Childress	29	SF	100	0.55	15	0.148
Tornike Shengelia	21	SF	93	0.46	23	0.244
Kris Joseph	24	SF	30	0.00	0	0.000

Player	DSG	DSG/M	AV	AV/M	LE	Roles
Deron Williams	-166	-0.058	1350	0.475	3.181	
Joe Johnson	-36	-0.014	976	0.369	3.212	
Brook Lopez	-35	-0.016	1260	0.559	2.999	
Gerald Wallace	-15	-0.007	512	0.246	3.061	
Reggie Evans	52	0.026	754	0.384	3.101	
Andray Blatche	71	0.046	963	0.619	3.497	
C.J. Watson	30	0.019	606	0.399	3.491	
Keith Bogans	-48	-0.034	165	0.117	3.323	
Kris Humphries	-50	-0.042	280	0.235	3.366	
MarShon Brooks	37	0.041	427	0.469	3.554	
Jerry Stackhouse	17	0.032	176	0.324	3.342	
Mirza Teletovic	6	0.013	163	0.327	3.566	SSB
Tyshawn Taylor	-9	-0.040	44	0.200	3.558	
Josh Childress	-1	-0.008	13	0.133	3.502	
Tornike Shengelia	18	0.191	58	0.627	3.177	
Kris Joseph	3	0.087	5	0.174	2.590	

Charlotte Bobcats

Record: 21-61

Team Stats

	Stat	Rank
Offensive Efficiency	.521	30
Point Balance	.956	10
Point Balance in the clutch	.912	17
Assist Balance	.898	17
Rebound Balance	.980	26
Lineup Entropy	5.939	24

EOP Player Spotlight: Gerald Henderson

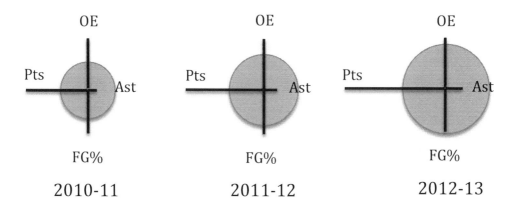

2010-11   2011-12   2012-13

Draft Pick Success

Year	Pick	First Name	Last Name	GP	EOP$^+$/G	Yield
2006	3	Adam	Morrison	161	5.65	-8.11
2006	50	Ryan	Hollins	374	4.12	1.81
2007	8	Brandan	Wright	227	7.45	-2.22
2007	22	Jared	Dudley	449	9.11	2.91
2008	9	D.J.	Augustin	358	10.40	0.31
2008	20	Alexis	Ajinca	71	2.18	-4.29
2008	38	Kyle	Weaver	73	5.02	2.40
2009	12	Gerald	Henderson	234	9.97	2.24
2009	40	Derrick	Brown	171	5.61	1.38
2009	54	Robert	Vaden	0	0.00	-1.60

Player Stats

Player	Age	Pos	Min	OE	EOP	EOP/M
Kemba Walker	22	PG	2859	0.54	1477	0.517
Bismack Biyombo	20	C	2186	0.71	444	0.203
Gerald Henderson	25	SG	2133	0.52	929	0.436
Michael Kidd-Gilchrist	19	SF	2025	0.57	684	0.338
Ramon Sessions	26	SG	1652	0.51	820	0.496
Ben Gordon	29	SG	1560	0.44	636	0.407
Jeff Taylor	23	SF	1507	0.51	404	0.268
Byron Mullens	23	PF	1428	0.46	437	0.306
Brendan Haywood	33	C	1162	0.72	259	0.223
Josh McRoberts	25	PF	802	0.68	303	0.378
Jeff Adrien	26	PF	713	0.64	230	0.323
Hakim Warrick	30	PF	482	0.46	147	0.305
Reggie Williams	26	SF	380	0.53	140	0.370
Tyrus Thomas	26	PF	360	0.43	91	0.252
Jannero Pargo	33	PG	292	0.47	125	0.429
DeSagana Diop	31	C	226	0.55	22	0.096
Cory Higgins	23	SG	32	0.48	13	0.403
Matt Carroll	32	SG	6	1.00	1	0.192

Player	DSG	DSG/M	AV	AV/M	LE	Roles
Kemba Walker	113	0.039	1703	0.596	3.485	
Bismack Biyombo	-32	-0.014	381	0.174	3.394	
Gerald Henderson	-11	-0.005	908	0.426	3.427	
Michael Kidd-Gilchrist	62	0.031	808	0.399	3.454	
Ramon Sessions	-13	-0.008	793	0.480	3.539	
Ben Gordon	-110	-0.070	416	0.267	3.668	
Jeff Taylor	38	0.025	479	0.318	3.639	3DW
Byron Mullens	-117	-0.082	203	0.142	3.269	SSB
Brendan Haywood	67	0.058	393	0.338	3.320	DB
Josh McRoberts	36	0.044	375	0.467	3.151	
Jeff Adrien	30	0.042	290	0.407	3.486	
Hakim Warrick	-1	-0.003	145	0.300	3.291	
Reggie Williams	-1	-0.004	138	0.362	3.870	
Tyrus Thomas	-4	-0.011	83	0.230	3.535	
Jannero Pargo	-12	-0.040	102	0.348	3.357	
DeSagana Diop	6	0.026	34	0.149	3.594	DB
Cory Higgins	-2	-0.050	10	0.304	3.324	
Matt Carroll	2	0.387	6	0.966	2.464	

Chicago Bulls

Record: 45-37

Team Stats

	Stat	Rank
Offensive Efficiency	.551	11
Point Balance	.967	20
Point Balance in the clutch	.978	29
Assist Balance	.948	27
Rebound Balance	.932	3
Lineup Entropy	5.618	15

EOP Player Spotlight: Joakim Noah

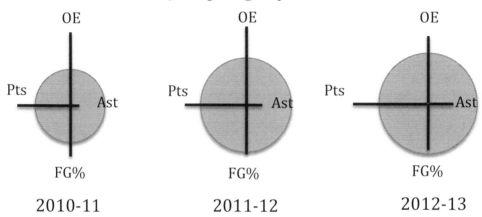

2010-11   2011-12   2012-13

Draft Pick Success

Year	Pick	First Name	Last Name	GP	EOP[+]/G	Yield
2006	2	LaMarcus	Aldridge	508	17.55	5.34
2006	16	Rodney	Carney	299	4.40	-2.51
2007	9	Joakim	Noah	396	12.89	2.80
2007	49	Aaron	Gray	281	4.43	1.78
2007	51	JamesOn	Curry	0	0.00	-1.48
2008	1	Derrick	Rose	279	22.40	5.95
2008	39	Sonny	Weems	140	7.06	3.65
2009	16	James	Johnson	219	5.88	-1.03
2009	26	Taj	Gibson	290	8.23	3.17
2010	17	Kevin	Seraphin	194	6.12	-0.47

Player Stats

Player	Age	Pos	Min	OE	EOP	EOP/M
Luol Deng	27	SF	2903	0.53	1131	0.389
Carlos Boozer	31	PF	2546	0.55	1177	0.462
Joakim Noah	27	C	2426	0.70	1042	0.430
Jimmy Butler	23	SF	2134	0.64	769	0.360
Nate Robinson	28	PG	2086	0.54	1108	0.531
Marco Belinelli	26	SG	1882	0.47	581	0.309
Kirk Hinrich	32	PG	1764	0.58	611	0.346
Taj Gibson	27	PF	1459	0.61	519	0.355
Richard Hamilton	34	SG	1088	0.49	429	0.395
Nazr Mohammed	35	C	693	0.59	165	0.238
Marquis Teague	19	PG	392	0.51	113	0.290
Daequan Cook	25	SG	276	0.31	42	0.154
Vladimir Radmanovic	32	PF	144	0.44	26	0.180
Malcolm Thomas	24	PF	36	0.88	18	0.498
Louis Amundson	30	PF	2	0.00	0	0.000

Player	DSG	DSG/M	AV	AV/M	LE	Roles
Luol Deng	4	0.001	1138	0.392	3.215	3DW
Carlos Boozer	-136	-0.053	905	0.356	3.133	
Joakim Noah	80	0.033	1202	0.496	3.042	DB
Jimmy Butler	35	0.017	840	0.394	3.370	3DW
Nate Robinson	-70	-0.034	968	0.464	3.177	
Marco Belinelli	-115	-0.061	351	0.186	3.117	
Kirk Hinrich	50	0.028	711	0.403	3.004	
Taj Gibson	70	0.048	658	0.451	3.185	DB
Richard Hamilton	11	0.010	452	0.415	2.773	
Nazr Mohammed	20	0.029	205	0.295	3.230	
Marquis Teague	13	0.033	140	0.356	3.234	
Daequan Cook	-1	-0.005	39	0.143	3.276	
Vladimir Radmanovic	-2	-0.013	22	0.154	3.157	
Malcolm Thomas	-4	-0.109	10	0.280	2.946	
Louis Amundson	0	-0.134	-1	-0.267	2.000	

Cleveland Cavaliers

Record: 24-58

Team Stats

	Stat	Rank
Offensive Efficiency	.536	28
Point Balance	.967	21
Point Balance in the clutch	.863	6
Assist Balance	.963	30
Rebound Balance	.941	8
Lineup Entropy	5.711	19

EOP Player Spotlight: Tristan Thompson

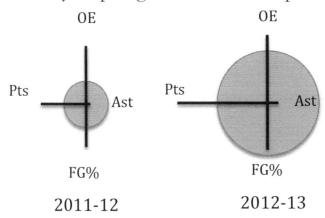

2011-12   2012-13

Draft Pick Success

Year	Pick	First Name	Last Name	GP	EOP$^+$/G	Yield
2002	34	Carlos	Boozer	714	17.66	14.14
2003	1	LeBron	James	765	28.92	12.47
2003	31	Jason	Kapono	509	5.40	1.14
2004	10	Luke	Jackson	73	2.78	-7.55
2006	25	Shannon	Brown	374	6.49	0.90
2006	42	Daniel	Gibson	397	7.08	4.46
2006	55	Ejike	Ugboaja	0	0.00	-2.34
2008	19	J.J.	Hickson	357	9.58	2.97
2009	30	Christian	Eyenga	51	4.66	-0.09
2009	46	Danny	Green	174	7.66	4.33

Player Stats

Player	Age	Pos	Min	OE	EOP	EOP/M
Tristan Thompson	21	PF	2564	0.69	1084	0.423
Alonzo Gee	25	SF	2541	0.47	671	0.264
Kyrie Irving	20	PG	2048	0.53	1276	0.623
Tyler Zeller	23	C	2033	0.58	598	0.294
Dion Waiters	21	SG	1756	0.47	741	0.422
C.J. Miles	25	SF	1364	0.44	519	0.380
Shaun Livingston	27	PG	1135	0.66	485	0.427
Wayne Ellington	25	SG	985	0.51	343	0.349
Daniel Gibson	26	PG	919	0.47	221	0.241
Anderson Varejao	30	C	901	0.80	503	0.558
Luke Walton	32	PF	857	0.64	290	0.339
Marreese Speights	25	C	721	0.54	340	0.472
Omri Casspi	24	SF	503	0.48	141	0.280
Jeremy Pargo	26	PG	447	0.49	183	0.410
Kevin Jones	23	PF	334	0.61	95	0.284
Donald Sloan	25	SG	257	0.51	85	0.330
Samardo Samuels	24	C	196	0.47	46	0.232
Jon Leuer	23	C	91	0.45	18	0.195
Chris Quinn	29	SG	78	0.43	11	0.142

Player	DSG	DSG/M	AV	AV/M	LE	Roles
Tristan Thompson	-40	-0.016	1003	0.391	3.507	
Alonzo Gee	-146	-0.057	379	0.149	3.434	
Kyrie Irving	-21	-0.010	1234	0.602	3.275	
Tyler Zeller	-74	-0.036	450	0.222	3.434	
Dion Waiters	-81	-0.046	579	0.330	3.415	
C.J. Miles	21	0.015	561	0.411	3.782	3DW
Shaun Livingston	10	0.009	505	0.445	3.506	
Wayne Ellington	-24	-0.024	296	0.300	3.343	
Daniel Gibson	17	0.018	255	0.277	3.930	
Anderson Varejao	14	0.015	530	0.588	3.198	
Luke Walton	26	0.030	342	0.399	3.628	SSB
Marreese Speights	1	0.002	343	0.475	3.475	
Omri Casspi	37	0.074	216	0.429	3.951	
Jeremy Pargo	13	0.029	210	0.469	3.302	
Kevin Jones	27	0.081	149	0.445	3.758	DB
Donald Sloan	8	0.032	101	0.393	3.425	
Samardo Samuels	17	0.085	79	0.402	3.590	
Jon Leuer	1	0.010	20	0.215	3.648	
Chris Quinn	20	0.257	51	0.656	2.942	

Dallas Mavericks

Record: 41-41

Team Stats

	Stat	Rank
Offensive Efficiency	.555	9
Point Balance	.969	24
Point Balance in the clutch	.894	15
Assist Balance	.916	22
Rebound Balance	.966	19
Lineup Entropy	6.007	27

EOP Player Spotlight: O. J. Mayo

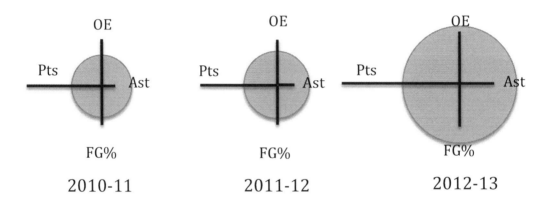

2010-11   2011-12   2012-13

Draft Pick Success

Year	Pick	First Name	Last Name	GP	EOP+/G	Yield
2004	50	Vassilis	Spanoulis	31	2.14	-0.17
2006	28	Maurice	Ager	82	1.21	-4.03
2006	58	J.R.	Pinnock	0	0.00	-1.44
2007	34	Nick	Fazekas	26	5.19	1.67
2007	50	Renaldas	Seibutis	0	0.00	-2.31
2007	60	Milovan	Rakovic	0	0.00	-2.02
2008	51	Shan	Foster	0	0.00	-1.48
2009	24	Byron	Mullens	144	6.66	-0.83
2009	56	Ahmad	Nivins	0	0.00	-1.70
2010	50	Solomon	Alabi	26	1.34	-0.97

Player Stats (minimum of 5 minutes played)

Player	Age	Pos	Min	OE	EOP	EOP/M
O.J. Mayo	25	SG	2913	0.53	1221	0.419
Darren Collison	25	PG	2372	0.59	1152	0.486
Vince Carter	36	SF	2093	0.52	967	0.462
Shawn Marion	34	PF	2010	0.64	907	0.451
Dirk Nowitzki	34	PF	1661	0.53	820	0.494
Elton Brand	33	C	1527	0.62	540	0.353
Chris Kaman	30	C	1363	0.54	599	0.440
Jae Crowder	22	SF	1353	0.49	348	0.257
Brandan Wright	25	C	1149	0.71	617	0.537
Mike James	37	PG	862	0.53	302	0.351
Dahntay Jones	32	SF	635	0.44	130	0.205
Rodrigue Beaubois	24	PG	549	0.52	195	0.355
Bernard James	27	C	457	0.79	162	0.354
Dominique Jones	24	PG	338	0.58	158	0.466
Troy Murphy	32	PF	256	0.43	45	0.178
Derek Fisher	38	PG	229	0.47	72	0.315
Anthony Morrow	27	SG	82	0.51	33	0.398
Chris Douglas-Roberts	26	SG	63	0.47	14	0.228
Jared Cunningham	21	SG	26	0.44	11	0.428
Eddy Curry	30	C	25	0.44	6	0.243
Josh Akognon	26	PG	9	0.60	5	0.582

Player	DSG	DSG/M	AV	AV/M	LE	Roles
O.J. Mayo	-122	-0.042	977	0.335	3.515	
Darren Collison	-109	-0.046	934	0.394	3.371	
Vince Carter	146	0.070	1259	0.601	3.616	3DW
Shawn Marion	-50	-0.025	808	0.402	3.403	SSB
Dirk Nowitzki	-3	-0.002	814	0.490	3.427	SSB
Elton Brand	-36	-0.023	469	0.307	3.409	
Chris Kaman	-16	-0.012	567	0.416	3.392	
Jae Crowder	55	0.041	458	0.339	3.802	3DW
Brandan Wright	-13	-0.012	590	0.514	3.509	
Mike James	-13	-0.015	276	0.320	3.262	
Dahntay Jones	-4	-0.007	122	0.192	3.796	
Rodrigue Beaubois	49	0.089	292	0.532	3.733	
Bernard James	10	0.022	182	0.397	3.736	
Dominique Jones	6	0.018	170	0.502	3.649	
Troy Murphy	6	0.023	57	0.225	3.398	DB
Derek Fisher	13	0.056	98	0.427	3.166	
Anthony Morrow	-10	-0.126	12	0.147	3.544	
Chris Douglas-Roberts	-2	-0.037	10	0.155	3.419	
Jared Cunningham	-1	-0.047	9	0.333	3.196	
Eddy Curry	0	-0.011	6	0.222	3.179	
Josh Akognon	0	-0.036	5	0.510	2.869	

Denver Nuggets

Record: 57-25

Team Stats

	Stat	Rank
Offensive Efficiency	.584	1
Point Balance	.998	30
Point Balance in the clutch	.965	26
Assist Balance	.821	2
Rebound Balance	.979	25
Lineup Entropy	5.501	11

AV Player Spotlight: 2012-13

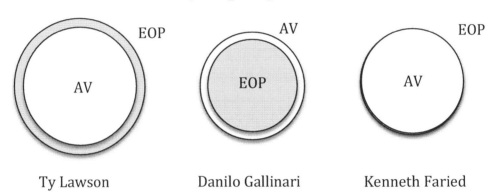

Ty Lawson   Danilo Gallinari   Kenneth Faried

Draft Pick Success

Year	Pick	First Name	Last Name	GP	EOP$^+$/G	Yield
2002	25	Frank	Williams	86	3.71	-1.88
2002	32	Vincent	Yarbrough	59	6.70	3.25
2003	3	Carmelo	Anthony	713	21.11	7.35
2003	46	Sani	Becirovic	0	0.00	-3.33
2004	20	Jameer	Nelson	583	14.25	7.78
2005	20	Julius	Hodge	23	1.74	-4.73
2005	22	Jarrett	Jack	611	12.21	6.01
2005	52	Axel	Hervelle	0	0.00	-2.33
2006	49	Leon	Powe	239	6.56	3.91
2009	34	Sergio	Llull	0	0.00	-3.52

Player Stats

Player	Age	Pos	Min	OE	EOP	EOP/M
Andre Iguodala	29	SG	2779	0.58	1197	0.431
Ty Lawson	25	PG	2513	0.59	1420	0.565
Danilo Gallinari	24	SF	2309	0.49	961	0.416
Kenneth Faried	23	PF	2248	0.74	1099	0.489
Andre Miller	36	PG	2151	0.64	1121	0.521
Corey Brewer	26	SF	2003	0.47	778	0.389
Kosta Koufos	23	C	1817	0.86	873	0.480
JaVale McGee	25	C	1433	0.68	755	0.527
Wilson Chandler	25	PF	1079	0.51	465	0.431
Evan Fournier	20	SG	428	0.54	191	0.447
Jordan Hamilton	22	SF	397	0.51	173	0.437
Timofey Mozgov	26	C	366	0.75	130	0.355
Anthony Randolph	23	PF	329	0.51	117	0.356
Julyan Stone	24	PG	28	1.00	13	0.461
Quincy Miller	20	SF	26	0.47	8	0.307

Player	DSG	DSG/M	AV	AV/M	LE	Roles
Andre Iguodala	141	0.051	1479	0.532	3.159	3DW
Ty Lawson	-96	-0.038	1228	0.489	3.106	
Danilo Gallinari	80	0.035	1121	0.485	3.005	3DW
Kenneth Faried	-5	-0.002	1088	0.484	3.015	
Andre Miller	-2	-0.001	1118	0.520	3.337	
Corey Brewer	-15	-0.008	747	0.373	3.331	
Kosta Koufos	69	0.038	1011	0.557	2.907	
JaVale McGee	-56	-0.039	643	0.449	3.154	
Wilson Chandler	30	0.028	525	0.486	3.176	DB, SSB
Evan Fournier	2	0.004	195	0.455	3.618	
Jordan Hamilton	-23	-0.058	127	0.320	3.535	
Timofey Mozgov	-24	-0.067	81	0.222	3.474	
Anthony Randolph	-11	-0.035	94	0.286	3.446	
Julyan Stone	-1	-0.036	11	0.388	3.162	
Quincy Miller	-1	-0.025	7	0.257	2.104	

Detroit Pistons

Record: 29-53

Team Stats

	Stat	Rank
Offensive Efficiency	.547	18
Point Balance	.986	29
Point Balance in the clutch	1.007	30
Assist Balance	.916	23
Rebound Balance	.941	9
Lineup Entropy	5.461	9

EOP Player Spotlight: Rodney Stuckey

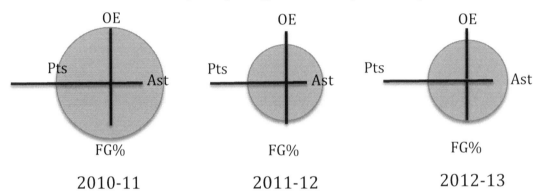

2010-11   2011-12   2012-13

Draft Pick Success

Year	Pick	First Name	Last Name	GP	EOP$^+$/G	Yield
2007	27	Arron	Afflalo	426	9.12	3.79
2007	57	Sammy	Mejia	0	0.00	-2.08
2008	29	D.J.	White	136	5.94	1.17
2008	59	Deron	Washington	0	0.00	-0.88
2009	15	Austin	Daye	237	4.48	-2.45
2009	35	DaJuan	Summers	83	2.34	-1.54
2009	39	Jonas	Jerebko	193	8.24	4.83
2009	44	Chase	Budinger	233	7.95	6.23
2010	7	Greg	Monroe	227	15.70	4.14
2010	36	Terrico	White	0	0.00	-4.07

Player Stats

Player	Age	Pos	Min	OE	EOP	EOP/M
Greg Monroe	22	C	2687	0.59	1363	0.507
Brandon Knight	21	PG	2365	0.50	924	0.391
Kyle Singler	24	SF	2293	0.50	587	0.256
Rodney Stuckey	26	SG	2171	0.52	849	0.391
Jason Maxiell	29	PF	1789	0.56	461	0.258
Tayshaun Prince	32	SF	1457	0.54	499	0.342
Andre Drummond	19	C	1243	0.92	692	0.557
Will Bynum	30	PG	1219	0.56	686	0.563
Charlie Villanueva	28	PF	1092	0.45	347	0.318
Jonas Jerebko	25	PF	892	0.56	345	0.387
Jose Calderon	31	PG	887	0.66	470	0.529
Khris Middleton	21	SG	475	0.51	144	0.304
Kim English	24	SG	407	0.46	96	0.236
Austin Daye	24	SF	348	0.53	111	0.318
Corey Maggette	33	SF	257	0.43	71	0.278
Viacheslav Kravtsov	25	C	224	0.93	119	0.530

Player	DSG	DSG/M	AV	AV/M	LE	Roles
Greg Monroe	39	0.015	1441	0.536	3.291	
Brandon Knight	112	0.047	1147	0.485	3.267	
Kyle Singler	66	0.029	718	0.313	3.405	3DW
Rodney Stuckey	-78	-0.036	692	0.319	3.615	
Jason Maxiell	-11	-0.006	439	0.245	2.964	
Tayshaun Prince	-40	-0.027	419	0.287	2.892	
Andre Drummond	7	0.006	707	0.568	3.498	DB
Will Bynum	-7	-0.006	672	0.551	3.652	
Charlie Villanueva	-20	-0.018	307	0.281	3.626	SSB
Jonas Jerebko	1	0.002	348	0.390	3.595	SSB
Jose Calderon	-27	-0.030	416	0.469	3.110	
Khris Middleton	8	0.017	160	0.337	3.429	
Kim English	-15	-0.036	66	0.163	3.588	
Austin Daye	18	0.053	147	0.423	3.076	
Corey Maggette	8	0.029	86	0.336	3.071	
Viacheslav Kravtsov	-3	-0.015	112	0.499	3.221	

Golden State Warriors

Record: 47-35

Team Stats

	Stat	Rank
Offensive Efficiency	.551	15
Point Balance	.913	3
Point Balance in the clutch	.871	9
Assist Balance	.851	6
Rebound Balance	.981	27
Lineup Entropy	5.194	5

AV Player Spotlight: 2012-13

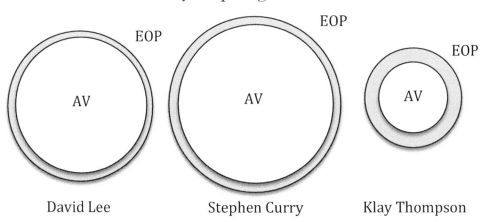

David Lee   Stephen Curry   Klay Thompson

Draft Pick Success

Year	Pick	First Name	Last Name	GP	EOP$^+$/G	Yield
2005	42	Chris	Taft	17	4.81	2005
2006	9	Patrick	O'Bryant	90	1.84	2006
2006	38	Kosta	Perovic	7	1.51	2006
2007	18	Marco	Belinelli	360	7.26	2007
2007	36	Jermareo	Davidson	52	2.48	2007
2007	46	Stephane	Lasme	15	4.67	2007
2008	14	Anthony	Randolph	209	6.63	2008
2008	49	Richard	Hendrix	0	0.00	2008
2009	7	Stephen	Curry	258	20.03	2009
2010	6	Ekpe	Udoh	195	4.91	2010

Player Stats

Player	Age	Pos	Min	OE	EOP	EOP/M
Stephen Curry	24	PG	2983	0.55	1840	0.617
Klay Thompson	22	SG	2936	0.46	1037	0.353
David Lee	29	PF	2907	0.62	1563	0.538
Jarrett Jack	29	SG	2349	0.58	1187	0.505
Harrison Barnes	20	SF	2058	0.48	603	0.293
Carl Landry	29	PF	1876	0.65	907	0.484
Festus Ezeli	23	C	1120	0.85	268	0.239
Draymond Green	22	SF	1061	0.45	183	0.173
Andrew Bogut	28	C	786	0.69	247	0.314
Richard Jefferson	32	SF	568	0.50	152	0.268
Andris Biedrins	26	C	495	1.60	84	0.170
Charles Jenkins	23	SG	291	0.50	78	0.269
Kent Bazemore	23	SG	267	0.43	91	0.342
Jeremy Tyler	21	C	63	0.40	14	0.219
Brandon Rush	27	SF	25	0.57	13	0.538
Malcolm Thomas	24	PF	21	0.50	3	0.163

Player	DSG	DSG/M	AV	AV/M	LE	Roles
Stephen Curry	-92	-0.031	1656	0.555	2.999	
Klay Thompson	-152	-0.052	734	0.250	3.025	
David Lee	-76	-0.026	1411	0.485	3.010	
Jarrett Jack	-55	-0.024	1076	0.458	3.208	
Harrison Barnes	-4	-0.002	595	0.289	3.043	
Carl Landry	-51	-0.027	804	0.429	3.165	
Festus Ezeli	-5	-0.004	258	0.230	3.040	
Draymond Green	55	0.051	292	0.275	3.376	
Andrew Bogut	-6	-0.008	235	0.299	2.462	
Richard Jefferson	27	0.047	206	0.362	3.399	
Andris Biedrins	-1	-0.002	82	0.165	3.092	
Charles Jenkins	23	0.079	124	0.426	3.284	
Kent Bazemore	23	0.087	138	0.516	3.447	
Jeremy Tyler	20	0.317	54	0.853	2.537	
Brandon Rush	5	0.191	23	0.921	2.983	
Malcolm Thomas	14	0.650	31	1.462	2.751	

Houston Rockets

Record: 45-37

Team Stats

	Stat	Rank
Offensive Efficiency	.551	13
Point Balance	.957	13
Point Balance in the clutch	.827	4
Assist Balance	.869	12
Rebound Balance	.958	16
Lineup Entropy	5.370	7

EOP Player Spotlight: Chandler Parsons

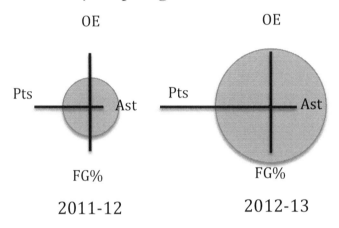

2011-12   2012-13

Draft Pick Success

Year	Pick	First Name	Last Name	GP	EOP+/G	Yield
2003	44	Malick	Badiane	0	0.00	-1.72
2004	55	Luis	Flores	16	2.09	-0.25
2005	24	Luther	Head	348	7.50	0.01
2006	8	Rudy	Gay	512	14.47	4.80
2006	32	Steve	Novak	360	4.01	0.56
2007	26	Aaron	Brooks	325	10.87	5.81
2007	54	Brad	Newley	0	0.00	-1.60
2008	25	Nicolas	Batum	328	10.60	5.01
2008	54	Maarty	Leunen	0	0.00	-1.60
2010	14	Patrick	Patterson	187	8.60	0.52

Player Stats

Player	Age	Pos	Min	OE	EOP	EOP/M
James Harden	23	SG	2985	0.51	1845	0.618
Chandler Parsons	24	SF	2758	0.57	1190	0.432
Jeremy Lin	24	PG	2640	0.56	1248	0.473
Omer Asik	26	C	2464	0.69	935	0.379
Carlos Delfino	30	SF	1689	0.48	586	0.347
Patrick Patterson	23	PF	1219	0.60	534	0.438
Marcus Morris	23	PF	1154	0.50	379	0.328
Greg Smith	22	C	1110	0.85	568	0.512
Toney Douglas	26	PG	913	0.49	346	0.379
Patrick Beverley	24	PG	713	0.64	309	0.433
Donatas Motiejunas	22	PF	538	0.52	217	0.403
Francisco Garcia	31	SF	319	0.48	96	0.300
James Anderson	23	SG	307	0.54	115	0.374
Terrence Jones	21	PF	276	0.62	108	0.391
Thomas Robinson	21	PF	247	0.56	79	0.319
Cole Aldrich	24	C	213	0.57	47	0.221
Daequan Cook	25	SG	165	0.44	42	0.255
Aaron Brooks	28	PG	38	0.45	10	0.264
Scott Machado	22	PG	21	0.45	9	0.408
Tim Ohlbrecht	24	C	12	0.25	1	0.119

Player	DSG	DSG/M	AV	AV/M	LE	Roles
James Harden	-114	-0.038	1617	0.542	3.315	
Chandler Parsons	52	0.019	1294	0.469	3.257	3DW
Jeremy Lin	-20	-0.007	1208	0.458	3.194	
Omer Asik	98	0.040	1130	0.459	3.156	DB
Carlos Delfino	36	0.021	659	0.390	3.538	3DW
Patrick Patterson	-45	-0.037	444	0.364	2.929	SSB
Marcus Morris	-10	-0.009	358	0.310	3.256	SSB
Greg Smith	-21	-0.019	527	0.474	3.581	
Toney Douglas	-39	-0.043	267	0.292	3.394	
Patrick Beverley	49	0.069	407	0.570	3.647	
Donatas Motiejunas	-7	-0.012	203	0.378	3.480	SSB
Francisco Garcia	14	0.042	123	0.384	3.393	
James Anderson	-1	-0.003	113	0.367	3.840	
Terrence Jones	-9	-0.032	91	0.328	3.785	
Thomas Robinson	13	0.054	105	0.427	3.339	
Cole Aldrich	-5	-0.023	37	0.174	3.451	
Daequan Cook	-6	-0.039	29	0.178	3.530	
Aaron Brooks	2	0.060	15	0.383	3.273	
Scott Machado	4	0.172	16	0.753	2.693	
Tim Ohlbrecht	1	0.109	4	0.336	2.869	

Indiana Pacers

Record: 49-32

Team Stats

	Stat	Rank
Offensive Efficiency	.537	27
Point Balance	.963	18
Point Balance in the clutch	.890	13
Assist Balance	.907	20
Rebound Balance	.970	21
Lineup Entropy	4.879	2

AV Player Spotlight: 2012-13

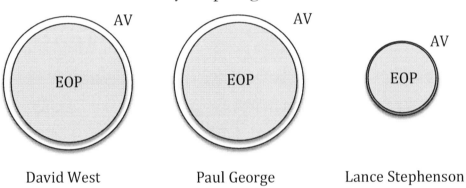

David West   Paul George   Lance Stephenson

Draft Pick Success

Year	Pick	First Name	Last Name	GP	EOP+/G	Yield
2005	46	Erazem	Lorbek	0	0.00	-3.33
2006	17	Shawne	Williams	215	4.62	-1.97
2006	45	Alexander	Johnson	102	3.76	-0.22
2008	11	Jerryd	Bayless	309	8.31	-0.02
2008	41	Nathan	Jawai	45	3.05	-0.38
2009	13	Tyler	Hansbrough	246	7.66	-1.13
2009	52	A.J.	Price	207	6.51	4.18
2010	10	Paul	George	206	11.42	1.09
2010	40	Lance	Stephenson	132	6.62	2.39
2010	57	Ryan	Reid	5	2.01	-0.07

Player Stats

Player	Age	Pos	Min	OE	EOP	EOP/M
Paul George	22	SF	2972	0.50	1226	0.413
George Hill	26	PG	2620	0.57	1168	0.446
David West	32	PF	2435	0.58	1240	0.509
Lance Stephenson	22	SG	2278	0.56	732	0.322
Roy Hibbert	26	C	2269	0.59	922	0.406
Tyler Hansbrough	27	PF	1366	0.59	532	0.389
Ian Mahinmi	26	C	1322	0.53	339	0.256
D.J. Augustin	25	PG	1226	0.53	392	0.320
Gerald Green	27	SF	1080	0.41	288	0.266
Sam Young	27	SG	693	0.51	144	0.208
Orlando Johnson	23	SG	619	0.50	183	0.295
Jeff Pendergraph	25	PF	369	0.56	134	0.362
Ben Hansbrough	25	PG	200	0.44	49	0.243
Danny Granger	29	SF	74	0.33	15	0.200
Miles Plumlee	24	C	55	0.50	11	0.200
Dominic McGuire	27	SF	12	0.33	0	0.032

Player	DSG	DSG/M	AV	AV/M	LE	Roles
Paul George	79	0.026	1384	0.466	3.110	3DW
George Hill	32	0.012	1232	0.470	2.914	
David West	75	0.031	1390	0.571	2.906	
Lance Stephenson	19	0.009	771	0.339	2.899	3DW
Roy Hibbert	8	0.003	937	0.413	2.773	DB
Tyler Hansbrough	-22	-0.016	489	0.358	3.375	
Ian Mahinmi	9	0.007	358	0.270	3.329	
D.J. Augustin	-12	-0.010	367	0.300	3.392	
Gerald Green	4	0.004	295	0.273	3.465	3DW
Sam Young	-35	-0.050	75	0.108	3.504	
Orlando Johnson	-9	-0.014	165	0.267	3.453	
Jeff Pendergraph	-12	-0.033	109	0.295	3.645	
Ben Hansbrough	0	0.001	49	0.246	3.345	
Danny Granger	-2	-0.025	11	0.151	3.066	
Miles Plumlee	-8	-0.145	-5	-0.090	2.762	
Dominic McGuire	2	0.132	4	0.296	3.098	

Los Angeles Clippers

Record: 56-26

Team Stats

	Stat	Rank
Offensive Efficiency	.580	2
Point Balance	.952	9
Point Balance in the clutch	.782	2
Assist Balance	.844	3
Rebound Balance	.940	6
Lineup Entropy	5.069	4

AV/EOP Player Spotlight: Blake Griffin

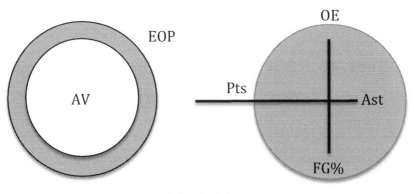

2012-13

Draft Pick Success

Year	Pick	First Name	Last Name	GP	EOP$^+$/G	Yield
2005	32	Daniel	Ewing	127	3.44	-0.01
2006	34	Paul	Davis	82	2.55	-0.97
2006	52	Guillermo	Diaz	6	0.95	-1.38
2007	14	Al	Thornton	296	9.64	1.56
2007	45	Jared	Jordan	0	0.00	-3.98
2008	7	Eric	Gordon	247	15.25	3.69
2008	35	DeAndre	Jordan	351	9.55	5.67
2009	1	Blake	Griffin	228	22.45	6.00
2010	8	Al-Farouq	Aminu	223	5.65	-4.02
2010	54	Willie	Warren	19	2.62	1.02

Player Stats

Player	Age	Pos	Min	OE	EOP	EOP/M
Blake Griffin	23	PF	2598	0.64	1616	0.622
Chris Paul	27	PG	2335	0.66	1714	0.734
Jamal Crawford	32	SG	2230	0.48	1017	0.456
Matt Barnes	32	SF	2058	0.56	777	0.378
DeAndre Jordan	24	C	2010	0.84	952	0.474
Caron Butler	32	SF	1879	0.46	611	0.325
Lamar Odom	33	PF	1616	0.60	401	0.248
Eric Bledsoe	23	PG	1553	0.57	703	0.452
Willie Green	31	SG	1188	0.51	382	0.321
Ronny Turiaf	30	C	701	0.72	162	0.231
Ryan Hollins	28	C	663	0.68	221	0.334
Grant Hill	40	SF	437	0.45	77	0.175
Chauncey Billups	36	SG	418	0.50	167	0.399
Maalik Wayns	21	PG	37	0.56	21	0.581
DaJuan Summers	25	PF	7	0.40	2	0.239

Player	DSG	DSG/M	AV	AV/M	LE	Roles
Blake Griffin	-198	-0.076	1221	0.470	3.121	
Chris Paul	-94	-0.040	1526	0.653	3.092	
Jamal Crawford	84	0.038	1185	0.531	3.256	3DW
Matt Barnes	107	0.052	991	0.482	3.254	3DW
DeAndre Jordan	-145	-0.072	663	0.330	2.897	
Caron Butler	-103	-0.055	404	0.215	2.942	
Lamar Odom	170	0.105	741	0.459	3.187	DB
Eric Bledsoe	93	0.060	888	0.572	3.225	
Willie Green	-37	-0.031	308	0.259	2.922	
Ronny Turiaf	43	0.061	247	0.353	2.981	DB
Ryan Hollins	9	0.013	239	0.360	3.115	DB
Grant Hill	-12	-0.026	53	0.122	3.280	
Chauncey Billups	-30	-0.071	108	0.258	2.695	
Maalik Wayns	6	0.158	33	0.896	3.119	
DaJuan Summers	0	0.055	2	0.350	2.237	

Los Angeles Lakers

Record: 45-37

Team Stats

	Stat	Rank
Offensive Efficiency	.555	8
Point Balance	.929	6
Point Balance in the clutch	.801	3
Assist Balance	.911	21
Rebound Balance	.941	10
Lineup Entropy	5.887	22

EOP Player Spotlight: Pau Gasol

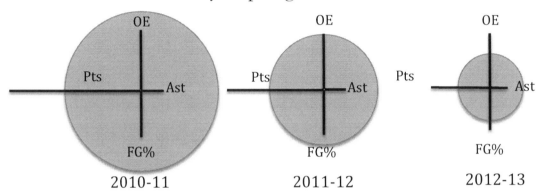

2010-11   2011-12   2012-13

Draft Pick Success

Year	Pick	First Name	Last Name	GP	EOP$^+$/G	Yield
2006	51	Cheikh	Samb	22	0.99	-0.49
2007	19	Javaris	Crittenton	113	5.47	-1.14
2007	40	Sun	Yue	10	0.35	-3.88
2007	48	Marc	Gasol	377	15.11	11.85
2008	58	Joe	Crawford	2	2.92	1.48
2009	29	Toney	Douglas	246	8.21	3.44
2009	42	Patrick	Beverley	41	7.53	4.91
2009	59	Chinemelu	Elonu	0	0.00	-0.88
2010	43	Devin	Ebanks	63	2.89	-1.18
2010	58	Derrick	Caracter	41	1.68	0.24

Player Stats

Player	Age	Pos	Min	OE	EOP	EOP/M
Kobe Bryant	34	SG	3013	0.53	1994	0.662
Dwight Howard	27	C	2722	0.65	1349	0.496
Metta World Peace	33	SF	2530	0.48	732	0.289
Jodie Meeks	25	SG	1663	0.45	454	0.273
Pau Gasol	32	PF	1655	0.61	762	0.460
Antawn Jamison	36	PF	1636	0.56	634	0.387
Steve Nash	38	PG	1627	0.63	845	0.519
Earl Clark	25	PF	1363	0.55	395	0.290
Steve Blake	32	PG	1175	0.59	412	0.351
Chris Duhon	30	PG	820	0.63	224	0.273
Darius Morris	22	PG	683	0.52	200	0.292
Jordan Hill	25	PF	458	0.80	248	0.542
Robert Sacre	23	C	203	0.44	31	0.155
Devin Ebanks	23	SF	197	0.40	45	0.226
Darius Johnson-Odom	23	SG	6	0.25	0	0.048
Andrew Goudelock	24	SG	6	0.00	0	0.000

Player	DSG	DSG/M	AV	AV/M	LE	Roles
Kobe Bryant	-153	-0.051	1689	0.561	3.338	
Dwight Howard	180	0.066	1710	0.628	3.283	DB
Metta World Peace	148	0.059	1028	0.406	3.292	3DW
Jodie Meeks	-3	-0.002	447	0.269	3.443	
Pau Gasol	-15	-0.009	732	0.442	3.264	
Antawn Jamison	-33	-0.020	568	0.347	3.427	SSB
Steve Nash	-23	-0.014	798	0.491	2.996	
Earl Clark	-53	-0.039	289	0.212	3.241	SSB
Steve Blake	15	0.013	442	0.376	3.118	
Chris Duhon	-33	-0.040	159	0.194	3.285	
Darius Morris	45	0.066	289	0.424	3.364	
Jordan Hill	-18	-0.039	213	0.465	3.370	
Robert Sacre	-3	-0.016	25	0.123	3.334	
Devin Ebanks	-2	-0.010	40	0.205	3.466	
Darius Johnson-Odom	0	-0.082	-1	-0.116	2.767	
Andrew Goudelock	-1	-0.204	-2	-0.408	2.423	

Memphis Grizzlies

Record: 56-26

Team Stats

	Stat	Rank
Offensive Efficiency	.552	10
Point Balance	.976	26
Point Balance in the clutch	.952	23
Assist Balance	.869	11
Rebound Balance	.944	11
Lineup Entropy	5.214	6

AV Player Spotlight: 2012-13

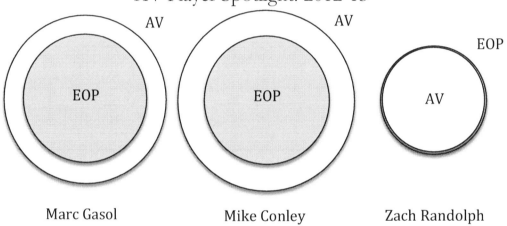

Marc Gasol   Mike Conley   Zach Randolph

Draft Pick Success

Year	Pick	First Name	Last Name	GP	EOP$^+$/G	Yield
2006	24	Kyle	Lowry	427	12.85	5.36
2007	4	Mike	Conley	438	14.35	1.83
2008	5	Kevin	Love	287	17.21	4.94
2008	28	Donte	Greene	253	4.53	-0.71
2009	2	Hasheem	Thabeet	201	2.95	-9.26
2009	27	DeMarre	Carroll	173	4.21	-1.12
2009	36	Sam	Young	249	4.72	0.65
2010	12	Xavier	Henry	133	3.35	-4.38
2010	25	Dominique	Jones	80	3.73	-1.86
2010	28	Greivis	Vasquez	214	11.90	6.66

Player Stats

Player	Age	Pos	Min	OE	EOP	EOP/M
Marc Gasol	28	C	2796	0.64	1336	0.478
Mike Conley	25	PG	2757	0.57	1336	0.485
Zach Randolph	31	PF	2607	0.60	1130	0.433
Tony Allen	31	SG	2109	0.54	637	0.302
Jerryd Bayless	24	PG	1765	0.53	722	0.409
Rudy Gay	26	SF	1541	0.46	563	0.365
Quincy Pondexter	24	SF	1243	0.53	336	0.271
Tayshaun Prince	32	SF	1174	0.54	317	0.270
Darrell Arthur	24	PF	970	0.53	312	0.321
Wayne Ellington	25	SG	676	0.47	179	0.265
Marreese Speights	25	C	579	0.55	231	0.400
Ed Davis	23	PF	544	0.73	212	0.390
Austin Daye	24	SF	328	0.48	102	0.312
Tony Wroten	19	SG	272	0.52	98	0.361
Chris Johnson	22	SF	102	0.52	24	0.236
Jon Leuer	23	PF	96	0.82	45	0.469
Hamed Haddadi	27	C	87	0.58	16	0.182
Keyon Dooling	32	PG	82	0.53	30	0.363
Josh Selby	21	PG	59	0.30	11	0.179
Dexter Pittman	24	C	20	0.25	1	0.038

Player	DSG	DSG/M	AV	AV/M	LE	Roles
Marc Gasol	210	0.075	1756	0.628	3.275	DB
Mike Conley	276	0.100	1888	0.685	3.190	
Zach Randolph	-22	-0.008	1087	0.417	3.212	
Tony Allen	180	0.085	996	0.472	3.026	
Jerryd Bayless	-138	-0.078	447	0.253	3.785	
Rudy Gay	6	0.004	575	0.373	2.978	3DW
Quincy Pondexter	-77	-0.062	183	0.147	3.654	
Tayshaun Prince	22	0.019	360	0.307	2.812	
Darrell Arthur	-59	-0.061	193	0.199	3.729	
Wayne Ellington	10	0.014	199	0.294	3.238	3DW
Marreese Speights	-24	-0.041	184	0.318	3.293	
Ed Davis	12	0.022	236	0.433	3.344	DB
Austin Daye	-19	-0.059	64	0.194	3.400	
Tony Wroten	-37	-0.136	24	0.090	3.769	
Chris Johnson	1	0.005	25	0.246	3.028	
Jon Leuer	-11	-0.117	22	0.234	3.492	
Hamed Haddadi	7	0.086	31	0.354	3.460	
Keyon Dooling	-1	-0.012	28	0.339	3.186	
Josh Selby	-7	-0.111	-3	-0.043	3.168	
Dexter Pittman	-5	-0.233	-9	-0.427	2.760	

Miami Heat

Record: 66-16

Team Stats

	Stat	Rank
Offensive Efficiency	.579	3
Point Balance	.912	2
Point Balance in the clutch	.886	12
Assist Balance	.857	9
Rebound Balance	.979	24
Lineup Entropy	5.433	8

AV Player Spotlight: 2012-13

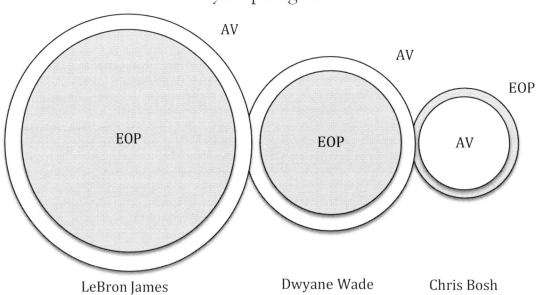

LeBron James   Dwyane Wade   Chris Bosh

Draft Pick Success

Year	Pick	First Name	Last Name	GP	EOP$^+$/G	Yield
2007	20	Jason	Smith	300	5.14	-1.33
2007	39	Stanko	Barac	0	0.00	-3.41
2008	2	Michael	Beasley	354	10.97	-1.24
2008	52	Darnell	Jackson	138	2.10	-0.23
2009	43	Marcus	Thornton	269	11.75	7.68
2009	60	Robert	Dozier	0	0.00	-2.02
2010	32	Dexter	Pittman	48	2.26	-1.19
2010	41	Jarvis	Varnado	13	0.51	-2.92
2010	42	Da'Sean	Butler	0	0.00	-2.62
2010	48	Latavious	Williams	0	0.00	-3.26

Player Stats

Player	Age	Pos	Min	OE	EOP	EOP/M
LeBron James	28	PF	2877	0.65	2408	0.837
Chris Bosh	28	C	2454	0.59	1190	0.485
Dwyane Wade	31	SG	2391	0.59	1556	0.651
Mario Chalmers	26	PG	2068	0.55	734	0.355
Ray Allen	37	SG	2035	0.50	736	0.362
Shane Battier	34	SF	1786	0.52	415	0.232
Norris Cole	24	PG	1590	0.51	439	0.276
Udonis Haslem	32	PF	1414	0.70	341	0.241
Mike Miller	32	SF	900	0.57	310	0.344
Rashard Lewis	33	PF	792	0.45	212	0.267
Chris Andersen	34	C	624	0.82	274	0.439
Joel Anthony	30	C	566	0.83	122	0.215
James Jones	32	SF	221	0.44	47	0.212
Juwan Howard	39	PF	51	0.55	21	0.419
Jarvis Varnado	24	PF	40	0.33	2	0.044
Josh Harrellson	23	C	31	0.44	7	0.217
Terrel Harris	25	SG	29	0.40	7	0.241
Dexter Pittman	24	C	12	1.00	9	0.758

Player	DSG	DSG/M	AV	AV/M	LE	Roles
LeBron James	186	0.065	2781	0.966	3.172	SSB
Chris Bosh	-92	-0.038	1005	0.410	3.075	SSB
Dwyane Wade	164	0.069	1884	0.788	3.123	
Mario Chalmers	108	0.052	949	0.459	2.971	
Ray Allen	-110	-0.054	516	0.253	3.394	
Shane Battier	-20	-0.011	375	0.210	3.229	
Norris Cole	-79	-0.050	281	0.177	3.476	
Udonis Haslem	89	0.063	520	0.367	2.962	
Mike Miller	-48	-0.054	213	0.237	3.523	
Rashard Lewis	-21	-0.026	171	0.216	3.570	SSB
Chris Andersen	21	0.034	316	0.507	3.010	DB
Joel Anthony	-17	-0.031	87	0.154	3.358	
James Jones	0	-0.002	46	0.208	3.505	
Juwan Howard	-12	-0.245	-4	-0.070	2.918	
Jarvis Varnado	-9	-0.215	-15	-0.385	2.849	
Josh Harrellson	-1	-0.042	4	0.133	3.454	
Terrel Harris	-5	-0.185	-4	-0.129	3.507	
Dexter Pittman	-3	-0.256	3	0.247	2.463	

Milwaukee Bucks

Record: 38-44

Team Stats

	Stat	Rank
Offensive Efficiency	.546	21
Point Balance	.956	11
Point Balance in the clutch	.890	14
Assist Balance	.855	8
Rebound Balance	.981	28
Lineup Entropy	5.746	20

EOP Player Spotlight: Brandon Jennings

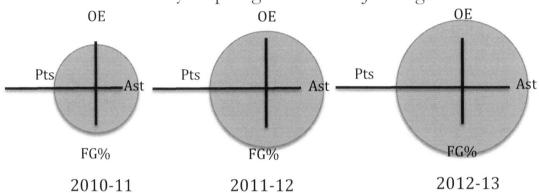

2010-11   2011-12   2012-13

Draft Pick Success

Year	Pick	First Name	Last Name	GP	EOP$^+$/G	Yield
2007	6	Yi	Jianlian	272	5.95	-3.32
2007	56	Ramon	Sessions	384	13.32	11.62
2008	8	Joe	Alexander	67	3.44	-6.23
2008	37	Luc	Mbah a Moute	335	7.33	2.77
2009	10	Brandon	Jennings	291	16.72	6.39
2009	41	Jodie	Meeks	278	6.01	2.58
2010	15	Larry	Sanders	183	6.63	-0.30
2010	37	Darington	Hobson	5	1.02	-3.54
2010	44	Jerome	Jordan	21	2.83	1.11
2010	47	Tiny	Gallon	0	0.00	-4.56

Player Stats

Player	Age	Pos	Min	OE	EOP	EOP/M
Monta Ellis	27	SG	3076	0.51	1513	0.492
Brandon Jennings	23	PG	2897	0.53	1447	0.500
Ersan Ilyasova	25	PF	2012	0.58	925	0.460
Mike Dunleavy	32	SF	1943	0.51	690	0.355
Larry Sanders	24	C	1937	0.71	813	0.420
Luc Mbah a Moute	26	SF	1326	0.50	324	0.245
Ekpe Udoh	25	C	1312	0.66	357	0.272
Marquis Daniels	32	SF	1085	0.48	270	0.249
John Henson	22	PF	827	0.65	396	0.479
J.J. Redick	28	SG	804	0.49	299	0.372
Samuel Dalembert	31	C	765	0.72	358	0.468
Beno Udrih	30	SG	719	0.61	340	0.473
Tobias Harris	20	SF	325	0.51	113	0.348
Doron Lamb	21	SG	280	0.41	59	0.209
Gustavo Ayon	27	C	163	0.86	78	0.481
Drew Gooden	31	C	151	0.41	35	0.234
Ishmael Smith	24	PG	138	0.57	53	0.383
Joel Przybilla	33	C	68	0.71	5	0.080

Player	DSG	DSG/M	AV	AV/M	LE	Roles
Monta Ellis	1	0.000	1515	0.493	3.466	3DW
Brandon Jennings	-279	-0.096	889	0.307	3.423	
Ersan Ilyasova	-10	-0.005	905	0.450	3.283	SSB
Mike Dunleavy	4	0.002	699	0.360	3.534	3DW
Larry Sanders	114	0.059	1041	0.537	3.117	DB
Luc Mbah a Moute	15	0.011	353	0.267	3.237	
Ekpe Udoh	31	0.024	419	0.320	3.471	
Marquis Daniels	44	0.040	358	0.330	3.509	
John Henson	-21	-0.026	354	0.428	3.670	
J.J. Redick	-31	-0.039	237	0.295	3.414	
Samuel Dalembert	-36	-0.047	287	0.375	3.368	
Beno Udrih	18	0.025	376	0.523	3.371	
Tobias Harris	-1	-0.002	112	0.345	3.231	
Doron Lamb	5	0.018	69	0.245	3.645	
Gustavo Ayon	24	0.146	126	0.773	3.172	
Drew Gooden	-2	-0.010	32	0.214	3.662	
Ishmael Smith	11	0.083	76	0.548	3.300	
Joel Przybilla	-21	-0.311	-37	-0.541	3.413	

Minnesota Timberwolves

Record: 31-51

Team Stats

	Stat	Rank
Offensive Efficiency	.544	23
Point Balance	.978	27
Point Balance in the clutch	.973	27
Assist Balance	.854	7
Rebound Balance	.987	30
Lineup Entropy	5.819	21

AV/EOP Player Spotlight: Ricky Rubio

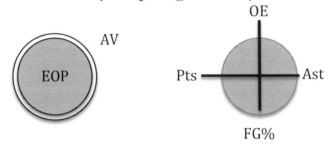

2012-13

Draft Pick Success

Year	Pick	First Name	Last Name	GP	EOP⁺/G	Yield
2009	6	Jonny	Flynn	163	9.19	-0.08
2009	18	Ty	Lawson	279	16.13	8.74
2009	28	Wayne	Ellington	267	5.52	0.28
2009	45	Nick	Calathes	0	0.00	-3.98
2009	47	Henk	Norel	0	0.00	-4.56
2010	4	Wesley	Johnson	194	6.02	-6.50
2010	16	Luke	Babbitt	126	2.69	-4.22
2010	23	Trevor	Booker	163	7.64	1.63
2010	45	Paulao	Prestes	0	0.00	-3.98
2010	56	Hamady	N'Diaye	19	0.73	-0.97

Player Stats

Player	Age	Pos	Min	OE	EOP	EOP/M
Luke Ridnour	31	SG	2474	0.56	998	0.403
Andrei Kirilenko	31	SF	2034	0.61	858	0.422
Dante Cunningham	25	SF	2010	0.58	661	0.329
Nikola Pekovic	27	C	1959	0.66	1050	0.536
Derrick Williams	21	PF	1916	0.46	673	0.351
Alexey Shved	24	SG	1840	0.51	680	0.370
Jose Barea	28	PG	1713	0.52	841	0.491
Ricky Rubio	22	PG	1691	0.57	798	0.472
Greg Stiemsma	27	C	1209	0.51	257	0.212
Mickael Gelabale	29	SF	644	0.66	200	0.311
Kevin Love	24	PF	618	0.47	256	0.414
Chase Budinger	24	SF	508	0.46	165	0.326
Malcolm Lee	22	SG	289	0.54	76	0.263
Chris Johnson	27	C	284	0.74	138	0.484
Josh Howard	32	SF	207	0.43	50	0.241
Louis Amundson	30	C	161	0.59	30	0.189
Brandon Roy	28	SG	122	0.55	39	0.317
Lazar Hayward	26	SF	31	0.38	7	0.231
Will Conroy	30	PG	20	0.00	0	0.000

Player	DSG	DSG/M	AV	AV/M	LE	Roles
Luke Ridnour	-67	-0.027	864	0.349	3.462	
Andrei Kirilenko	-7	-0.004	843	0.415	3.369	
Dante Cunningham	79	0.039	819	0.407	3.540	
Nikola Pekovic	-95	-0.048	860	0.439	3.295	
Derrick Williams	-55	-0.029	563	0.294	3.386	
Alexey Shved	-4	-0.002	671	0.365	3.568	
Jose Barea	44	0.026	930	0.543	3.519	
Ricky Rubio	50	0.030	899	0.532	3.227	
Greg Stiemsma	71	0.059	400	0.330	3.357	
Mickael Gelabale	-16	-0.024	169	0.262	3.279	
Kevin Love	-14	-0.022	228	0.370	2.988	SSB
Chase Budinger	31	0.062	228	0.449	3.229	
Malcolm Lee	16	0.055	108	0.373	3.234	
Chris Johnson	-31	-0.109	76	0.267	3.189	
Josh Howard	2	0.008	53	0.258	3.206	
Louis Amundson	-3	-0.020	24	0.149	3.650	
Brandon Roy	-8	-0.066	22	0.184	2.588	
Lazar Hayward	-4	-0.120	0	-0.008	2.801	
Will Conroy	-7	-0.332	-13	-0.664	2.607	

New Orleans Pelicans (Hornets)

Record: 27-55

Team Stats

	Stat	Rank
Offensive Efficiency	.549	16
Point Balance	.950	8
Point Balance in the clutch	.949	21
Assist Balance	.811	1
Rebound Balance	.940	7
Lineup Entropy	5.638	16

AV Player Spotlight: 2012-13

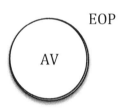

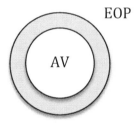

Anthony Davis   Al-Farouq Aminu   Ryan Anderson

Draft Pick Success

Year	Pick	First Name	Last Name	GP	EOP+/G	Yield
2005	4	Chris	Paul	555	25.38	12.86
2005	33	Brandon	Bass	476	7.83	3.84
2006	12	Hilton	Armstrong	277	3.07	-4.66
2006	15	Cedric	Simmons	75	1.87	-5.06
2006	43	Marcus	Vinicius	26	1.52	-2.55
2007	13	Julian	Wright	231	4.09	-4.70
2007	43	Adam	Haluska	0	0.00	-4.07
2008	27	Darrell	Arthur	247	5.90	0.57
2009	21	Darren	Collison	296	14.02	7.00
2010	11	Cole	Aldrich	89	2.12	-6.21

Player Stats

Player	Age	Pos	Min	OE	EOP	EOP/M
Greivis Vasquez	26	PG	2685	0.59	1459	0.543
Ryan Anderson	24	PF	2503	0.51	1067	0.426
Robin Lopez	24	C	2136	0.67	996	0.466
Al-Farouq Aminu	22	SF	2066	0.59	569	0.275
Anthony Davis	19	PF	1846	0.62	862	0.467
Austin Rivers	20	SG	1418	0.47	340	0.240
Brian Roberts	27	PG	1324	0.55	603	0.455
Eric Gordon	24	SG	1264	0.45	557	0.440
Roger Mason	32	SG	1219	0.49	317	0.260
Jason Smith	26	C	876	0.55	371	0.424
Darius Miller	22	SF	694	0.53	121	0.174
Lance Thomas	24	SF	646	0.75	185	0.286
Xavier Henry	21	SF	625	0.43	133	0.212
Louis Amundson	30	C	209	0.76	58	0.278
Dominic McGuire	27	SF	145	0.64	25	0.174
Terrel Harris	25	SG	108	0.23	4	0.033
Hakim Warrick	30	PF	7	0.50	3	0.433
Donald Sloan	25	PG	6	0.50	1	0.096
Henry Sims	22	C	5	1.00	6	1.213

Player	DSG	DSG/M	AV	AV/M	LE	Roles
Greivis Vasquez	-191	-0.071	1077	0.401	3.324	
Ryan Anderson	-168	-0.067	731	0.292	3.624	SSB
Robin Lopez	4	0.002	1003	0.470	3.257	
Al-Farouq Aminu	76	0.037	721	0.349	3.160	
Anthony Davis	-12	-0.007	838	0.454	3.337	
Austin Rivers	-23	-0.016	294	0.207	3.411	
Brian Roberts	18	0.013	638	0.482	3.675	
Eric Gordon	-10	-0.008	536	0.424	2.929	
Roger Mason	-23	-0.019	270	0.222	3.484	
Jason Smith	30	0.034	431	0.492	3.380	DB
Darius Miller	45	0.065	211	0.305	3.570	
Lance Thomas	13	0.021	212	0.327	3.473	
Xavier Henry	13	0.022	160	0.256	3.582	
Louis Amundson	9	0.045	77	0.368	3.255	
Dominic McGuire	-4	-0.030	16	0.113	3.197	
Terrel Harris	29	0.266	61	0.565	3.072	
Hakim Warrick	3	0.363	8	1.160	2.431	
Donald Sloan	1	0.121	2	0.338	2.629	
Henry Sims	1	0.185	8	1.582	3.124	

New York Knicks

Record: 54-28

Team Stats

	Stat	Rank
Offensive Efficiency	.547	20
Point Balance	.926	5
Point Balance in the clutch	.867	8
Assist Balance	.868	10
Rebound Balance	.984	29
Lineup Entropy	5.987	25

EOP Player Spotlight: Raymond Felton

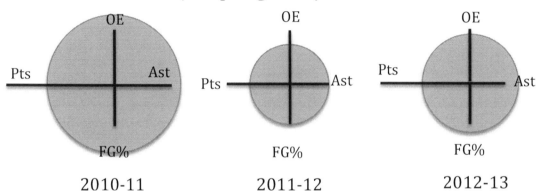

2010-11   2011-12   2012-13

Draft Pick Success

Year	Pick	First Name	Last Name	GP	EOP+/G	Yield
2005	8	Channing	Frye	500	8.15	-1.52
2005	30	David	Lee	577	16.92	12.17
2005	54	Dijon	Thompson	16	2.33	0.73
2006	20	Renaldo	Balkman	221	4.82	-1.65
2006	29	Mardy	Collins	189	4.03	-0.74
2007	23	Wilson	Chandler	305	11.42	5.41
2008	6	Danilo	Gallinari	285	11.74	2.47
2009	8	Jordan	Hill	187	6.05	-3.62
2010	38	Andy	Rautins	5	1.09	-1.53
2010	39	Landry	Fields	199	8.56	5.15

Player Stats

Player	Age	Pos	Min	OE	EOP	EOP/M
J.R. Smith	27	SG	2678	0.48	1185	0.442
Carmelo Anthony	28	PF	2482	0.49	1535	0.618
Raymond Felton	28	PG	2313	0.55	1029	0.445
Tyson Chandler	30	C	2164	1.13	1264	0.584
Jason Kidd	39	SG	2043	0.59	575	0.282
Steve Novak	29	SF	1641	0.46	394	0.240
Pablo Prigioni	35	PG	1263	0.67	462	0.366
Iman Shumpert	22	SG	996	0.52	284	0.285
Chris Copeland	28	PF	862	0.49	379	0.440
Ronnie Brewer	27	SF	711	0.52	155	0.218
Amar'e Stoudemire	30	PF	682	0.62	397	0.582
James White	30	SF	435	0.50	112	0.258
Kenyon Martin	35	C	431	0.77	158	0.366
Kurt Thomas	40	PF	392	0.75	128	0.328
Rasheed Wallace	38	C	296	0.41	95	0.320
Marcus Camby	38	PF	250	0.53	43	0.171
Earl Barron	31	C	37	0.64	12	0.327
Quentin Richardson	32	SF	29	0.22	2	0.067
Solomon Jones	28	PF	26	0.00	0	0.000

Player	DSG	DSG/M	AV	AV/M	LE	Roles
J.R. Smith	86	0.032	1356	0.506	3.519	3DW
Carmelo Anthony	-64	-0.026	1408	0.567	3.357	SSB
Raymond Felton	-78	-0.034	872	0.377	3.378	
Tyson Chandler	-20	-0.009	1224	0.566	3.266	
Jason Kidd	24	0.012	624	0.305	3.422	3DW
Steve Novak	21	0.013	436	0.266	3.638	3DW
Pablo Prigioni	77	0.061	615	0.487	3.667	
Iman Shumpert	-33	-0.033	219	0.219	3.483	
Chris Copeland	-17	-0.020	345	0.400	3.635	SSB
Ronnie Brewer	2	0.003	159	0.223	3.253	
Amar'e Stoudemire	1	0.001	398	0.583	3.149	
James White	-27	-0.062	58	0.134	3.683	
Kenyon Martin	11	0.026	180	0.418	3.190	
Kurt Thomas	-5	-0.012	119	0.304	3.552	
Rasheed Wallace	12	0.041	119	0.402	3.204	DB, SSB
Marcus Camby	9	0.037	61	0.245	3.357	DB
Earl Barron	-1	-0.033	10	0.260	2.494	
Quentin Richardson	-1	-0.033	0	0.001	2.406	
Solomon Jones	1	0.058	3	0.115	2.833	

Oklahoma City Thunder

Record: 60-22

Team Stats

	Stat	Rank
Offensive Efficiency	.564	5
Point Balance	.886	1
Point Balance in the clutch	.735	1
Assist Balance	.848	5
Rebound Balance	.970	20
Lineup Entropy	4.573	1

AV/EOP Player Spotlight: Russell Westbrook

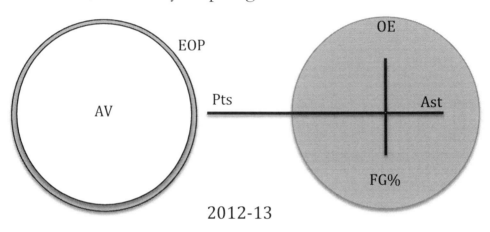

2012-13

Draft Pick Success

Year	Pick	First Name	Last Name	GP	EOP$^+$/G	Yield
2008	32	Walter	Sharpe	8	0.54	-2.91
2008	46	Trent	Plaisted	0	0.00	-3.33
2008	50	DeVon	Hardin	0	0.00	-2.31
2008	56	Sasha	Kaun	0	0.00	-1.70
2009	3	James	Harden	298	14.73	0.97
2009	25	Rodrigue	Beaubois	182	6.90	1.31
2010	18	Eric	Bledsoe	197	7.52	0.13
2010	21	Craig	Brackins	17	1.36	-5.66
2010	26	Quincy	Pondexter	189	3.97	-1.09
2010	51	Magnum	Rolle	0	0.00	-1.48

Player Stats

Player	Age	Pos	Min	OE	EOP	EOP/M
Kevin Durant	24	SF	3119	0.54	2105	0.675
Russell Westbrook	24	PG	2861	0.56	1992	0.696
Serge Ibaka	23	PF	2486	0.68	1114	0.448
Thabo Sefolosha	28	SG	2229	0.58	628	0.282
Kevin Martin	29	SG	2136	0.48	839	0.393
Kendrick Perkins	28	C	1954	0.60	377	0.193
Nick Collison	32	C	1583	0.82	625	0.395
Reggie Jackson	22	PG	993	0.57	400	0.403
Hasheem Thabeet	25	C	770	0.84	215	0.279
Eric Maynor	25	PG	391	0.51	123	0.315
Derek Fisher	38	SG	346	0.39	66	0.190
DeAndre Liggins	24	SG	290	0.57	60	0.207
Perry Jones	21	SF	280	0.44	63	0.226
Jeremy Lamb	20	SF	147	0.39	44	0.302
Ronnie Brewer	27	SF	142	0.67	21	0.147
Daniel Orton	22	C	104	0.76	42	0.400

Player	DSG	DSG/M	AV	AV/M	LE	Roles
Kevin Durant	-142	-0.046	1821	0.584	2.978	
Russell Westbrook	-55	-0.019	1881	0.657	2.790	
Serge Ibaka	-47	-0.019	1019	0.410	2.705	SSB
Thabo Sefolosha	40	0.018	708	0.318	2.797	3DW
Kevin Martin	-17	-0.008	805	0.377	3.293	
Kendrick Perkins	-2	-0.001	374	0.191	2.417	
Nick Collison	35	0.022	695	0.439	3.303	
Reggie Jackson	27	0.027	454	0.457	3.557	
Hasheem Thabeet	57	0.074	329	0.428	3.453	DB
Eric Maynor	-13	-0.033	97	0.249	3.185	
Derek Fisher	2	0.005	69	0.200	3.104	
DeAndre Liggins	4	0.015	69	0.238	3.548	
Perry Jones	4	0.016	72	0.258	3.374	
Jeremy Lamb	-18	-0.122	9	0.059	3.294	
Ronnie Brewer	-9	-0.063	3	0.020	3.408	
Daniel Orton	0	0.000	42	0.401	3.392	

Orlando Magic

Record: 20-62

Team Stats

	Stat	Rank
Offensive Efficiency	.547	19
Point Balance	.972	25
Point Balance in the clutch	.953	24
Assist Balance	.934	25
Rebound Balance	.945	12
Lineup Entropy	5.999	26

EOP Player Spotlight: Nikola Vucevic

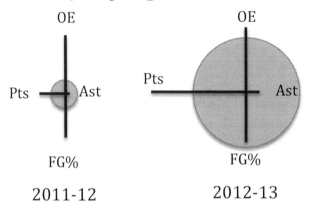

2011-12   2012-13

Draft Pick Success

Year	Pick	First Name	Last Name	GP	EOP+/G	Yield
2005	11	Fran	Vasquez	0	0.00	-8.33
2005	38	Travis	Diener	179	5.70	3.08
2005	44	Martynas	Andriuskevicius	6	0.00	-1.72
2006	11	J.J.	Redick	424	8.45	0.12
2006	41	James	Augustine	27	1.90	-1.53
2006	44	Lior	Eliyahu	0	0.00	-1.72
2007	44	Reyshawn	Terry	0	0.00	-1.72
2008	22	Courtney	Lee	365	8.11	1.91
2010	29	Daniel	Orton	29	3.96	-0.81
2010	59	Stanley	Robinson	0	0.00	-0.88

Player Stats

Player	Age	Pos	Min	OE	EOP	EOP/M
Nikola Vucevic	22	C	2559	0.67	1136	0.444
Arron Afflalo	27	SF	2307	0.49	909	0.394
Jameer Nelson	30	PG	1977	0.54	935	0.473
Maurice Harkless	19	SF	1974	0.55	556	0.281
E'Twaun Moore	23	SG	1682	0.51	581	0.345
J.J. Redick	28	SG	1575	0.54	751	0.477
Andrew Nicholson	23	PF	1249	0.56	523	0.418
Glen Davis	27	PF	1064	0.51	437	0.411
Tobias Harris	20	PF	974	0.53	410	0.421
DeQuan Jones	22	SF	803	0.45	167	0.208
Beno Udrih	30	PG	738	0.59	359	0.487
Josh McRoberts	25	PF	685	0.62	199	0.291
Kyle O'Quinn	22	C	638	0.69	285	0.447
Gustavo Ayon	27	C	571	0.69	208	0.364
Ishmael Smith	24	PG	378	0.51	99	0.261
Doron Lamb	21	SG	297	0.46	59	0.199
Hedo Turkoglu	33	SF	189	0.44	33	0.175
Al Harrington	32	C	119	0.44	39	0.329

Player	DSG	DSG/M	AV	AV/M	LE	Roles
Nikola Vucevic	-38	-0.015	1061	0.415	3.558	
Arron Afflalo	-70	-0.030	770	0.334	3.469	
Jameer Nelson	37	0.019	1009	0.510	3.409	
Maurice Harkless	-12	-0.006	532	0.269	3.687	
E'Twaun Moore	-9	-0.006	562	0.334	3.789	
J.J. Redick	-35	-0.022	682	0.433	3.391	
Andrew Nicholson	71	0.057	665	0.532	3.680	DB
Glen Davis	59	0.056	555	0.522	3.018	DB
Tobias Harris	24	0.024	457	0.469	3.234	SSB
DeQuan Jones	-40	-0.049	88	0.110	3.876	
Beno Udrih	3	0.003	364	0.494	3.227	
Josh McRoberts	-12	-0.017	175	0.256	3.477	
Kyle O'Quinn	-3	-0.004	280	0.439	3.669	
Gustavo Ayon	6	0.010	219	0.384	3.398	
Ishmael Smith	13	0.035	125	0.331	3.509	
Doron Lamb	-1	-0.005	56	0.190	3.133	
Hedo Turkoglu	-17	-0.090	-1	-0.004	3.495	
Al Harrington	-9	-0.079	20	0.170	3.130	

Philadelphia 76ers

Record: 34-48

Team Stats

	Stat	Rank
Offensive Efficiency	.551	12
Point Balance	.961	15
Point Balance in the clutch	.861	5
Assist Balance	.871	13
Rebound Balance	.946	13
Lineup Entropy	5.490	10

EOP Player Spotlight: Evan Turner

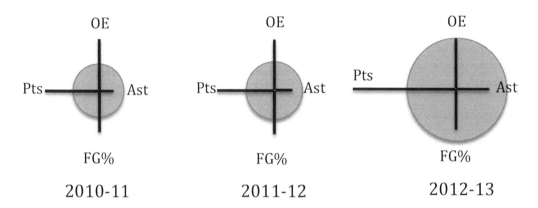

2010-11   2011-12   2012-13

Draft Pick Success

Year	Pick	First Name	Last Name	GP	EOP+/G	Yield
2004	9	Andre	Iguodala	695	16.34	6.25
2005	45	Louis	Williams	494	10.89	6.91
2006	13	Thabo	Sefolosha	490	5.76	-3.03
2007	12	Thaddeus	Young	437	12.50	4.77
2007	21	Daequan	Cook	328	4.41	-2.61
2007	30	Petteri	Koponen	0	0.00	-4.75
2007	38	Kyrylo	Fesenko	135	2.37	-0.25
2008	16	Marreese	Speights	344	7.09	0.18
2009	17	Jrue	Holiday	298	15.19	8.60
2010	2	Evan	Turner	225	9.88	-2.33

Player Stats

Player	Age	Pos	Min	OE	EOP	EOP/M
Jrue Holiday	22	PG	2926	0.56	1571	0.537
Evan Turner	24	SF	2892	0.52	1068	0.369
Thaddeus Young	24	PF	2629	0.64	1185	0.451
Spencer Hawes	24	C	2233	0.59	930	0.416
Dorell Wright	27	SF	1783	0.50	642	0.360
Lavoy Allen	23	C	1669	0.66	511	0.306
Nick Young	27	SG	1411	0.47	496	0.351
Damien Wilkins	33	SG	1095	0.56	386	0.352
Jason Richardson	32	SG	936	0.47	276	0.295
Royal Ivey	31	SG	698	0.52	154	0.220
Arnett Moultrie	22	PF	542	1.01	279	0.514
Kwame Brown	30	C	269	0.84	61	0.226
Jeremy Pargo	26	SG	208	0.50	69	0.332
Maalik Wayns	21	PG	165	0.38	40	0.245
Charles Jenkins	23	PG	150	0.57	36	0.241
Justin Holiday	23	SG	142	0.43	35	0.246
Shelvin Mack	23	SG	7	0.40	2	0.239

Player	DSG	DSG/M	AV	AV/M	LE	Roles
Jrue Holiday	184	0.063	1939	0.663	3.262	
Evan Turner	-123	-0.043	822	0.284	3.316	
Thaddeus Young	95	0.036	1376	0.523	3.211	
Spencer Hawes	-21	-0.010	887	0.397	3.248	SSB
Dorell Wright	-24	-0.013	594	0.333	3.475	
Lavoy Allen	47	0.028	604	0.362	3.322	DB
Nick Young	-14	-0.010	468	0.332	3.324	
Damien Wilkins	-40	-0.037	306	0.279	3.228	
Jason Richardson	21	0.023	319	0.341	2.922	3DW
Royal Ivey	30	0.043	214	0.306	3.335	3DW
Arnett Moultrie	-20	-0.037	239	0.440	3.539	
Kwame Brown	6	0.024	74	0.274	2.987	
Jeremy Pargo	-18	-0.089	32	0.155	3.228	
Maalik Wayns	-30	-0.185	-20	-0.124	3.322	
Charles Jenkins	8	0.051	51	0.343	3.277	
Justin Holiday	-2	-0.013	31	0.219	3.156	
Shelvin Mack	-1	-0.076	1	0.086	3.101	

Phoenix Suns

Record: 25-57

Team Stats

	Stat	Rank
Offensive Efficiency	.541	25
Point Balance	.979	28
Point Balance in the clutch	.974	28
Assist Balance	.906	19
Rebound Balance	.964	18
Lineup Entropy	5.683	18

AV Player Spotlight: 2012-13

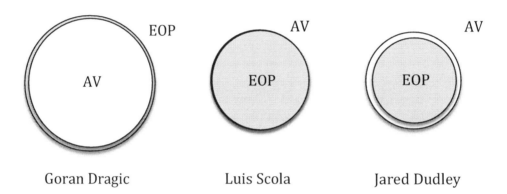

Goran Dragic   Luis Scola   Jared Dudley

Draft Pick Success

Year	Pick	First Name	Last Name	GP	EOP$^+$/G	Yield
2007	24	Rudy	Fernandez	249	8.15	0.66
2007	29	Alando	Tucker	51	3.23	-1.54
2007	59	D.J.	Strawberry	33	2.04	1.16
2008	15	Robin	Lopez	324	7.36	0.43
2008	48	Malik	Hairston	62	2.51	-0.75
2009	14	Earl	Clark	197	3.66	-4.42
2009	48	Taylor	Griffin	8	0.83	-2.43
2009	57	Emir	Preldzic	0	0.00	-2.08
2010	46	Gani	Lawal	0	0.00	-3.33
2010	60	Dwayne	Collins	0	0.00	-2.02

Player Stats

Player	Age	Pos	Min	OE	EOP	EOP/M
Goran Dragic	26	PG	2581	0.60	1416	0.549
Luis Scola	32	PF	2184	0.58	1037	0.475
Jared Dudley	27	SF	2170	0.58	889	0.409
P.J. Tucker	27	SG	1910	0.65	584	0.306
Marcin Gortat	28	C	1876	0.60	676	0.360
Markieff Morris	23	PF	1837	0.51	581	0.316
Michael Beasley	24	SF	1554	0.43	556	0.358
Shannon Brown	27	SG	1402	0.49	520	0.371
Jermaine O'Neal	34	C	1029	0.55	403	0.392
Wesley Johnson	25	SF	953	0.43	275	0.288
Sebastian Telfair	27	PG	795	0.52	284	0.357
Kendall Marshall	21	PG	702	0.57	219	0.312
Marcus Morris	23	SF	370	0.45	96	0.260
Hamed Haddadi	27	C	235	0.57	65	0.277
Diante Garrett	24	PG	149	0.52	50	0.334
Luke Zeller	25	C	58	0.43	14	0.238

Player	DSG	DSG/M	AV	AV/M	LE	Roles
Goran Dragic	-36	-0.014	1345	0.521	3.303	
Luis Scola	5	0.002	1047	0.479	3.332	
Jared Dudley	61	0.028	1011	0.466	3.367	3DW
P.J. Tucker	105	0.055	794	0.415	3.429	
Marcin Gortat	-29	-0.016	617	0.329	3.072	
Markieff Morris	-72	-0.039	437	0.238	3.600	SSB
Michael Beasley	-88	-0.057	379	0.244	3.574	
Shannon Brown	-68	-0.048	384	0.274	3.343	
Jermaine O'Neal	36	0.035	476	0.463	3.487	DB
Wesley Johnson	6	0.006	286	0.301	3.506	3DW
Sebastian Telfair	60	0.076	404	0.509	3.225	
Kendall Marshall	-22	-0.032	174	0.248	3.595	
Marcus Morris	5	0.013	106	0.287	3.429	
Hamed Haddadi	18	0.075	100	0.427	3.285	DB
Diante Garrett	1	0.008	52	0.349	3.676	
Luke Zeller	-6	-0.101	2	0.037	3.215	

Portland Trail Blazers

Record: 33-49

Team Stats

	Stat	Rank
Offensive Efficiency	.543	24
Point Balance	.925	4
Point Balance in the clutch	.957	25
Assist Balance	.892	16
Rebound Balance	.932	2
Lineup Entropy	4.890	3

AV Player Spotlight: 2012-13

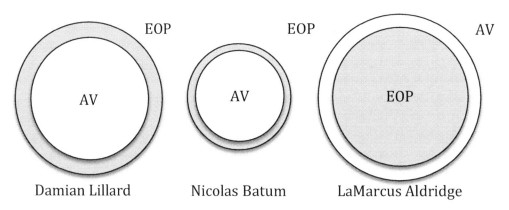

Damian Lillard   Nicolas Batum   LaMarcus Aldridge

Draft Pick Success

Year	Pick	First Name	Last Name	GP	EOP+/G	Yield
2008	13	Brandon	Rush	291	7.25	-1.54
2008	33	Joey	Dorsey	61	4.10	0.11
2008	36	Omer	Asik	230	6.86	2.79
2008	55	Mike	Taylor	51	5.52	3.18
2009	22	Victor	Claver	49	3.26	-2.94
2009	33	Dante	Cunningham	285	6.08	2.09
2009	38	Jon	Brockman	150	4.85	2.23
2009	55	Patrick	Mills	148	5.32	2.98
2010	22	Elliot	Williams	24	3.34	-2.86
2010	34	Armon	Johnson	47	3.39	-0.13

Player Stats

Player	Age	Pos	Min	OE	EOP	EOP/M
Damian Lillard	22	PG	3167	0.54	1599	0.505
Nicolas Batum	24	SF	2807	0.55	1109	0.395
LaMarcus Aldridge	27	PF	2790	0.56	1453	0.521
Wesley Matthews	26	SG	2403	0.50	872	0.363
J.J. Hickson	24	C	2323	0.71	1171	0.504
Meyers Leonard	20	C	1206	0.66	402	0.333
Will Barton	22	SG	894	0.45	231	0.259
Victor Claver	24	SF	812	0.48	160	0.197
Luke Babbitt	23	PF	730	0.43	172	0.235
Eric Maynor	25	SG	572	0.56	230	0.401
Sasha Pavlovic	29	SG	528	0.47	90	0.171
Ronnie Price	29	PG	510	0.52	127	0.250
Joel Freeland	25	PF	477	0.53	116	0.242
Jared Jeffries	31	PF	350	0.51	42	0.120
Nolan Smith	24	PG	288	0.45	93	0.324

Player	DSG	DSG/M	AV	AV/M	LE	Roles
Damian Lillard	-161	-0.051	1278	0.403	3.219	
Nicolas Batum	-80	-0.028	949	0.338	3.143	
LaMarcus Aldridge	145	0.052	1742	0.624	3.142	
Wesley Matthews	-63	-0.026	746	0.311	3.037	
J.J. Hickson	-92	-0.040	987	0.425	2.952	
Meyers Leonard	-18	-0.015	365	0.303	3.559	
Will Barton	9	0.010	250	0.280	3.633	
Victor Claver	-34	-0.041	92	0.114	3.450	
Luke Babbitt	27	0.037	226	0.309	3.605	DB, SSB
Eric Maynor	-46	-0.080	138	0.241	3.353	
Sasha Pavlovic	31	0.059	153	0.290	3.568	
Ronnie Price	34	0.066	195	0.382	3.450	
Joel Freeland	11	0.023	138	0.289	3.640	DB
Jared Jeffries	24	0.068	90	0.257	3.417	DB
Nolan Smith	43	0.149	179	0.621	3.453	

Sacramento Kings

Record: 28-54

Team Stats

	Stat	Rank
Offensive Efficiency	.541	26
Point Balance	.962	17
Point Balance in the clutch	.942	20
Assist Balance	.949	28
Rebound Balance	.947	14
Lineup Entropy	5.560	12

EOP Player Spotlight: DeMarcus Cousins

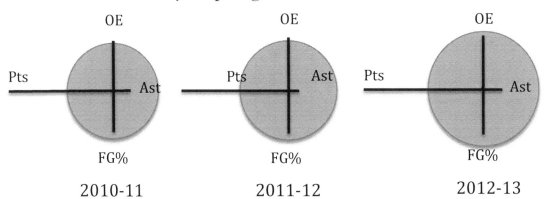

2010-11   2011-12   2012-13

Draft Pick Success

Year	Pick	First Name	Last Name	GP	EOP⁺/G	Yield
2006	19	Quincy	Douby	143	3.01	-3.60
2007	10	Spencer	Hawes	420	9.01	-1.32
2008	12	Jason	Thompson	378	10.96	3.23
2008	42	Sean	Singletary	37	2.14	-0.48
2008	43	Patrick	Ewing	7	0.28	-3.79
2009	4	Tyreke	Evans	257	17.20	4.68
2009	23	Omri	Casspi	256	6.47	0.46
2009	31	Jeff	Pendergraph	96	3.12	-1.14
2010	5	DeMarcus	Cousins	220	14.72	2.45
2010	33	Hassan	Whiteside	18	1.90	-2.09

Player Stats

Player	Age	Pos	Min	OE	EOP	EOP/M
DeMarcus Cousins	22	C	2289	0.55	1194	0.522
Jason Thompson	26	PF	2285	0.60	875	0.383
John Salmons	33	SF	2278	0.53	676	0.297
Isaiah Thomas	23	PG	2122	0.54	1101	0.519
Tyreke Evans	23	SG	2016	0.56	983	0.487
Marcus Thornton	25	SG	1726	0.48	716	0.415
Chuck Hayes	29	C	1209	0.84	361	0.299
Jimmer Fredette	23	SG	967	0.48	410	0.424
Aaron Brooks	28	PG	959	0.53	363	0.379
James Johnson	25	SF	878	0.49	236	0.269
Thomas Robinson	21	PF	809	0.55	229	0.284
Francisco Garcia	31	SG	710	0.46	166	0.234
Patrick Patterson	23	PF	556	0.64	209	0.376
Travis Outlaw	28	SF	444	0.48	156	0.350
Toney Douglas	26	PG	376	0.58	156	0.415
Cole Aldrich	24	C	175	0.77	61	0.351
Tyler Honeycutt	22	SF	32	0.33	5	0.150

Player	DSG	DSG/M	AV	AV/M	LE	Roles
DeMarcus Cousins	-33	-0.015	1127	0.492	3.294	
Jason Thompson	5	0.002	885	0.387	3.326	
John Salmons	46	0.020	768	0.337	3.351	3DW
Isaiah Thomas	30	0.014	1160	0.547	3.310	
Tyreke Evans	19	0.009	1020	0.506	3.321	3DW
Marcus Thornton	-40	-0.023	636	0.368	3.731	
Chuck Hayes	82	0.068	524	0.434	3.669	DB
Jimmer Fredette	-34	-0.035	343	0.354	3.794	
Aaron Brooks	-32	-0.033	300	0.312	3.362	
James Johnson	-18	-0.021	199	0.227	3.620	
Thomas Robinson	-10	-0.013	209	0.258	3.497	
Francisco Garcia	1	0.001	168	0.237	3.430	3DW
Patrick Patterson	-21	-0.038	167	0.300	3.445	
Travis Outlaw	-20	-0.044	116	0.262	3.844	
Toney Douglas	40	0.106	236	0.628	3.388	
Cole Aldrich	11	0.061	83	0.473	3.262	
Tyler Honeycutt	-1	-0.019	4	0.112	3.079	

San Antonio Spurs

Record: 58-24

Team Stats

	Stat	Rank
Offensive Efficiency	.568	4
Point Balance	.967	22
Point Balance in the clutch	.879	11
Assist Balance	.932	24
Rebound Balance	.953	15
Lineup Entropy	5.927	23

AV Player Spotlight: 2012-13

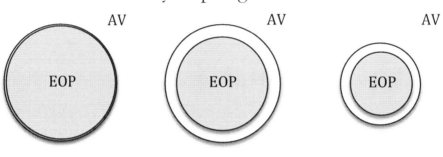

Tim Duncan   Tiago Splitter   Kawhi Leonard

Draft Pick Success

Year	Pick	First Name	Last Name	GP	EOP$^+$/G	Yield
2007	33	Marcus	Williams	0	0.00	-3.99
2007	58	Giorgos	Printezis	0	0.00	-1.44
2008	26	George	Hill	357	10.91	5.85
2008	45	Goran	Dragic	348	11.19	7.21
2008	57	James	Gist	0	0.00	-2.08
2009	37	DeJuan	Blair	288	8.70	4.14
2009	51	Jack	McClinton	0	0.00	-1.48
2009	53	Nando	De Colo	72	4.46	2.37
2010	20	James	Anderson	116	3.29	-3.18
2010	49	Ryan	Richards	0	0.00	-2.65

Player Stats

Player	Age	Pos	Min	OE	EOP	EOP/M
Danny Green	25	SG	2201	0.51	728	0.331
Tony Parker	30	PG	2174	0.62	1613	0.742
Tim Duncan	36	C	2078	0.57	1181	0.568
Tiago Splitter	28	PF	1997	0.69	974	0.488
Kawhi Leonard	21	SF	1810	0.57	658	0.364
Boris Diaw	30	PF	1709	0.68	587	0.344
Gary Neal	28	SG	1484	0.48	540	0.364
Manu Ginobili	35	SG	1393	0.55	761	0.546
Stephen Jackson	34	SF	1075	0.44	266	0.247
Nando De Colo	25	SG	920	0.56	321	0.349
Matt Bonner	32	PF	909	0.58	275	0.303
DeJuan Blair	23	PF	851	0.63	343	0.404
Patrick Mills	24	PG	656	0.53	272	0.414
Cory Joseph	21	PG	388	0.60	152	0.393
Aron Baynes	26	C	141	0.58	41	0.289
James Anderson	23	SF	94	0.53	33	0.347

Player	DSG	DSG/M	AV	AV/M	LE	Roles
Danny Green	-2	-0.001	725	0.329	3.398	
Tony Parker	53	0.024	1719	0.791	3.229	
Tim Duncan	19	0.009	1219	0.587	3.315	DB
Tiago Splitter	127	0.064	1229	0.615	3.455	DB
Kawhi Leonard	97	0.054	852	0.471	3.280	3DW
Boris Diaw	-40	-0.024	507	0.296	3.512	SSB
Gary Neal	-70	-0.047	399	0.269	3.663	
Manu Ginobili	18	0.013	798	0.573	3.543	3DW
Stephen Jackson	5	0.004	275	0.256	3.621	3DW
Nando De Colo	-28	-0.031	265	0.288	3.707	
Matt Bonner	-18	-0.020	240	0.264	3.739	SSB
DeJuan Blair	-27	-0.031	290	0.341	3.691	
Patrick Mills	-35	-0.053	202	0.308	3.715	
Cory Joseph	-14	-0.037	124	0.319	3.695	
Aron Baynes	1	0.006	43	0.302	3.438	
James Anderson	3	0.035	39	0.417	3.244	

Toronto Raptors

Record: 34-48

Team Stats

	Stat	Rank
Offensive Efficiency	.545	22
Point Balance	.968	23
Point Balance in the clutch	.913	19
Assist Balance	.891	15
Rebound Balance	.970	22
Lineup Entropy	6.042	28

AV Player Spotlight: 2012-13

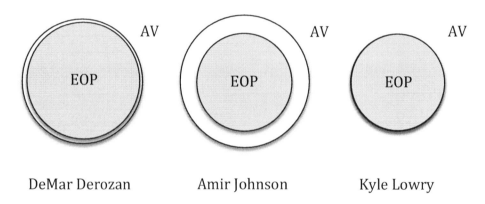

DeMar Derozan   Amir Johnson   Kyle Lowry

Draft Pick Success

Year	Pick	First Name	Last Name	GP	EOP$^+$/G	Yield
2005	7	Charlie	Villanueva	510	9.47	-2.09
2005	16	Joey	Graham	377	5.08	-1.83
2005	41	Roko	Ukic	85	4.44	1.01
2005	58	Uros	Slokar	20	1.52	0.08
2006	1	Andrea	Bargnani	433	11.26	-5.19
2006	35	P.J.	Tucker	96	6.44	2.56
2006	56	Edin	Bavcic	0	0.00	-1.70
2008	17	Roy	Hibbert	376	11.19	4.60
2009	9	DeMar	DeRozan	304	12.36	2.27
2010	13	Ed	Davis	212	9.08	0.29

Player Stats

Player	Age	Pos	Min	OE	EOP	EOP/M
DeMar DeRozan	23	SG	3013	0.49	1216	0.404
Amir Johnson	25	PF	2325	0.74	1018	0.438
Kyle Lowry	26	PG	2020	0.59	1005	0.498
Alan Anderson	30	SF	1495	0.44	518	0.347
Jonas Valanciunas	20	C	1482	0.65	578	0.390
Jose Calderon	31	PG	1273	0.66	750	0.589
Terrence Ross	21	SG	1239	0.46	351	0.284
Rudy Gay	26	SF	1146	0.47	510	0.445
Ed Davis	23	C	1087	0.70	510	0.469
Landry Fields	24	SF	1037	0.61	264	0.254
Andrea Bargnani	27	PF	1003	0.42	302	0.302
John Lucas	30	PG	827	0.51	320	0.388
Aaron Gray	28	C	513	0.73	159	0.311
Mickael Pietrus	30	SF	386	0.36	59	0.153
Linas Kleiza	23	SF	376	0.39	95	0.252
Quincy Acy	25	PF	342	0.73	137	0.400
Dominic McGuire	26	SF	230	0.66	40	0.172
Sebastian Telfair	30	PG	185	0.51	67	0.360

Player	DSG	DSG/M	AV	AV/M	LE	Roles
DeMar DeRozan	41	0.014	1297	0.431	3.726	3DW
Amir Johnson	181	0.078	1379	0.593	3.661	DB
Kyle Lowry	2	0.001	1010	0.500	3.447	
Alan Anderson	-38	-0.025	443	0.296	3.686	
Jonas Valanciunas	-21	-0.014	536	0.362	3.542	
Jose Calderon	-13	-0.010	723	0.568	3.503	
Terrence Ross	-11	-0.008	330	0.267	3.786	
Rudy Gay	58	0.050	625	0.545	3.126	3DW
Ed Davis	-12	-0.011	486	0.447	3.441	
Landry Fields	-47	-0.045	170	0.164	3.594	
Andrea Bargnani	-26	-0.026	250	0.250	3.504	SSB
John Lucas	-36	-0.044	248	0.300	3.665	
Aaron Gray	3	0.005	165	0.321	3.621	
Mickael Pietrus	2	0.006	64	0.165	3.123	
Linas Kleiza	-16	-0.042	63	0.169	3.385	
Quincy Acy	26	0.076	189	0.552	3.528	DB
Dominic McGuire	-9	-0.041	21	0.090	3.092	
Sebastian Telfair	41	0.014	103	0.555	3.154	

Utah Jazz

Record: 43-39

Team Stats

	Stat	Rank
Offensive Efficiency	.558	7
Point Balance	.957	12
Point Balance in the clutch	.909	16
Assist Balance	.954	29
Rebound Balance	.934	5
Lineup Entropy	5.668	17

AV Player Spotlight: 2012-13

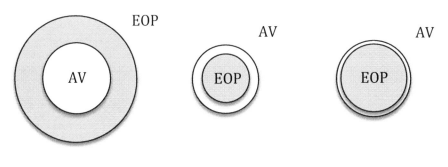

Al Jefferson   Enes Kanter   Derrick Favors

Draft Pick Success

Year	Pick	First Name	Last Name	GP	EOP+/G	Yield
2006	47	Paul	Millsap	540	13.46	8.90
2007	25	Morris	Almond	38	2.09	-3.50
2007	55	Herbert	Hill	0	0.00	-2.34
2008	23	Kosta	Koufos	263	6.36	0.35
2008	44	Ante	Tomic	0	0.00	-1.72
2008	53	Tadija	Dragicevic	0	0.00	-2.09
2009	20	Eric	Maynor	236	5.90	-0.57
2009	50	Goran	Suton	0	0.00	-2.31
2010	9	Gordon	Hayward	210	10.15	0.06
2010	55	Jeremy	Evans	115	4.18	1.84

Player Stats

Player	Age	Pos	Min	OE	EOP	EOP/M
Al Jefferson	28	C	2578	0.57	1320	0.512
Paul Millsap	27	PF	2375	0.61	1186	0.499
Randy Foye	29	SG	2249	0.47	718	0.319
Gordon Hayward	22	SF	2104	0.52	930	0.442
Derrick Favors	21	PF	1787	0.59	706	0.395
Marvin Williams	26	SF	1727	0.50	445	0.258
Mo Williams	30	PG	1418	0.56	686	0.484
Jamaal Tinsley	34	PG	1221	0.61	418	0.342
Alec Burks	21	SG	1137	0.49	390	0.343
DeMarre Carroll	26	SF	1111	0.63	421	0.379
Enes Kanter	20	C	1078	0.63	506	0.469
Earl Watson	33	PG	829	0.64	232	0.280
Jeremy Evans	25	PF	215	1.03	130	0.604
Kevin Murphy	22	SG	52	0.27	7	0.131

Player	DSG	DSG/M	AV	AV/M	LE	Roles
Al Jefferson	-290	-0.113	740	0.287	3.155	
Paul Millsap	-71	-0.030	1045	0.440	3.178	
Randy Foye	-146	-0.065	425	0.189	3.210	
Gordon Hayward	78	0.037	1086	0.516	3.423	3DW
Derrick Favors	44	0.025	794	0.444	3.466	DB
Marvin Williams	-47	-0.027	351	0.203	3.187	
Mo Williams	-36	-0.025	614	0.433	2.855	
Jamaal Tinsley	-17	-0.014	383	0.314	3.076	
Alec Burks	62	0.055	514	0.452	3.453	3DW
DeMarre Carroll	91	0.082	603	0.543	3.445	
Enes Kanter	103	0.096	712	0.661	3.359	DB
Earl Watson	8	0.010	249	0.300	3.193	
Jeremy Evans	6	0.026	141	0.656	3.287	DB
Kevin Murphy	-12	-0.238	-18	-0.345	2.557	

Washington Wizards

Record: 29-53

Team Stats

	Stat	Rank
Offensive Efficiency	.531	29
Point Balance	.960	14
Point Balance in the clutch	.951	22
Assist Balance	.935	26
Rebound Balance	.958	17
Lineup Entropy	6.052	29

AV/EOP Player Spotlight: Bradley Beal

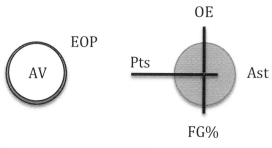

2012-13

Draft Pick Success

Year	Pick	First Name	Last Name	GP	EOP+/G	Yield
2006	18	Oleksiy	Pecherov	111	2.74	-4.65
2006	48	Vladimir	Veremeenko	0	0.00	-3.26
2007	16	Nick	Young	416	8.21	1.30
2007	47	Dominic	McGuire	342	3.63	-0.93
2008	18	JaVale	McGee	354	9.03	1.64
2008	47	Bill	Walker	157	4.91	0.35
2009	32	Jermaine	Taylor	65	4.36	0.91
2010	1	John	Wall	184	19.57	3.12
2010	30	Lazar	Hayward	72	2.16	-2.59
2010	35	Nemanja	Bjelica	0	0.00	-3.88

Player Stats

Player	Age	Pos	Min	OE	EOP	EOP/M
Martell Webster	26	SF	2200	0.52	770	0.350
Emeka Okafor	30	C	2052	0.61	775	0.378
Bradley Beal	19	SG	1745	0.48	645	0.370
Kevin Seraphin	23	C	1721	0.49	563	0.327
Nene Hilario	30	PF	1659	0.57	780	0.470
John Wall	22	PG	1602	0.57	1022	0.638
Trevor Ariza	27	SF	1471	0.50	465	0.316
A.J. Price	26	PG	1278	0.55	500	0.391
Garrett Temple	26	SG	1156	0.54	288	0.249
Jordan Crawford	24	SG	1127	0.50	525	0.466
Chris Singleton	23	PF	924	0.47	186	0.202
Trevor Booker	25	PF	887	0.77	333	0.375
Cartier Martin	28	SF	694	0.40	171	0.247
Jan Vesely	22	PF	601	0.67	151	0.251
Shaun Livingston	27	PG	320	0.52	73	0.227
Shelvin Mack	23	PG	141	0.57	47	0.336
Earl Barron	31	C	122	0.47	22	0.177
Jannero Pargo	33	PG	102	0.41	20	0.192
Jason Collins	34	C	54	0.33	3	0.052

Player	DSG	DSG/M	AV	AV/M	LE	Roles
Martell Webster	-47	-0.021	676	0.307	3.662	
Emeka Okafor	-17	-0.008	741	0.361	3.550	
Bradley Beal	-25	-0.014	595	0.341	3.669	
Kevin Seraphin	-45	-0.026	473	0.275	3.861	
Nene Hilario	80	0.048	939	0.566	3.493	
John Wall	22	0.014	1067	0.666	3.430	
Trevor Ariza	22	0.015	509	0.346	3.549	3DW
A.J. Price	-8	-0.007	483	0.378	3.550	
Garrett Temple	40	0.034	367	0.317	3.522	
Jordan Crawford	-1	-0.001	523	0.464	3.823	
Chris Singleton	2	0.002	190	0.205	3.825	
Trevor Booker	-51	-0.057	232	0.261	3.588	
Cartier Martin	4	0.006	180	0.259	3.809	3DW
Jan Vesely	-23	-0.038	105	0.175	3.828	
Shaun Livingston	-6	-0.018	61	0.191	3.348	
Shelvin Mack	-14	-0.097	20	0.142	3.191	
Earl Barron	14	0.112	49	0.400	3.469	
Jannero Pargo	13	0.130	46	0.451	3.009	
Jason Collins	12	0.216	26	0.484	3.013	

Appendix

Table A1: Top 100 EOP for 2012-13

Rank	Player	Pos	Age	Tm	PTS	OE	EOP
1	LeBron James	PF	28	MIA	2036	0.65	2408
2	Kevin Durant	SF	24	OKC	2280	0.54	2105
3	Kobe Bryant	SG	34	LAL	2133	0.53	1994
4	Russell Westbrook	PG	24	OKC	1903	0.56	1992
5	James Harden	SG	23	HOU	2023	0.51	1845
6	Stephen Curry	PG	24	GSW	1786	0.55	1840
7	Chris Paul	PG	27	LAC	1186	0.66	1714
8	Deron Williams	PG	28	BRK	1476	0.57	1682
9	Blake Griffin	PF	23	LAC	1440	0.64	1616
10	Tony Parker	PG	30	SAS	1341	0.62	1613
11	Damian Lillard	PG	22	POR	1562	0.54	1599
12	Jrue Holiday	PG	22	PHI	1383	0.56	1571
13	David Lee	PF	29	GSW	1459	0.62	1563
14	Dwyane Wade	SG	31	MIA	1463	0.59	1556
15	Carmelo Anthony	PF	28	NYK	1920	0.49	1535
16	Monta Ellis	SG	27	MIL	1577	0.51	1513
17	Kemba Walker	PG	22	CHA	1455	0.54	1477
18	Greivis Vasquez	PG	26	NOH	1083	0.59	1459
19	Al Horford	C	26	ATL	1289	0.65	1454
20	LaMarcus Aldridge	PF	27	POR	1560	0.56	1453
21	Brandon Jennings	PG	23	MIL	1397	0.53	1447
22	Ty Lawson	PG	25	DEN	1216	0.59	1420
23	Goran Dragic	PG	26	PHO	1134	0.60	1416
24	Jeff Teague	PG	24	ATL	1166	0.58	1410
25	Greg Monroe	C	22	DET	1298	0.59	1363
26	Dwight Howard	C	27	LAL	1296	0.65	1349
27	Paul Pierce	SF	35	BOS	1430	0.52	1346
28	Marc Gasol	C	28	MEM	1127	0.64	1336
29	Mike Conley	PG	25	MEM	1168	0.57	1336
30	Brook Lopez	C	24	BRK	1437	0.59	1330
31	Al Jefferson	C	28	UTA	1391	0.57	1320
32	Josh Smith	PF	27	ATL	1327	0.55	1300
33	Kyrie Irving	PG	20	CLE	1325	0.53	1276
34	Tyson Chandler	C	30	NYK	689	1.13	1264
35	Jeremy Lin	PG	24	HOU	1095	0.56	1248

Rank	Player	Pos	Age	Tm	PTS	OE	EOP
36	David West	PF	32	IND	1250	0.58	1240
37	Paul George	SF	22	IND	1377	0.50	1226
38	O.J. Mayo	SG	25	DAL	1255	0.53	1221
39	Jose Calderon	PG	31	TOT	826	0.66	1219
40	DeMar DeRozan	SG	23	TOR	1485	0.49	1216
41	Andre Iguodala	SG	29	DEN	1038	0.58	1197
42	DeMarcus Cousins	C	22	SAC	1280	0.55	1194
43	Chandler Parsons	SF	24	HOU	1177	0.57	1190
44	Chris Bosh	C	28	MIA	1232	0.59	1190
45	Jarrett Jack	SG	29	GSW	1023	0.58	1187
46	Paul Millsap	PF	27	UTA	1135	0.61	1186
47	Thaddeus Young	PF	24	PHI	1127	0.64	1185
48	J.R. Smith	SG	27	NYK	1446	0.48	1185
49	Tim Duncan	C	36	SAS	1227	0.57	1181
50	Carlos Boozer	PF	31	CHI	1281	0.55	1177
51	J.J. Hickson	C	24	POR	1018	0.71	1171
52	George Hill	PG	26	IND	1076	0.57	1168
53	Darren Collison	PG	25	DAL	972	0.59	1152
54	Nikola Vucevic	C	22	ORL	1008	0.67	1136
55	Luol Deng	SF	27	CHI	1237	0.53	1131
56	Zach Randolph	PF	31	MEM	1169	0.60	1130
57	Andre Miller	PG	36	DEN	786	0.64	1121
58	Serge Ibaka	PF	23	OKC	1055	0.68	1114
59	Nicolas Batum	SF	24	POR	1047	0.55	1109
60	Nate Robinson	PG	28	CHI	1074	0.54	1108
61	Isaiah Thomas	PG	23	SAC	1100	0.54	1101
62	Kenneth Faried	PF	23	DEN	923	0.74	1099
63	Tristan Thompson	PF	21	CLE	957	0.69	1084
64	Rudy Gay	SF	26	TOT	1366	0.47	1072
65	Evan Turner	SF	24	PHI	1094	0.52	1068
66	Ryan Anderson	PF	24	NOH	1309	0.51	1067
67	J.J. Redick	SG	28	TOT	1100	0.52	1050
68	Nikola Pekovic	C	27	MIN	1011	0.66	1050
69	Joe Johnson	SG	31	BRK	1170	0.51	1049
70	Joakim Noah	C	27	CHI	784	0.70	1042
71	Klay Thompson	SG	22	GSW	1359	0.46	1037
72	Luis Scola	PF	32	PHO	1048	0.58	1037
73	Raymond Felton	PG	28	NYK	948	0.55	1029
74	John Wall	PG	22	WAS	906	0.57	1022
75	Amir Johnson	PF	25	TOR	813	0.74	1018
76	Jamal Crawford	SG	32	LAC	1255	0.48	1017
77	Kyle Lowry	PG	26	TOR	791	0.59	1005
78	Luke Ridnour	SG	31	MIN	939	0.56	998
79	Robin Lopez	C	24	NOH	929	0.67	996
80	Tyreke Evans	SG	23	SAC	987	0.56	983
81	Tiago Splitter	PF	28	SAS	838	0.69	974

Rank	Player	Pos	Age	Tm	PTS	OE	EOP
82	Vince Carter	SF	36	DAL	1088	0.52	967
83	Danilo Gallinari	SF	24	DEN	1149	0.49	961
84	DeAndre Jordan	C	24	LAC	724	0.84	952
85	Kevin Garnett	C	36	BOS	1004	0.56	949
86	Jameer Nelson	PG	30	ORL	822	0.54	935
87	Omer Asik	C	26	HOU	832	0.69	935
88	Gordon Hayward	SF	22	UTA	1017	0.52	930
89	Spencer Hawes	C	24	PHI	905	0.59	930
90	Gerald Henderson	SG	25	CHA	1055	0.52	929
91	Ersan Ilyasova	PF	25	MIL	962	0.58	925
92	Brandon Knight	PG	21	DET	999	0.50	924
93	Roy Hibbert	C	26	IND	937	0.59	922
94	Arron Afflalo	SF	27	ORL	1057	0.49	909
95	Shawn Marion	PF	34	DAL	812	0.64	907
96	Carl Landry	PF	29	GSW	874	0.65	907
97	Jared Dudley	SF	27	PHO	861	0.58	889
98	Jason Thompson	PF	26	SAC	891	0.60	875
99	Kosta Koufos	C	23	DEN	648	0.86	873
100	Wesley Matthews	SG	26	POR	1022	0.50	872

Table A2: LeBron James' Career OE and EOP

Season	Age	Tm	FG	FGA	AST	TOV	PTS	OE	EOP
2003-04	19	CLE	622	1492	465	273	1654	0.51	1579
2004-05	20	CLE	795	1684	577	262	2175	0.57	2269
2005-06	21	CLE	875	1823	521	260	2478	0.55	2431
2006-07	22	CLE	772	1621	470	250	2132	0.55	2086
2007-08	23	CLE	794	1642	539	255	2250	0.58	2316
2008-09	24	CLE	789	1613	587	241	2304	0.59	2470
2009-10	25	CLE	768	1528	651	261	2258	0.60	2509
2010-11	26	MIA	758	1485	554	284	2111	0.58	2247
2011-12	27	MIA	621	1169	387	213	1683	0.60	1834
2012-13	28	MIA	765	1354	551	226	2036	0.65	2408
Career			7559	15411	5302	2525	21081	0.58	22149

Table A3: Top 100 EOP for 1991-92

Rank	Player	Pos	Age	Tm	PTS	OE	EOP
1	Michael Jordan	SG	28	CHI	2404	0.59	2363
2	Tim Hardaway	PG	25	GSW	1893	0.60	2146
3	John Stockton	PG	29	UTA	1297	0.69	2138
4	Karl Malone	PF	28	UTA	2272	0.58	2058
5	Kevin Johnson	PG	25	PHO	1536	0.63	1974
6	Scottie Pippen	SF	26	CHI	1720	0.63	1949
7	Clyde Drexler	SG	29	POR	1903	0.58	1925
8	Chris Mullin	SF	28	GSW	2074	0.57	1888
9	Charles Barkley	PF	28	PHI	1730	0.67	1876
10	Patrick Ewing	C	29	NYK	1970	0.57	1718
11	Jeff Hornacek	SG	28	PHO	1632	0.61	1703
12	Larry Johnson	PF	22	CHH	1576	0.65	1690
13	Brad Daugherty	C	26	CLE	1566	0.66	1678
14	Horace Grant	PF	26	CHI	1149	0.89	1671
15	Pooh Richardson	PG	25	MIN	1350	0.62	1660
16	Danny Manning	PF	25	LAC	1579	0.64	1646
17	Dennis Rodman	PF	30	DET	800	1.20	1633
18	Otis Thorpe	PF	29	HOU	1420	0.71	1632
19	David Robinson	C	26	SAS	1578	0.66	1619
20	Mitch Richmond	SG	26	SAC	1803	0.53	1616
21	Reggie Miller	SG	26	IND	1695	0.58	1611
22	Micheal Williams	PG	25	IND	1188	0.64	1548
23	Larry Nance	PF	32	CLE	1375	0.69	1543
24	Detlef Schrempf	PF	29	IND	1380	0.66	1531
25	Terry Porter	PG	28	POR	1485	0.57	1519
26	Kendall Gill	SG	23	CHH	1622	0.56	1510
27	Sedale Threatt	PG	30	LAL	1240	0.62	1509
28	Isiah Thomas	PG	30	DET	1445	0.56	1504
29	Kevin Willis	PF	29	ATL	1480	0.65	1504
30	Mark Price	PG	27	CLE	1247	0.63	1488
31	Joe Dumars	SG	28	DET	1635	0.54	1476
32	Drazen Petrovic	SG	27	NJN	1691	0.55	1476
33	Reggie Lewis	SG	26	BOS	1703	0.55	1469
34	Michael Adams	PG	29	WSB	1408	0.54	1454
35	Chuck Person	SF	27	IND	1497	0.56	1449
36	Mark Jackson	PG	26	NYK	916	0.68	1413
37	Ricky Pierce	SG	32	SEA	1690	0.52	1410
38	Glen Rice	SF	24	MIA	1765	0.51	1396
39	Dan Majerle	SF	26	PHO	1418	0.60	1395
40	Ron Harper	SG	28	LAC	1495	0.54	1394
41	Hakeem Olajuwon	C	29	HOU	1510	0.59	1373
42	Jeff Malone	SG	30	UTA	1639	0.54	1368
43	Spud Webb	PG	28	SAC	1231	0.57	1343
44	Kenny Smith	PG	26	HOU	1137	0.60	1341

Rank	Player	Pos	Age	Tm	PTS	OE	EOP
45	Pervis Ellison	C	24	WSB	1322	0.62	1312
46	Muggsy Bogues	PG	27	CHH	730	0.70	1303
47	Reggie Williams	SF	27	DEN	1474	0.54	1288
48	Sarunas Marciulionis	SG	27	GSW	1361	0.57	1273
49	Grant Long	PF	25	MIA	1212	0.64	1269
50	Hersey Hawkins	SG	25	PHI	1536	0.51	1260
51	Lionel Simmons	SF	23	SAC	1336	0.55	1260
52	Armen Gilliam	PF	27	PHI	1367	0.60	1254
53	Sean Elliott	SF	23	SAS	1338	0.58	1242
54	Johnny Dawkins	PG	28	PHI	988	0.60	1216
55	Moses Malone	C	36	MIL	1279	0.63	1213
56	Doug West	SG	24	MIN	1116	0.63	1196
57	Billy Owens	PF	22	GSW	1141	0.65	1192
58	A.C. Green	PF	28	LAL	1116	0.69	1191
59	Jay Humphries	PG	29	MIL	991	0.61	1186
60	Scott Skiles	PG	27	ORL	1057	0.56	1185
61	Derrick Coleman	PF	24	NJN	1289	0.57	1182
62	Mookie Blaylock	PG	24	NJN	996	0.60	1180
63	Rony Seikaly	C	26	MIA	1296	0.59	1174
64	Buck Williams	PF	31	POR	901	0.83	1169
65	Hot Rod Williams	C	29	CLE	952	0.74	1165
66	Tony Campbell	SF	29	MIN	1307	0.54	1157
67	Rumeal Robinson	PG	25	ATL	1055	0.57	1148
68	Vernon Maxwell	SG	26	HOU	1372	0.49	1144
69	Derek Harper	PG	30	DAL	1152	0.55	1137
70	Dikembe Mutombo	C	25	DEN	1177	0.61	1131
71	Rolando Blackman	SG	32	DAL	1374	0.51	1127
72	Eddie Johnson	SF	32	SEA	1386	0.52	1126
73	Kevin Gamble	SF	26	BOS	1108	0.61	1118
74	Terry Cummings	PF	30	SAS	1210	0.60	1113
75	Terry Catledge	PF	28	ORL	1154	0.62	1102
76	Rod Strickland	PG	25	SAS	787	0.65	1082
77	Byron Scott	SG	30	LAL	1218	0.54	1073
78	Gary Payton	PG	23	SEA	764	0.65	1069
79	Harvey Grant	SF	26	WSB	1155	0.58	1062
80	Jerome Kersey	SF	29	POR	971	0.64	1059
81	Robert Parish	C	38	BOS	1115	0.63	1054
82	Stacey Augmon	SG	23	ATL	1094	0.59	1053
83	Alvin Robertson	SG	29	MIL	1010	0.57	1048
84	John Starks	SG	26	NYK	1139	0.53	1028
85	Kenny Gattison	PF	27	CHH	1042	0.62	1017
86	Dell Curry	SG	27	CHH	1209	0.53	1017
87	Michael Cage	PF	30	SEA	720	0.89	1015
88	Wayman Tisdale	PF	27	SAC	1195	0.55	1011
89	Dominique Wilkins	SF	32	ATL	1179	0.53	995

Rank	Player	Pos	Age	Tm	PTS	OE	EOP
90	Xavier McDaniel	SF	28	NYK	1125	0.56	993
91	Nick Anderson	SG	24	ORL	1196	0.52	992
92	James Worthy	SF	30	LAL	1075	0.55	991
93	Sam Perkins	PF	30	LAL	1041	0.60	991
94	Tim Perry	PF	26	PHO	982	0.64	990
95	Dale Ellis	SF	31	MIL	1272	0.51	981
96	Shawn Kemp	PF	22	SEA	994	0.64	979
97	Winston Garland	PG	27	DEN	846	0.59	975
98	Sam Bowie	C	30	NJN	1062	0.56	971
99	Ed Pinckney	PF	28	BOS	613	1.02	963
100	Larry Bird	SF	35	BOS	908	0.58	944

Table A4: Michael Jordan's Career OE and EOP

Season	Age	Tm	FG	FGA	AST	TOV	PTS	OE	EOP
1984-85	21	CHI	837	1625	481	291	2313	0.59	2264
1985-86	22	CHI	150	328	53	45	408	0.50	325
1986-87	23	CHI	1098	2279	377	272	3041	0.53	2543
1987-88	24	CHI	1069	1998	485	252	2868	0.60	2775
1988-89	25	CHI	966	1795	650	290	2633	0.62	2834
1989-90	26	CHI	1034	1964	519	247	2753	0.60	2733
1990-91	27	CHI	990	1837	453	202	2580	0.61	2567
1991-92	28	CHI	943	1818	489	200	2404	0.59	2363
1992-93	29	CHI	992	2003	428	207	2541	0.57	2350
1994-95	31	CHI	166	404	90	35	457	0.51	393
1995-96	32	CHI	916	1850	352	197	2491	0.56	2316
1996-97	33	CHI	920	1892	352	166	2431	0.55	2247
1997-98	34	CHI	881	1893	283	185	2357	0.52	2009
2001-02	38	WAS	551	1324	310	162	1375	0.49	1204
2002-03	39	WAS	679	1527	311	173	1640	0.51	1471
Career			12192	24537	5633	2924	32292	0.57	30393

Table A5: Top 100 EOP for 1984-85

Rank	Player	Pos	Age	Tm	PTS	OE	EOP
1	Isiah Thomas	PG	23	DET	1720	0.65	2392
2	Larry Bird	SF	28	BOS	2295	0.61	2354
3	Michael Jordan	SG	21	CHI	2313	0.59	2264
4	Magic Johnson	PG	25	LAL	1406	0.71	2165
5	Alex English	SF	31	DEN	2262	0.58	2100
6	Micheal Ray Richardson	PG	29	NJN	1649	0.61	1878
7	Kareem Abdul-Jabbar	C	37	LAL	1735	0.65	1794
8	Calvin Natt	PF	28	DEN	1817	0.63	1789
9	Mark Aguirre	SF	25	DAL	2055	0.55	1777
10	Hakeem Olajuwon	C	22	HOU	1692	0.68	1721
11	Dominique Wilkins	SF	25	ATL	2217	0.50	1707
12	Purvis Short	SF	27	GSW	2186	0.50	1696
13	Terry Cummings	PF	23	MIL	1861	0.58	1683
14	Norm Nixon	PG	29	LAC	1395	0.59	1637
15	Gus Williams	PG	31	WSB	1578	0.56	1628
16	Moses Malone	C	29	PHI	1941	0.56	1623
17	Eddie Johnson	SF	25	KCK	1876	0.54	1623
18	Reggie Theus	SG	27	KCK	1341	0.61	1614
19	Derek Smith	SG	23	LAC	1767	0.58	1607
20	Sidney Moncrief	PG	27	MIL	1585	0.60	1601
21	Paul Pressey	SF	26	MIL	1284	0.65	1582
22	Kevin McHale	PF	27	BOS	1565	0.66	1577
23	Orlando Woolridge	SF	25	CHI	1767	0.59	1577
24	Bernard King	SF	28	NYK	1809	0.56	1574
25	Johnny Moore	PG	26	SAS	1046	0.66	1571
26	Artis Gilmore	C	35	SAS	1548	0.67	1570
27	Clyde Drexler	SG	22	POR	1377	0.63	1544
28	Ralph Sampson	PF	24	HOU	1809	0.54	1517
29	Rolando Blackman	SG	25	DAL	1598	0.58	1509
30	Mike Mitchell	SF	29	SAS	1824	0.54	1503
31	Buck Williams	PF	24	NJN	1491	0.64	1470
32	Bill Laimbeer	C	27	DET	1438	0.64	1429
33	Dennis Johnson	PG	30	BOS	1254	0.60	1427
34	World B. Free	SG	31	CLE	1597	0.54	1416
35	Tom Chambers	PF	25	SEA	1739	0.52	1415
36	Rodney McCray	SF	23	HOU	1183	0.68	1413
37	Sleepy Floyd	SG	24	GSW	1598	0.52	1408
38	James Worthy	SF	23	LAL	1410	0.63	1398
39	Julius Erving	SF	34	PHI	1561	0.56	1392
40	Darrell Griffith	SG	26	UTA	1764	0.50	1381
41	Eddie Johnson	SG	29	ATL	1193	0.59	1377
42	Maurice Cheeks	PG	28	PHI	1025	0.69	1377
43	Clark Kellogg	PF	23	IND	1432	0.59	1368
44	Adrian Dantley	SF	28	UTA	1462	0.60	1364

Rank	Player	Pos	Age	Tm	PTS	OE	EOP
45	Fat Lever	PG	24	DEN	1051	0.63	1360
46	Robert Parish	C	31	BOS	1394	0.64	1353
47	Kiki Vandeweghe	SF	26	POR	1616	0.55	1345
48	Mychal Thompson	PF	30	POR	1451	0.58	1336
49	Rickey Green	PG	30	UTA	1000	0.64	1324
50	Larry Nance	PF	25	PHO	1211	0.69	1314
51	Gerald Henderson	PG	29	SEA	1062	0.61	1302
52	Jack Sikma	C	29	SEA	1259	0.61	1286
53	John Bagley	PG	24	CLE	804	0.67	1279
54	Alvan Adams	PF	30	PHO	1202	0.62	1271
55	Larry Drew	PG	26	KCK	1075	0.61	1263
56	Brad Davis	PG	29	DAL	825	0.70	1262
57	Byron Scott	SG	23	LAL	1295	0.59	1251
58	George Gervin	SG	32	SAS	1524	0.53	1248
59	Jay Vincent	PF	25	DAL	1441	0.55	1240
60	Jeff Malone	SG	23	WSB	1436	0.55	1231
61	Jim Paxson	SG	27	POR	1218	0.60	1213
62	Andrew Toney	SG	27	PHI	1245	0.55	1206
63	Charles Barkley	PF	21	PHI	1148	0.66	1196
64	Danny Ainge	SG	25	BOS	971	0.65	1179
65	Herb Williams	C	26	IND	1375	0.53	1177
66	Larry Smith	PF	27	GSW	887	0.85	1172
67	Darrell Walker	PG	23	NYK	1103	0.57	1149
68	Rory Sparrow	PG	26	NYK	781	0.66	1142
69	Darnell Valentine	PG	25	POR	872	0.63	1140
70	Al Wood	SG	26	SEA	1203	0.57	1126
71	Doc Rivers	PG	23	ATL	974	0.61	1120
72	Lewis Lloyd	SG	25	HOU	1077	0.60	1107
73	Vinnie Johnson	SG	28	DET	1051	0.59	1102
74	Otis Birdsong	SG	29	NJN	1155	0.58	1101
75	Marques Johnson	SF	28	LAC	1181	0.56	1092
76	Phil Hubbard	SF	28	CLE	1201	0.59	1082
77	Mike Woodson	SG	26	KCK	1329	0.53	1080
78	Otis Thorpe	PF	22	KCK	1052	0.66	1065
79	Vern Fleming	PG	22	IND	1126	0.56	1049
80	Greg Ballard	SF	30	WSB	1072	0.59	1043
81	Thurl Bailey	PF	23	UTA	1212	0.55	1037
82	Johnny Davis	PG	29	CLE	941	0.57	1034
83	Quintin Dailey	SG	24	CHI	1262	0.51	1030
84	LaSalle Thompson	C	23	KCK	965	0.66	1008
85	Craig Hodges	SG	24	MIL	871	0.62	1007
86	Mike Gminski	C	25	NJN	1036	0.61	1007
87	Steve Stipanovich	C	24	IND	1126	0.55	1006
88	Derek Harper	PG	23	DAL	790	0.64	980
89	Roy Hinson	PF	23	CLE	1201	0.54	976

Rank	Player	Pos	Age	Tm	PTS	OE	EOP
90	Gene Banks	SF	25	SAS	778	0.71	1360
91	Louis Orr	PF	26	NYK	1007	0.58	1353
92	Michael Cooper	SG	28	LAL	702	0.63	1345
93	Junior Bridgeman	SF	31	LAC	1115	0.52	1336
94	Sam Bowie	C	23	POR	758	0.70	1324
95	Kyle Macy	PG	27	PHO	714	0.64	1314
96	James Edwards	C	29	PHO	1044	0.54	1302
97	Jerome Whitehead	C	28	GSW	1026	0.59	1286
98	Mark Olberding	PF	28	KCK	823	0.62	1279
99	Sam Perkins	PF	23	DAL	903	0.61	1271
100	Jim Thomas	SG	24	IND	885	0.57	1263

Table A6: Larry Bird's Career OE and EOP

Season	Age	Tm	FG	FGA	AST	TOV	PTS	OE	EOP
1979-80	23	BOS	693	1463	370	263	1745	0.57	1666
1980-81	24	BOS	719	1503	451	289	1741	0.57	1721
1981-82	25	BOS	711	1414	447	254	1761	0.60	1826
1982-83	26	BOS	747	1481	458	240	1867	0.61	1944
1983-84	27	BOS	758	1542	520	237	1908	0.60	1984
1984-85	28	BOS	918	1760	531	248	2295	0.61	2354
1985-86	29	BOS	796	1606	557	266	2115	0.60	2208
1986-87	30	BOS	786	1497	566	240	2076	0.62	2225
1987-88	31	BOS	881	1672	467	213	2275	0.60	2263
1988-89	32	BOS	49	104	29	11	116	0.55	109
1989-90	33	BOS	718	1517	562	243	1820	0.57	1864
1990-91	34	BOS	462	1017	431	187	1164	0.56	1216
1991-92	35	BOS	353	758	306	125	908	0.58	944
Career			8591	17334	5695	2816	21791	0.59	22325

Table A7: Top 90 in EOPP for 2012-13

Rnk	First	Last	Pos	EOPP	Rnk	First	Last	Pos	EOPP
1	LeBron	James	PF	1605	46	Rudy	Gay	SF	416
2	Kevin	Durant	SF	1449	47	Evan	Turner	SF	412
3	Kobe	Bryant	SG	1240	48	J.J.	Hickson	C	407
4	James	Harden	SG	1090	49	Paul	Millsap	PF	383
5	Russell	Westbrook	PG	1011	50	Thaddeus	Young	PF	382
6	Stephen	Curry	PG	860	51	Carlos	Boozer	PF	374
7	Blake	Griffin	PF	813	52	Nikola	Vucevic	C	373
8	Dwyane	Wade	SG	802	53	Mike	Conley	PG	356
9	David	Lee	PF	760	54	Zach	Randolph	PF	327
10	Monta	Ellis	SG	758	55	Serge	Ibaka	PF	311
11	Chris	Paul	PG	734	56	Vince	Carter	SF	310
12	Carmelo	Anthony	PF	732	57	Danilo	Gallinari	SF	305
13	Deron	Williams	PG	702	58	J.J.	Redick	SG	296
14	Al	Horford	C	691	59	Kenneth	Faried	PF	296
15	Paul	Pierce	SF	690	60	Kyrie	Irving	PG	296
16	LaMarcus	Aldridge	PF	650	61	Joe	Johnson	SG	294
17	Tony	Parker	PG	633	62	Nikola	Pekovic	C	286
18	Damian	Lillard	PG	619	63	Klay	Thompson	SG	283
19	Greg	Monroe	C	599	64	Tristan	Thompson	PF	281
20	Jrue	Holiday	PG	591	65	Joakim	Noah	C	279
21	Dwight	Howard	C	586	66	Gordon	Hayward	SF	274
22	Marc	Gasol	C	573	67	Jeremy	Lin	PG	268
23	Paul	George	SF	570	68	Ryan	Anderson	PF	264
24	Brook	Lopez	C	567	69	Jamal	Crawford	SG	263
25	Al	Jefferson	C	557	70	Arron	Afflalo	SF	253
26	Chandler	Parsons	SF	534	71	Luke	Ridnour	SG	243
27	Tyson	Chandler	C	500	72	Jose	Calderon	PG	239
28	Kemba	Walker	PG	497	73	Luis	Scola	PF	234
29	Josh	Smith	PF	497	74	Jared	Dudley	SF	232
30	Greivis	Vasquez	PG	479	75	Robin	Lopez	C	232
31	Luol	Deng	SF	474	76	Tyreke	Evans	SG	228
32	Brandon	Jennings	PG	467	77	Amir	Johnson	PF	215
33	O.J.	Mayo	SG	467	78	Andrei	Kirilenko	SF	202
34	DeMar	DeRozan	SG	462	79	DeAndre	Jordan	C	188
35	Nicolas	Batum	SF	452	80	George	Hill	PG	187
36	Andre	Iguodala	SG	442	81	Kevin	Garnett	C	186
37	Ty	Lawson	PG	440	82	Gerald	Henderson	SG	175
38	David	West	PF	437	83	Darren	Collison	PG	172
39	Goran	Dragic	PG	436	84	Omer	Asik	C	171
40	Jarrett	Jack	SG	432	85	Tiago	Splitter	PF	171
41	J.R.	Smith	SG	430	86	Spencer	Hawes	C	166
42	DeMarcus	Cousins	C	430	87	Tayshaun	Prince	SF	159
43	Jeff	Teague	PG	430	88	Roy	Hibbert	C	158
44	Chris	Bosh	C	426	89	Andre	Miller	PG	141
45	Tim	Duncan	C	417	90	Nate	Robinson	PG	128

Table A8: Top EOP in the Clutch for 2012-13

Rank	Player	Min	FGM	FGA	AST	TO	OE	EOP
1	LeBron James (MIA)	161	42	95	50	9	0.65	166
2	Kobe Bryant (LAL)	140	45	106	17	10	0.48	121
3	Chris Paul (LAC)	110	31	63	16	9	0.55	110
4	Tony Parker (SAS)	158	40	85	23	5	0.57	109
5	Kyrie Irving (CLE)	130	49	105	18	27	0.45	107
6	Ty Lawson (DEN)	177	39	84	24	16	0.53	102
7	Chris Bosh (MIA)	162	27	35	3	6	0.86	102
8	Jrue Holiday (PHI)	120	38	81	26	15	0.56	101
9	Paul Pierce (BOS)	218	36	105	34	14	0.47	101
10	Monta Ellis (MIL)	169	44	105	15	9	0.47	100
11	James Harden (HOU)	143	33	82	16	14	0.45	98
12	O.J. Mayo (DAL)	203	40	88	16	14	0.49	97
13	Amir Johnson (TOR)	149	19	29	6	5	1.19	97
14	Kevin Durant (OKC)	145	38	97	9	15	0.39	96
15	Carlos Boozer (CHI)	126	26	45	8	7	0.85	94
16	Kenneth Faried (DEN)	122	19	34	4	1	1.15	91
17	Jarrett Jack (GSW)	141	22	58	19	4	0.53	89
18	Al Horford (ATL)	151	30	51	12	5	0.70	88
19	Al Jefferson (UTA)	157	39	79	8	7	0.55	86
20	Larry Sanders (MIL)	125	20	35	5	0	1.19	84
21	Tim Duncan (SAS)	159	32	67	12	6	0.59	84
22	Kevin Garnett (BOS)	200	38	91	12	5	0.49	83
23	Andre Iguodala (DEN)	174	28	55	15	9	0.60	82
24	Andre Miller (DEN)	165	24	62	23	11	0.53	81
25	George Hill (IND)	161	28	65	22	16	0.51	81
26	Dwyane Wade (MIA)	147	30	60	16	11	0.58	80
27	Damian Lillard (POR)	178	36	87	17	16	0.46	79
28	Nicolas Batum (POR)	170	23	60	20	7	0.57	78
29	Joakim Noah (CHI)	125	15	37	18	5	0.87	77
30	Stephen Curry (GSW)	148	25	67	16	12	0.44	77
31	Kemba Walker (CHA)	147	28	75	23	12	0.49	75
32	Josh Smith (ATL)	139	30	67	23	22	0.52	75
33	LaMarcus Aldridge (POR)	170	31	70	12	7	0.56	75
34	Russell Westbrook (OKC)	145	28	79	14	11	0.43	74
35	Goran Dragic (PHX)	138	21	44	18	6	0.59	74
36	Luol Deng (CHI)	151	25	61	9	4	0.56	73
37	Brandon Jennings (MIL)	145	20	63	30	13	0.48	70
38	JJ Redick (MIL)	161	24	61	15	5	0.48	70
39	Tristan Thompson (CLE)	143	18	27	3	5	0.91	70
40	David West (IND)	164	30	78	11	12	0.51	69
41	JJ Hickson (POR)	138	11	26	6	3	0.94	68
42	Ray Allen (MIA)	158	25	51	4	3	0.53	68
43	Mike Conley (MEM)	158	22	65	18	9	0.45	67
44	Paul Millsap (UTA)	148	24	54	6	4	0.53	65

Rank	Player	Min	FGM	FGA	AST	TO	OE	EOP
45	Jamal Crawford (LAC)	102	23	45	7	4	0.55	65
46	Marc Gasol (MEM)	143	16	32	9	9	0.68	63
47	Dirk Nowitzki (DAL)	124	28	59	6	10	0.47	63
48	Wesley Matthews (POR)	150	19	46	12	7	0.50	60
49	Darren Collison (DAL)	148	14	38	20	9	0.53	60
50	Danilo Gallinari (DEN)	171	23	59	5	5	0.44	60
51	Serge Ibaka (OKC)	120	8	19	2	4	1.43	57
52	Paul George (IND)	157	22	59	6	8	0.42	57
53	Nikola Vucevic (ORL)	120	20	35	4	2	0.80	57
54	Deron Williams (BKN)	158	15	55	18	14	0.38	56
55	Zach Randolph (MEM)	148	21	55	4	8	0.54	55
56	Kyle Lowry (TOR)	154	16	57	23	10	0.47	55
57	Nene (WAS)	121	17	34	12	10	0.63	55
58	Dwight Howard (LAL)	131	10	15	4	4	0.78	54
59	Greivis Vasquez (NOH)	147	22	78	25	8	0.43	54
60	Vince Carter (DAL)	172	22	61	15	10	0.45	53
61	Rudy Gay (TOR)	155	32	88	5	15	0.38	53
62	Jeff Teague (ATL)	125	18	48	18	12	0.47	52
63	Jameer Nelson (ORL)	121	17	50	21	9	0.49	52
64	Ryan Anderson (NOH)	136	20	45	6	2	0.58	51
65	Ramon Sessions (CHA)	107	17	39	9	7	0.48	51
66	Kawhi Leonard (SAS)	106	14	29	7	2	0.68	51
67	David Lee (GSW)	143	17	39	14	7	0.61	50
68	Brandon Knight (DET)	111	18	38	10	7	0.58	50
69	Thaddeus Young (PHI)	120	19	30	2	2	0.81	48
70	Carmelo Anthony (NYK)	104	26	69	0	10	0.38	48
71	Joe Johnson (BKN)	149	22	55	7	8	0.42	48
72	Dion Waiters (CLE)	122	22	59	9	3	0.46	48
73	Jeff Green (BOS)	121	18	32	3	5	0.57	48
74	Jeremy Lin (HOU)	108	16	33	7	7	0.50	46
75	Randy Foye (UTA)	109	9	20	10	4	0.58	46
76	Brook Lopez (BKN)	115	23	52	0	8	0.43	45
77	Manu Ginobili (SAS)	106	16	41	10	7	0.49	45
78	Jason Kidd (NYK)	114	11	22	9	4	0.63	44
79	Jimmy Butler (CHI)	118	11	22	4	2	0.68	43
80	Jose Calderon (DET)	123	9	31	22	6	0.54	42
81	Jason Terry (BOS)	160	16	46	9	4	0.43	42
82	Greg Monroe (DET)	118	14	33	10	7	0.55	41
83	DeMar DeRozan (TOR)	208	23	82	6	8	0.32	39
84	DeMarcus Cousins (SAC)	112	17	49	7	9	0.41	38
85	Gordon Hayward (UTA)	120	13	30	10	8	0.52	37
86	J.R. Smith (NYK)	133	21	65	7	7	0.38	37
87	Blake Griffin (LAC)	122	16	30	5	11	0.55	37
88	Mike Dunleavy (MIL)	109	13	29	9	8	0.51	36
89	Alan Anderson (TOR)	104	17	45	5	5	0.42	35

Rank	Player	Min	FGM	FGA	AST	TO	OE	EOP
90	Raymond Felton (NYK)	108	12	39	16	9	0.47	35
91	Alonzo Gee (CLE)	153	13	26	6	3	0.68	34
92	Chandler Parsons (HOU)	124	12	28	7	6	0.49	33
93	Ersan Ilyasova (MIL)	122	13	32	4	8	0.55	32
94	Rodney Stuckey (DET)	103	15	42	8	8	0.41	32
95	Shawn Marion (DAL)	110	10	21	8	2	0.67	32
96	Tayshaun Prince (MEM)	145	15	32	5	12	0.47	31
97	Roy Hibbert (IND)	140	10	34	3	3	0.68	30
98	Kyle Korver (ATL)	127	10	22	1	4	0.46	30
99	Lance Stephenson (IND)	125	8	17	10	4	0.62	29
100	Arron Afflalo (ORL)	120	14	47	4	9	0.31	27
101	Evan Turner (PHI)	107	13	33	7	9	0.43	27
102	Dante Cunningham (MIN)	102	10	24	3	3	0.54	23
103	Klay Thompson (GSW)	138	11	38	5	3	0.36	23
104	Brandon Bass (BOS)	103	9	25	2	2	0.61	22
105	Bradley Beal (WAS)	116	9	36	3	7	0.29	20
106	Gerald Wallace (BKN)	121	7	23	5	6	0.43	19
107	Jared Dudley (PHX)	102	6	30	12	2	0.43	19
108	Danny Green (SAS)	112	11	36	4	4	0.36	18
109	Martell Webster (WAS)	125	9	27	2	4	0.38	17
110	Metta World Peace (LAL)	114	9	24	2	5	0.39	16
111	Omer Asik (HOU)	107	6	19	2	3	0.62	14
112	Avery Bradley (BOS)	101	4	13	2	0	0.50	9
113	Tyson Chandler (NYK)	116	7	8	2	1	-9.00	-362

*Clutch means last five minutes of a game with the difference in score no greater than five. To qualify, players must have played at least 100 minutes in this setting.

Table A9: Top 90 in Approximate Value (AV) for 2012-13

Rnk	Player	Tm	AV	Rnk	Player	Tm	AV
1	LeBron James	MIA	2781	46	Joakim Noah	CHI	1202
2	Jrue Holiday	PHI	1939	47	Jamal Crawford	LAC	1185
3	Mike Conley	MEM	1888	48	Isaiah Thomas	SAC	1160
4	Dwyane Wade	MIA	1884	49	Brandon Knight	DET	1147
5	Russell Westbrook	OKC	1881	50	Luol Deng	CHI	1138
6	Kevin Durant	OKC	1821	51	Omer Asik	HOU	1130
7	Marc Gasol	MEM	1756	52	DeMarcus Cousins	SAC	1127
8	LaMarcus Aldridge	POR	1742	53	Danilo Gallinari	DEN	1121
9	Tony Parker	SAS	1719	54	Andre Miller	DEN	1118
10	Dwight Howard	LAL	1710	55	Kenneth Faried	DEN	1088
11	Kemba Walker	CHA	1703	56	Zach Randolph	MEM	1087
12	Kobe Bryant	LAL	1689	57	Gordon Hayward	UTA	1086
13	Stephen Curry	GSW	1656	58	Greivis Vasquez	NOH	1077
14	James Harden	HOU	1617	59	Jarrett Jack	GSW	1076
15	Chris Paul	LAC	1526	60	John Wall	WAS	1067
16	Monta Ellis	MIL	1515	61	Nikola Vucevic	ORL	1061
17	Andre Iguodala	DEN	1479	62	Luis Scola	PHO	1047
18	Greg Monroe	DET	1441	63	Paul Millsap	UTA	1045
19	Paul Pierce	BOS	1423	64	Larry Sanders	MIL	1041
20	David Lee	GSW	1411	65	Metta World Peace	LAL	1028
21	Carmelo Anthony	NYK	1408	66	Tyreke Evans	SAC	1020
22	Kevin Garnett	BOS	1400	67	Serge Ibaka	OKC	1019
23	David West	IND	1390	68	Kosta Koufos	DEN	1011
24	Paul George	IND	1384	69	Jared Dudley	PHO	1011
25	Amir Johnson	TOR	1379	70	Kyle Lowry	TOR	1010
26	Thaddeus Young	PHI	1376	71	Jameer Nelson	ORL	1009
27	Josh Smith	ATL	1357	72	Chris Bosh	MIA	1005
28	J.R. Smith	NYK	1356	73	Tristan Thompson	CLE	1003
29	Deron Williams	BKN	1350	74	Robin Lopez	NOH	1003
30	Goran Dragic	PHO	1345	75	Tony Allen	MEM	996
31	Jeff Teague	ATL	1338	76	Matt Barnes	LAC	991
32	Al Horford	ATL	1329	77	J.J. Hickson	POR	987
33	DeMar DeRozan	TOR	1297	78	O.J. Mayo	DAL	977
34	Chandler Parsons	HOU	1294	79	Joe Johnson	BKN	976
35	Damian Lillard	POR	1278	80	Nate Robinson	CHI	968
36	Brook Lopez	BKN	1260	81	Andray Blatche	BKN	963
37	Vince Carter	DAL	1259	82	Mario Chalmers	MIA	949
38	Kyrie Irving	CLE	1234	83	Nicolas Batum	POR	949
39	George Hill	IND	1232	84	Nene Hilario	WAS	939
40	Tiago Splitter	SAS	1229	85	Roy Hibbert	IND	937
41	Ty Lawson	DEN	1228	86	Darren Collison	DAL	934
42	Tyson Chandler	NYK	1224	87	Jose Barea	MIN	930
43	Blake Griffin	LAC	1221	88	Gerald Henderson	CHA	908
44	Tim Duncan	SAS	1219	89	Carlos Boozer	CHI	905
45	Jeremy Lin	HOU	1208	90	Ersan Ilyasova	MIL	905

Table A10: Top 40 Draft Picks for Value

Rank	Year	Pick	First	Last	Team	EOP$^+$/G	Yield*
1	2001	30	Gilbert	Arenas	GSW	19.38	14.63
2	1996	13	Kobe	Bryant	CHH	23.35	14.56
3	2001	28	Tony	Parker	SAS	19.48	14.24
4	1985	13	Karl	Malone	UTA	22.99	14.20
5	2002	34	Carlos	Boozer	CLE	17.66	14.14
6	2005	40	Monta	Ellis	GSW	18.36	14.13
7	1984	16	John	Stockton	UTA	20.77	13.86
8	1996	15	Steve	Nash	PHO	20.50	13.57
9	1978	6	Larry	Bird	BOS	22.45	13.18
10	2003	5	Dwyane	Wade	MIA	25.35	13.08
11	1984	3	Michael	Jordan	CHI	26.73	12.97
12	1999	57	Manu	Ginobili	SAS	15.02	12.94
13	2005	4	Chris	Paul	NOH	25.38	12.86
14	2003	1	LeBron	James	CLE	28.92	12.47
15	1986	46	Jeff	Hornacek	PHO	15.66	12.33
16	2005	30	David	Lee	NYK	16.92	12.17
17	2000	43	Michael	Redd	MIL	16.00	11.93
18	1993	37	Nick	Van Exel	LAL	16.46	11.90
19	1983	14	Clyde	Drexler	POR	19.98	11.90
20	1989	14	Tim	Hardaway	GSW	19.94	11.86
21	2007	48	Marc	Gasol	LAL	15.11	11.85
22	1988	53	Anthony	Mason	POR	13.74	11.65
23	2007	56	Ramon	Sessions	MIL	13.32	11.62
24	2002	55	Luis	Scola	SAS	13.95	11.61
25	1977	49	Eddie	Johnson	ATL	13.98	11.33
26	1977	22	Norm	Nixon	LAL	17.44	11.24
27	1986	25	Mark	Price	DAL	16.76	11.17
28	1984	5	Charles	Barkley	PHI	23.04	10.77
29	1980	25	Jeff	Ruland	GSW	16.16	10.57
30	1986	60	Drazen	Petrovic	POR	12.53	10.51
31	1993	24	Sam	Cassell	HOU	17.92	10.43
32	1988	19	Rod	Strickland	NYK	16.99	10.38
33	1998	41	Cuttino	Mobley	HOU	13.74	10.31
34	2006	21	Rajon	Rondo	PHO	17.30	10.28
35	1997	42	Stephen	Jackson	PHO	12.86	10.24
36	1987	7	Kevin	Johnson	CLE	21.74	10.18
37	1978	36	Maurice	Cheeks	PHI	14.11	10.04
38	2003	47	Mo	Williams	UTA	14.52	9.96
39	1989	40	Dino	Radja	BOS	14.17	9.94
40	1998	32	Rashard	Lewis	SEA	13.34	9.89

*Yield is the EOP/G of the player minus the average EOP/G of all players from 1977 through 2010 drafted at the same pick number.

Index